T5-ASN-568

MAX LEOPOLD MARGOLIS

SOCIETY OF BIBLICAL LITERATURE
BIBLICAL SCHOLARSHIP IN NORTH AMERICA

Kent Harold Richards, Editor

LEONARD GREENSPOON

MAX LEOPOLD MARGOLIS
A Scholar's Scholar

Scholars Press
Atlanta, Georgia

SOCIETY OF BIBLICAL LITERATURE
CENTENNIAL PUBLICATIONS

Editorial Board

Paul J. Achtemeier, Union Theological Seminary, Richmond, Virginia
Adela Yarbro Collins, McCormick Theological Seminary, Chicago, Illinois
Eldon Jay Epp, Case Western Reserve University, Cleveland, Ohio
Edwin S. Gaustad, University of California, Riverside, California
E. Brooks Holifield, Emory University, Atlanta, Georgia
Douglas A. Knight, Vanderbilt Divinity School, Nashville, Tennessee
George W. MacRae, Harvard Divinity School, Cambridge, Massachusetts
Harry M. Orlinsky, Hebrew Union College-Jewish Institute of Religion, New York
Kent Harold Richards, Chair, The Iliff School of Theology, Denver, Colorado
Gene M. Tucker, Candler School of Theology, Atlanta, Georgia
Maurya P. Horgan, Associate Editor, Denver
Paul J. Kobelski, Associate Editor, Denver

The Society of Biblical Literature gratefully acknowledges a grant from the National Endowment for the Humanities to underwrite certain editorial and research expenses of the Centennial Publications Series. Published results and interpretations do not necessarily represent the view of the Endowment.

BM
755
.M332
G74
1987

© 1987
Society of Biblical Literature

Library of Congress Cataloging-in-Publication Data

Greenspoon, Leonard J.
  Max Leopold Margolis.

  (Biblical scholarship in North America ; no. 15)
  Includes bibliographical references.
  1. Margolis, Max Leopold, 1866-1932. 2. Scholars,
Jewish—United States—Biography. 3. Old Testament
scholars—United States—Biography. I. Title.
II. Series.
BM755.M332G74   1987   221'.092'4 [B]   87-9899
ISBN 1-55540-146-5 (alk. paper)
ISBN 1-55540-147-3 (pbk. : alk. paper)

Printed in the United States of America
on acid-free paper

JESUIT - KRAUSS - McCORMICK - LIBRARY
1100 EAST 55th STREET
CHICAGO, ILLINOIS 60615

To My Father:

Alvin Louis Greenspoon

CONTENTS

Max Leopold Margolis

PREFACE

Writing in the *B'nai B'rith News* of June 1915, Max L. Margolis offered one of his favorite descriptions of the relationship between a scholar and his scholarship (see below, in chapter 2, for Cyrus H. Gordon's recollection of this same description):

> Scholarship is made up of two assets: a prerequisite knowledge of where to look for things and a ready acquaintance with the things to be looked for. A moneyed man may have a fat bank-account; but to buy groceries you have to have ready change. In the region of learning, the knowledge of sources is a valuable bank-account; but the possession of the knowledge drawn from many obscure sources is the ready cash. And that knowledge is found only in men of experience, who have behind them and not ahead of them the preparation.

When Margolis wrote of this ideal scholar, who possessed both "ready cash" and a "fat bank-account," he was not describing any particular individual. On the contrary, he was bemoaning the scarcity of such scholars in a world where far too many were willing to draw upon the bank accounts of others instead of building up their own assets through firsthand acquaintance with the sources themselves. (And is it all that different in the 1980s?) In my opinion, Max Margolis exemplifies the ideal. Morever, his contributions are to be measured by the qualities he displayed as much as by the quantities he produced. Margolis possessed a rare integrity that impelled him to expose the counterfeit and debased products that were accepted so facilely by others as the unalloyed "coin of the realm." At the same time, he scrupulously assessed his own assets and liabilities according to the same exacting standards he imposed on others. It is for these reasons that I feel that Max Leopold Margolis is, in the words of this book's subtitle, truly "a scholar's scholar."

The course of Margolis' professional career is closely connected with his personal and family life. With this in mind, I have organized this book largely in terms of a biography. The first chapter begins with Margolis' birth in 1866 and traces his life from a small village in Eastern Europe to a controversial two years (1905—1907) at Hebrew Union College in Cincinnati. The second chapter recounts Margolis' career from 1907 until his death in April 1932. The setting for most of this period is Philadelphia, where Margolis served as a professor at Dropsie College for over two decades. Within the chronological framework of these first two chapters, reference is made to Margolis' major scholarly work as well as to significant events in his personal life. Two of his most lasting achievements in the field of Biblical studies are dealt with separately in individual chapters: his editorship of the Jewish Publication Society of America's Bible translation (chapter 3) and his research as a textual critic, particularly in the Greek traditions of the book of Joshua (chapter 4). The fifth and final chapter of this biography summarizes Margolis' views on Biblical scholarship within the Jewish community as well as in the larger community of scholars. In these chapters also, the activties and concerns of Margolis' private life are shown to spill over into the academic, scholarly, and communal achievements through which he distinguished himself in public life.

I have been working on this book for several years. During that time, I have badgered countless archivists, bored numerous colleagues, and bewildered family and a dwindling circle of friends. Remarkably enough, I have yet to be barred from any archives, scholarly meetings, or family gatherings. In all seriousness, I have been the recipient of more help and support than I would have thought possible, and I have attempted to thank each individual in an appropriate and personal way. At this point, I add a public and collective thank you.

There are some gentlemen (and I use this word in its narrower definition: "polite, gracious, and considerate men") for whom even the warmest collective thank you is insufficient. First of all, I am most grateful to Philip Margolis, Max Margolis' surviving son, whose interest in this project, particularly in its later stages, has been very encouraging. And then I wish to express my very deepest gratitude to Robert Gordis, Cyrus H. Gordon, Simon Greenberg, Louis L. Kaplan, and Harry M. Orlinsky. These men, who constitute something of a "Who's Who" among senior scholars in Biblical and Jewish studies, share two characteristics that helped give shape and substance to this book. First, they were all students of Margolis' at Dropsie. And secondly, they all graciously allowed me to interview them about their experiences with Margolis and their thoughts concerning him as a scholar, teacher, and human being. The numerous citations to my oral interviews with them (especially in chapter 2) is partial evidence of the debt I owe them. Lastly, I single out one of these men, Harry M. Orlinsky, who first suggested a volume on Margolis for this Series and then went out on a limb to recommend me as its author. Anyone who has known Professor Orlinsky treasures, as I do, a voluminous correspondence with him, which in my case is filled with his insightful comments on this manuscript, on future research projects related to Margolis, and on life in general. More than anything else, I have endeavored to repay Professor Orlinsky for the trust he placed in me.

In the introduction to a volume entitled *Max Leopold Margolis: Scholar and Teacher* (Philadelphia: Dropsie College, 1952), Evelyn Aronson Margolis wrote:

> My husband was a born teacher and he loved to teach. But more than teaching, he reverenced scholarship. No sacrifice was too great, personal or economic, to uphold the integrity of scholarship. These ideals he passed on to you, his pupils.

From the careers of the gentlemen mentioned above and others, it is clear that Max L. Margolis succeeded in passing on these ideals to his students. Through this biography, I hope to be part of the process by which Margolis' ideals are kept alive for the benefit of the present and future generations.

1. FROM EASTERN EUROPE TO THE AMERICAN MIDWEST (1866-1907)

Max Leopold Margolis was born on October 15, 1866, in the village of Meretz (also Merecz or Merech), located in the Russian province of Vilna (in present-day Lithuania).[1] On his father's side he was a descendant of a famous rabbi and scholar, Yom Tov Lippman Heller, from whom Margolis' Hebrew name was taken.[2]

Margolis' father Isaac, who was in his mid-20s at the time of his son's birth, was also a rabbi. He came to this position after an earlier unsuccessful career in business. Whatever losses Isaac Margolis suffered in business were more than offset by his notable achievements in scholarship, and these not limited to Jewish learning. Apparently on his own, he acquired sufficient knowledge in classical languages, mathematics,

[1] The most important sources of information on the life of Margolis are Cyrus Adler, "Address of Doctor Adler at the Meeting in Memory of Max L. Margolis. May 9, 1932," typescript, 9pp., found in the Dropsie College Archives; idem, "Max Leopold Margolis," American Jewish Yearbook 35 (1933), 139–144 (Adler also prepared the entry on Margolis for the Dictionary of American Biography); David J. Galter, "Max L. Margolis—Distinguished American Scholar and Author: A Biographical Appreciation," The Jewish Exponent (Philadelphia) April 8, 1932, 1 and 8 (p. 8 also contains tributes to Margolis); idem, "Max Margolis: Lover of the Book," B'nai B'rith Magazine May 1932, 246 and 254; Robert Gordis, "The Life of Professor Max Leopold Margolis: An Appreciation," Max Leopold Margolis: Scholar and Teacher (Philadelphia: Alumni Association, Dropsie College for Hebrew and Cognate Learning, 1952), 1–16 (Gordis also prepared the entry on Margolis for the Encyclopaedia Judaica); Richard Gottheil, A. V. Williams Jackson, and Ludlow S. Bull (Committee on Resolutions), "The Life and Work of Max Leopold Margolis," JAOS 52 (1932), 106–109; Alexander Marx, "In Memoriam: Prof. Max Leopold Margolis," Proceedings of the Rabbinical Assembly of America 4 (1932), 368–380; reprinted (with minor changes) in idem, Studies in Jewish History and Booklore (New York, 1944), 418–430, and Essays in Jewish Biography (Philadelphia: Jewish Publication Society of America, 1947), 265–279. When compared, these sources do not agree at all points. In attempting to construct a consistent account, I have drawn on the material listed above and, in addition, on a one page autobiographical statement in Latin that Margolis appended to his Ph.D. dissertation (Columbia University, 1892 [see below]) and on a detailed five page form, completed after Margolis' death, for the National Cyclopedia of American Biography. For the period prior to 1892, I have not cited particular references when the information comes from one or more of the above sources. Specific citations for this early period of Margolis' life are largely limited to one or two autobiographical reminiscences that Margolis included in some of his popular presentations.

[2] For more on Heller, who lived from 1579–1654, see the entry "Heller, Yom Tov Lipmann ben Nathan ha-Levi" in the Encyclopaedia Judaica, vol. 8, 311–314. The Encyclopaedia may also be consulted for further information on other Jewish individuals and institutions mentioned in this and later chapters.

and science to write learned articles on those topics. This breadth of knowledge, which complemented his mastery of classical Jewish learning, was passed on to his son, whose earliest education he supervised.

Accounts of Max Margolis as a child are sketchy and sometimes contradictory. It should come as no surprise to anyone familiar with him that these accounts agree in depicting him as a precocious and strong-willed boy. One story tells of Margolis' first day at the local Jewish elementary school (Heder): after but one hour's exposure to the teacher (Melamed), Margolis pronounced him an ignoramous (Am ha-Aretz) and stalked out of the school, never to return. So well did he profit from his father's tutelage that by the age of seven he was chanting from the Torah scroll in synagogue. Just four years later he was able to read from any part of the Hebrew Bible. By that time he was also well on his way toward becoming an expert scribe. The precise, meticulous penmanship characteristic of the mature Margolis had its antecedents in such boyhood experience.

Margolis tells a story about his own childhood that reveals another side of his developing personality.[3] When he was about five years old, he recalls, his father was reading to him the book of Ruth on the eve of the festival of Shavuot. After his father had finished the first chapter, the child burst out in tears. Not knowing that the story was destined for a happy ending, he begged his father to stop reading. Looking back on this incident, Margolis was of the opinion that he was none the worse for the tears shed. This sensitive side of Margolis' nature lies just below the surface of much of his work and of his approach to it.

For several years before his Bar Mitzvah, in addition to being taught by his father, Margolis was the student of a priest of Meretz. From him Margolis received further instruction in secular subjects of the sort that had also attracted his father. Following his Bar Mitzvah, it appears, the young Margolis ran away from his hometown, ending up at the home of his maternal grandfather in Berlin. This stay in the big city was short; he returned to Meretz to continue study under the guidance of his father. Both religious and secular topics occupied father and son during these years. Isaac Margolis went so far as to prepare a Hebrew textbook on trigonometry and logarithms for his son.

In late 1881, Margolis accompanied his father, who was then offering private instruction as a tutor, to Warsaw. There, in December of that year, Margolis and his father were forced to hide for three days to escape the wrath of a mob during a pogrom. Emerging from their place of confinement on the Shabbat, Margolis saw with his own eyes devastation and widespread looting. He noticed a proliferation of ikons over the doors

---

[3] Max L. Margolis, "The Religious content of Biblical History. Lecture I," n.d. Typescript found in office of Harry M. Orlinsky.

of many undisturbed houses; these images, his father explained, had been hastily produced to mark the dwellings as non-Jewish.[4] As a result of this incident, which may have been Margolis' first encounter with the growing phenomenon of anti-Semitism, he determined never to go back to Russia. And, although he did return to his native village in the eastern European region controlled by the Russians, Margolis' future lay in the West.

Several years after the events in Warsaw, Margolis' parents decided that their son was now ready to take advantage of the opportunities available in Berlin. So Margolis, with his family's blessing, went again to the home of his mother's father, David Bernstein, who was a prosperous merchant in that city. This path, also taken by many other Russian youths, led Margolis to seek admission to the highly-regarded Leibnitz Gymnasium, where he was duly enrolled after passing qualifying examinations.

Accounts of Margolis' years as a student in Berlin emphasize two aspects of this experience—his brilliance and his exposure to ever-widening fields of knowledge, particularly in the area of classical studies. For several terms, it is reported, Margolis was the top student in Greek. This thorough acquaintance with classical languages and literature, topics which had engaged Margolis' interest even as a child, was a probable factor in the eventual decision to concentrate his efforts on the Septuagint. Success in such intellectual endeavors was, in addition, the result of Margolis' introduction to the scientific methods that characterized German education at that time. Orderly thinking, thorough marshalling of the evidence, uncompromising academic integrity—these are among the scholarly rigors that Margolis submitted to, and made part of his own life.

Neither Margolis' brilliance nor his exposure was limited to secular subjects. He continued his studies in traditional Jewish lore and earned money giving Hebrew lessons. He also came into contact with Berlin's reform synagogues and the distinctly untraditional thinkers who gravitated toward them. In the third-person description that follows, Margolis was presumably narrating some of the changes he, himself, underwent in Germany:

He may have become lax in certain religious observances; but withal he is supremely the Jew, albeit after the fashion of Berlin Jewry; he has tasted of a superior culture; he has humanized and modernized himself; the crude life of Lithuania he has cast far behind him, even as in his

---

[4] Max L. Margolis, "Upon the Doorposts of Thy House," n.d. Typescript found in office of Harry M. Orlinsky.

speech he has exchanged the uncouth jargon with its rapid tempo for the slow diction of the compatriots of Lessing and Mendelssohn.[5]

These encounters with German culture profoundly affected Margolis, but they did not blind him to German anti-Semitism. No pogroms of the sort Margolis had earlier witnessed in Warsaw were to scratch the veneer of civilized urban life in Berlin of the 1880s; nevertheless, anti-Semitic rhetoric was no stranger even within the halls of the Gymnasium. Margolis' subsequent acute sensitivity to the stirrings of American anti-Jewish feeling, which likewise found a home in cultured circles, owes something to his Berlin years. It is unclear to what extent, if any, Margolis came into contact with early Zionist leaders who were in Berlin at the same time as he. Perhaps, Margolis' Zionism, which was later to become a passionate commitment on his part, still lay beneath the surface prior to his coming to America.

Margolis graduated from the Leibnitz Gymnasium in 1889. Three years earlier his parents and the rest of his family had emigrated to America.[6] They settled in New York City, where Margolis' father became rabbi of the Kalvarier Schul. A year later, in 1887, Isaac Margolis died; his son had seen him for the last time when the family passed through Berlin on its way to America. There is a small detail, almost a footnote, that illuminates the high esteem in which Margolis held his father. After Margolis' death in April 1932, an inventory of his personal library revealed that he had kept in his possession, for approximately half a century, three manuscripts written by his father.

The death of Margolis' father must have been a severe blow to the remaining members of the family. Concern for the economic well-being of his family, along with the desire to pursue a university education, determined the course of Margolis' immediate future: Upon graduation from Gymnasium he followed his family to America. The next three years were to be dominated by these dual concerns—pursuit of a university education, at Columbia, and providing some income for his family, through a series of jobs usually associated with academic life or the Jewish community.

Margolis enrolled at Columbia College (as the University was then

[5] Max L. Margolis, "Orientation," *The Jewish Forum* May 1918, 212. This article (pp. 208–215) contains numerous other glimpses of Margolis' life from Lithuanian village through his arrival and early years in New York City.

[6] At the death of Margolis' mother, Mrs. Hinde Margolis, in 1912, *The American Hebrew* 92 (November 15, 1912), 65, listed her as "mother of Prof. Max L. Margolis, Rabbi Elias Margolis, Mrs. Lina Ginsberg, Miss Bertha Margolis and Barnett Margolis." That list is, however, only partially correct. As shown on a family tree drawn up by Elias Margolis, Max and Elias were the only brothers. There were four sisters: Anna, Lena, Ida, and Bertha. Ida remained single; Bertha married a man with the last name of Barnett (whence the "Barnett" of *The American Hebrew* notice). Anna and then Lena both married the same man; his last name was Ginsberg.

called) in the fall of 1889, not long after his arrival in New York City. The following year he earned an M.A.; just one year later, in 1891, he received his Ph.D. In the brief autobiography he appended to his dissertation he lists four professors with whom he studied at Columbia: Gottheil, in Semitics; Peck, in Latin; Butler and Catell, in philosophy. It was the first-named of these professors that had the strongest influence on Margolis, who was more and more drawn to the study of Semitics.

Margolis' dissertation was titled *Commentarius Isaacidis quatenus ad textum talmudis investigandum adhiberi possit tractatu 'Erubhin ostenditur* ("The commentary of Rashi in the Tractate Erubin viewed insofar as it is possible to be applied for the investigation of the talmudic text").[7] This dissertation, for which Margolis was awarded the first doctorate granted by Columbia's Oriental Department, was written entirely in Latin. His choice of that language may have been in imitation of prevailing European academic usage, but it also shows the immigrant scholar's greater confidence in a classical language over against his still developing mastery of English. In years to come, Margolis, who never lost the interest in classical studies that he had begun to acquire as a youth, was to become a much praised master of the English tongue.

Margolis' choice of language, then, points both backwards and forwards, to what he had already accomplished and to what he was to achieve. This same dual orientation is discernible in Margolis' choice of subject matter. The dissertation was a textual study, in which he sought to demonstrate the value of Rashi's commentary for constructing a critical edition of the Talmud. In achieving his goal, Margolis analyzed, in minute detail, the differing textual traditions of Rashi and numerous manuscripts of the Talmud. Margolis understood his work as but a small part of the total effort necessary to restore the authentic text of the Talmud, for Rashi was only one source that would have to be mined and Erubin was but one tractate. Margolis' philological training, his exposure to traditional Jewish learning, and his growing interest in the academic study of Semitics all bore fruit in this labor. His later text critical work in the Septuagint would require the same skills he was perfecting at this time. Grand theories had their place, but they must be preceded and supported by scrupulous analysis of every single detail that might shed light on the proper relationship among the masses of data painstakingly collated.

The fact that this dissertation was accepted by Columbia is firm evidence of the high regard in which Margolis' work was held by interested scholars. This estimation was, however, not unanimous: a dissent of

---

[7] This English translation of the title is found in Frank Zimmermann, "The Contributions of M. L. Margolis to the Fields of Bible and Rabbinics," *Max Leopold Margolis: Scholar and Teacher* (Philadelphia: Dropsie College, 1952), 17.

sorts' was entered by Kaufmann Kohler—not a criticism of Margolis' erudition or methodology, but rather an unhappiness with his choice of emphasis. This is the thrust of the remarks Kohler addressed to Margolis in a postcard dated June 5, 1891:[8]

> Of what benefit can it be to know whether *Raschi* used this or that word since there is actually no direct result for the *Talmudical* text to be derived from the number of *Variae Lectionae* which I have thus far looked over. I have not been so entirely estranged from Talmudical studies as not to appreciate the value of a *critical* edition even of so uninteresting a treatise as in the whole is *Raschi* to *Erubin*. But . . . . at present I must say: Cuius bono. What a waste of time, of labor, and of paper. . . See what men like Schechter or [Solomon] Buber do!

Kohler may have missed the point of what Margolis was doing; indeed, less than a month later he admits that "I was too hasty in my remarks" and offers his "hearty congratulations to your Ph.D. degree!"[9]

Still, Kohler did not entirely recant, and his remarks have a familiar ring: Several of Margolis' former students, all of whom are among his staunchest admirers, bemoan the fact that their professor so involved himself in technical minutiae that he never produced the broad, synthetic studies that would have been more valuable to a larger audience. Their words, spoken more in lament than criticism, relate especially to their teacher's preoccupation with the book of Joshua during the last part of his life.

After graduation Margolis remained at Columbia for another year as a University fellow in Semitic languages. He spent a portion of that year collating a Talmudic manuscript, which contained part of tractate Megilla, with several other manuscripts. This study resulted in Margolis' *The Columbia College Ms. of Meghilla* (Babylonian Talmud), in which he listed over 1700 variant readings in the ten folio pages the manuscript covered. Industry and thoroughness, these Margolis never lacked!

Margolis' energy found other outlets also, for he had to be a breadwinner as well as a scholar. For a while he was a censustaker, but most frequently his jobs related to his academic interests. Among these was his stint as secretary to Felix Adler, the founder of the Ethical Culture Society. Margolis was attracted by Adler's intellectual honesty, and he gave a series of lectures on the sages of the Talmud at the Society's summer school in Plymouth, Massachusetts. Margolis did not, however,

---

[8] I found this postcard in the office of Harry M. Orlinsky. As far as I can determine, this postcard is the earliest record of any sort of relationship between Kohler, who was then a rabbi in New York City, and Margolis.

[9] Letter of Kaufmann Kohler to Max L. Margolis, July 1891. This letter was found in office of Harry M. Orlinsky.

join the movement itself.[10] He also worked for the Baron de Hirsch Fund.

From Columbia, Margolis went to Professor Thomas Davidson's Glenmore School of Culture Sciences at Keene, NY, where in July and August of 1892 he delivered a series of lectures on Jewish literature.[11] During that summer Margolis faced a dilemma all too common among young academicians—where to secure one's first permanent teaching position.[12] It was at this time that he learned of a position at Hebrew Union College in Cincinnati. He applied, and was hired by the Institution's founder and president, Rabbi Isaac Mayer Wise. During the last week of August, Margolis left New York City for Cincinnati, a locale that he, with perhaps a typical New Yorker's view of American geography, described as the *far* West.[13] Before embarking on the westward journey he was guest of honor at a reception arranged by the Russian-American Hebrew Association. Cincinnati's Russian-Jewish community also embraced Margolis as one of their own.[14] In spite of his years in Berlin, Margolis appears to have enjoyed this attention.

Published sources indicate that Margolis was first appointed instructor, later assistant professor of Hebrew and Biblical Exegesis at Hebrew Union College. In a letter written in September 1892, Margolis explained that "my title is quite lengthy—*Precepter* in Exegesis and Talmud and *Instructor* in Syriac (as modified by me; the original is irreproducible)."[15]

Whatever the precise title, this position led Margolis directly into what was for him a new field of advanced research and teaching—the Bible. In the late 19th and early 20th century Biblical studies was not marked out as a Jewish subject; the Bible had not been a major concern of *Juedische Wissenschaft*. The non-Jewish status of Biblical studies was underscored by remarks Wise made to Margolis when the young instructor arrived in Cincinnati: "We have plenty of Talmud teachers, we have no Bible scholars among us Jews."[16]

---

[10] In "Orientation," Margolis wrote, again presumably about himself, that "he was captivated by the leader of the movement, but his Jewish training, overlaid though it was by German humanistic studies, kept him from accepting the movement itself."

[11] The Yale University Library contains a series of six letters that Margolis wrote to Davidson during the months of June and August, 1892.

[12] On Margolis' feelings during this period, see his letter to Davidson, dated August 26, 1892 (Yale University Library), and a letter addressed to "Dick" and dated August 23, 1892 (this letter is found at both the American Jewish Archives and the Archives of the American Jewish Historical Society). "Dick" is Stephen S. Wise.

[13] Margolis to Dick, August 26, 1892 (Archives of the American Jewish Historical Society).

[14] Margolis to Dick, September 2, 1892 (American Jewish Archives) and September 19, 1892 (American Jewish Archives and the Archives of the American Jewish Historical Society).

[15] Margolis to Dick, September 19, 1892 (see preceding fn.).

[16] Margolis related this anecdote in "The Jewish Defense of the Bible," *B'nai B'rith News*

By training, Margolis was uniquely well qualified to fill the gap. By temperament and inclination, so it appears, this was also the case. Cyrus Adler, with whom Margolis was later to have a long professional relationship, speaks of "an element of mysticism" in Margolis' make-up:

> He felt himself, in a way, a sort of successor to Samuel David Luzzatto who was called upon to carry on biblical study with the hope of continuing this Jewish influence upon all students of the Bible. Margolis was a proud spirit and he wished to show the Biblical scholars of the non-Jewish world that a Jew could also deal with the Greek versions.[17]

While Adler may have erred in his analysis of what motivated Margolis, he was clearly on the mark in highlighting the importance Margolis attached to his being a *Jewish* scholar of the Bible:

> If Christian scholars . . . bluntly assert that their exegesis of the OT is and must be Christian, then—and I have never repudiated it before my University classes—my understanding of the OT is and must be Jewish.[18]

The record of Margolis' career shows that Robert Gordis' characterization of him as "the greatest Jewish master of Biblical learning yet arisen in America [this statement was made in 1952]" was no exaggeration.[19]

Margolis had been in Cincinnati hardly a year before he began to establish that career through the publication of an important work, *An Elementary Text-Book of Hebrew Accidence Arranged in Typical Examples with Concise Explanations referring especially to the Modification of Sounds*.[20] Already in January 1893, Margolis informed a friend that

> I am writing a grammar which in manuscript form I use in my classes. The main novelty of my method consists in the fact that I teach grammar by pictures, typical forms, examples—of which each stands for its class, for a multitude of phenomena of one kind. Thus instead of giving a long rule in beautiful grammar language, that while the guttural ה after the article doesn't take the dageš forte assimilationis it does admit of a virtual doubling, I simply put down on the board or

---

June 1915, 10. See also Gordis, "An Appreciation," *Max Leopold Margolis*, 2, and, in a broader context, Nahum M. Sarna, "Abraham Geiger and Biblical Scholarship," *New Perspectives on Abraham Geiger*, ed. J. J. Petuchowski (Cincinnati: Hebrew Union College, 1975), 17–30.

[17] Cyrus Adler, "Max Leopold Margolis," *American Jewish Year Book* 35 (1933), 140.

[18] Max L. Margolis to Kaufmann Kohler, April 1905 (American Jewish Archives). Issues related to Margolis' exegetical attitude will be discussed in chapter 5.

[19] Gordis, "An Appreciation," *Max Leopold Margolis*, 1.

[20] This work was published by Hebrew Union College in 1893.

rather into the heads of my pupils the picture הַחֹרֶשׁ. This tells the rule. Advantages of my system: It is short and practical. It does not encourage thoughtlessness and mechanical study. The pupil who has in his mind a certain typical form has not the rule in his possession unless he read it off the example; he thus is obliged to re-think the whole process. The experiment works splendidly in my classes. Of course it devolves a good deal of work upon my shoulders.[21]

In his preface to *An Elementary Text-Book* Margolis also commented upon the pedagogical value of his paradigmatic method for training students to discern underlying linguistic principles:

No rule can be applied, unless it be reproduced by the aid of the example . . . the student . . . will in each case have to retrace the whole process of observation by which he was first led to *understand* the example, to *discover* the rule . . . *Thoughtlessness is rendered impossible by the present method.*[22]

Margolis aimed to produce a practical work, but one which

may be at the same time safely lay claim to a scientific character. The results of modern comparative philology are embodied throughout the book. . . . Even the beginner must be made to understand that there is law and order in what appears to the uninitiated as a *chaos* of facts, a *lawless mass* which may be committed to memory and occasionally marveled at, but never understood.[23]

Or, as he wrote elsewhere,

My method is first to *visualise* their knowledge of Hebrew. Thus every new word, every new form must be presented to them 'weis auf schwarz' with chalk on the blackboard. As beginners, they must not hear but see Hebrew. Secondly, while I use certain textbooks, I follow the strictly scientific method. . . . While beginners must not be encumbered with exceptions, the principal rules they must know. Grammatical rules must be understood as necessary never as arbitrary.[24]

Margolis' remark on the "scientific" character of his work calls to mind the discipline of his own earlier education, the rigors of which he vowed to introduce at HUC: "The College lacks a scientific spirit. So far as I am

[21] Margolis to "my dear friend" (Dick), January 29, 1893 (Archives of the American Jewish Historical Society).

[22] Preface to *An Elementary Text-Book,* v.

[23] Preface to *An Elementary Text-Book,* vii.

[24] Margolis to Dick, September 19, 1892 (American Jewish Archives and Archives of the American Jewish Historical Society).

concerned it is going to get it. The boys must be trained to speak and think logically before they begin to preach."[25]

It took Margolis only a few weeks to acquaint his "boys" with the "scientific spirit" he desired to introduce into the College. At the same time, Margolis was mindful of other factors that enhanced learning within the fairly formal structure of the classroom:

> The boys like me. Proof: I wanted to give them last Friday an extra hour in grammar (in grammar, mind you), and they all said: Yes, Do give us another hour. . . . I endeavor to arouse interest in my pupils, as when I said the other day to a boy who said of a verbal suffix that it was a nominal one, that he is *phe-nomenal*, whereupon the class was in a roar of laughter. I am both strict and lenient at the same time. Although I have 18 boys in the lowest class, they are all manageable, and show great interest. I think I have succeeded in impressing them that I stand for something, and this something is thoroughness. In reading the Bible, every form is analyzed. At the same time, the higher sense is paid attention to, as e.g. in the Psalms.[26]

As the previous paragraphs suggest, Margolis was largely engaged in the training of rabbis at Cincinnati. In nineteenth century Europe, rabbis like Isaac Margolis had combined erudite scholarship with the duties of leading a congregation. In America, Margolis came to observe, such was not the case. For most rabbis, the responsibilities of communal leadership crowded out whatever time they might have devoted to pure scholarship. Margolis' interest in learning led him to view many rabbis and rabbinical students with suspicion, even hostility. This attitude had a significant, if unpleasant, effect on how he treated clerics in the class-room later in his career. At Dropsie, for example, where he began teaching in 1909, he sacrificed nothing of his characteristic thoroughness nor did he deviate from his avowed goal of promoting the "scientific spirit" among all his students. His genial and gentle humor, however, was prone to turn caustic and cruel on the many occasions when he sensed opposition to his pedagogical program from student/rabbis who lacked the requisite preparation and seriousness.[27]

Margolis remained at Hebrew Union College until 1897. His profes-sional interests during this period are visible in two articles he published on Semitic grammar and one on a "Haggadic" element in the Sep-tuagint[28]; this latter article is apparently the first explicit indication of Margolis' interest in Greek Biblical translations, a field that was to

---

[25] *Ibid.*

[26] *Ibid.*

[27] See the following chapter.

[28] Max L. Margolis, "Notes on Semitic Grammar. I: The First Vowel of the Imperfect Tense-Stem," *Hebraica* 10 (1893/94), 188–192; "Notes on Semitic Grammar. II: The Feminine Ending

become his chief scholarly preoccupation. It would be incomplete, however, to portray only the academic side of even so earnest a man as
Margolis. Although no full picture of his social life in Cincinnati emerges,
hints appear in a passing comment or two: "A nice little Kneipe . . .
where I am supplied with beer" and "There are a number of girls in the
professional families, who are more or less refined, educated, etc., who
do not answer however my ideal."[29]

Margolis left Cincinnati in 1897 to become assistant professor of Semitic Languages and Literature at the University of California in Berkeley.
He appears to have been attracted to the position by the far wider range
of course offerings and research opportunities possible at an institution
like Berkeley.[30] For the most part Margolis enjoyed the support of
Berkeley's president, Benjamin Ide Wheeler, under whom he offered
such courses as general introduction to the study of language, fundamental problems of linguistics, and elementary Coptic. He directed a thesis
on "The Hebraisms in the Grammar of Biblical Aramaic" and aided in the
direction of at least one other, on the morphology of the Hupa language.[31] After one year at Berkeley, Margolis became an associate professor, and in 1902 he was, in addition, named acting head of the
Department of Semitic Languages. In late spring 1905, Margolis told
Wheeler that he had received an offer for another position; so highly did
Wheeler esteem Margolis that the inducements he offered him to stay
included the (permanent) headship of the Semitics department, a full
professorship, and an immediate increase in salary.[32] Despite Wheeler's
best efforts, Margolis did not stay, but chose instead to return to Hebrew
Union College. His second term in Cincinnati was to be a stormy one.

In contrast, Margolis' years in California were relatively tranquil and
very productive, personally not less than professionally. In fact, an account of this period can appropriately begin with the former, for it was at
this time that Margolis finally met a "refined, educated" girl who apparently "answered" his "ideal." This woman was Evelyn Aronson, whose
mother Caroline Goldwater was a member of the family that later produced a famous Republican senator from Arizona. In the 1850s the
Goldwater and Aronson families (Mrs. Margolis' father was Philip Aronson) had both come to San Francisco from England. Each of the two

---

T in Hebrew," *AJSL* 12 (1895/96), 197–229; "Another Haggadic Element in the Septuagint,"
AJSL 12 (1895/96), 267.

[29] Margolis to Dick, September 19, 1892.

[30] Margolis had been at Berkeley only a few months when Wise attempted to lure him back to
Cincinnati. Negotions toward that end, however, proved unsuccessful on this occasion.

[31] Approximately two dozen letters to or from Margolis have been preserved in the University
Archives at Berkeley. The most informative ones were written in 1905 and relate to Margolis'
departure from this institution (see below).

[32] Benjamin Ide Wheeler to Margolis, May 23, 1905 (University Archives, Berkeley).

families established stores and other commercial enterprises; they both prospered and were prominent among the Jews who lived in the Bay Area. Evelyn Aronson received a B.A. degree in history and economics from Berkeley in 1900 and afterwards traveled extensively in Europe. She and Max Margolis became engaged in 1905. The European-born scholar, who was by then in his late 30s, was apparently won over by his future wife's combination of upbringing, achievement, and personality. Their marriage did not take place until June 1906. During the interval between engagement and marriage there occurred the great San Francisco earthquake and Margolis' first year back at HUC, itself something of a disaster.[33]

The work produced by Margolis during his years at Berkeley provides evidence of his growing stature as a scholar and of the direction his primary research would take over the next three decades. He continued to make contributions to Semitic grammar, most notably in his article on the plural of segholates.[34] Scattered Biblical passages attracted his attention; he was drawn in particular to some textual problems in Ecclesiasticus, a book for which he could have produced a masterful commentary.[35]

[33] In the preceding paragraph most of the details concerning Evelyn Aronson Margolis and her family are taken from a pamphlet produced for a celebration on the occasion of her 75th birthday: *Mrs. Max L. Margolis: A Biographical Appreciation on her Seventy-fifth Birthday* (Wednesday, January 21, 1953, Ritz Carlton Hotel, Philadelphia). Mrs. Margolis' apparent emphasis on the *English* background of her family is technically correct (her mother, definitely, and her father, apparently, were born in England), although—as both Nahum and Jonathan Sarna pointed out to me—the Goldwater clan as a whole hailed from the same small Polish town as the Sarna family. One of Caroline Goldwater's brothers, Baron, was the father of Senator Barry Goldwater, who is thus a first cousin of Evelyn's. In the summer of 1981 I wrote to Senator Goldwater concerning this family connection with Max Margolis. In his response (dated July 27, 1981), he wrote:

> Max Margolis was married to one of my first cousins, Evelyn, but to say that I knew him would be stretching the point. I can remember him, I remember seeing him once or twice in the summers when they visited the rest of the family on Long Island and once I remember being in their home in Philadelphis. . . . [Max Margolis] was a very highly respected man and those of us in the family have always been proud of his great contributions to the translation of the Bible and in this I believe he was a premier in the world. . . .

[34] Max L. Margolis, "The Plural of Segholates," *Proceedings of the American Philological Association* 35 (1904), liii–liv. An assessment of this article, which is almost as long as the article itself, is found in Ephraim A. Speiser, "The Contribution of Max Leopold Margolis to Semitic Linguistics," *Max Leopold Margolis: Scholar and Teacher* (Philadelphia: Dropsie, 1952), 29–30. Other articles from this period that deal with grammar and linguistics are "Dogmatic Influences in our Vocalization," *AJSL* 14 (1897/98), 208; "Accents in Hebrew," *Jewish Encyclopedia* vol. 1, 149–58; and "Notes on Semitic Grammar. III: An Abnormal Hebrew Form," *AJSL* 19 (1902/03), 45–48.

[35] Between 1901 and 1905 Margolis published four short articles on Ecclesiasticus, all of which appeared in *Zeitschrift für die alttestamentliche Wissenschaft*: "A Passage in Eccle-

In his short discussions of these passages Margolis affords a glimpse of his continuing interest in the Septuagint. That interest, full-blown, was rapidly becoming a dominant concern of Margolis', as can be seen in a series of programmatic studies written during these years and published in 1905 and 1906. These articles aimed at correcting and improving a basic reference tool for Septuagintal research, *A Concordance to the Septuagint* by Hatch and Redpath, which was then being published by Oxford.[36] Margolis encountered many difficulties in using this work; among his chief complaints—"equivalents for the Greek translations other than LXX are entirely lacking; and for the LXX, they are lacking for particles and for words like *einai*," there are "questionable and false identifications," Hebrew philology is not dealt with.[37]

In Margolis' opinion these deficiencies could not be remedied by anything other than a new edition of Hatch-Redpath, something he himself proposed in the 1905 article. In that publication, and in two subsequent ones, he provided samples of how material would appear in the revision he contemplated. He chose as his examples three Greek verbs: μενειν, χαιειν, λαμβανειν. His volume, as these listings show, would eliminate false identifications, indicate false Greek readings, make note of variants, list equivalents according to their relative frequency, include compound forms under the simple root word, make use of all the Greek evidence, cite pertinent bibliographical data, and conclude with a Hebrew-Aramaic index. A grand plan, indeed, fully justifying Orlinsky's judgment that Margolis was from the beginning

[the] sober textual critic: His very first published article in matters septuagintal indicated clearly that his Greek-Hebrew methodology was

---

siasticus," *ZAW* 21 (1901), 271–272; "Ecclus. 3, 25," *ZAW* 25 (1905), 199–200; "Ecclus. 6, 4," *ZAW* 25 (1905), 320–322; "Ecclus. 7, 6d," *ZAW* 25 (1905), 323. (For Ecclesiasticus, see also his lengthy review of J. H. A. Hart, *Ecclesiasticus. The Greek Text of Codex 248* [*JQR* n.s. 1 (1910/11), 403–418].) He also wrote on the books of Amos and Judges: "Notes on Some Passages in Amos," *AJSL* 17 (1900/01), 170–171; "Judg. 11, 37," *ZAW* 21 (1901), 272.

[36] Edwin Hatch and Henry A. Redpath, *A Concordance to the Septuagint and the Other Greek Versions of the Old Testament (Including the Apocryphal Books)* (Oxford: Clarendon Press). Margolis' articles are "Entwurf zu einer revidierten Ausgabe der hebräisch-aramäischen Äquivalente in der Oxforder Concordance to the Septuagint and the other Greek Versions of the Old Testament," *ZAW* 25 (1905), 311–319; " χαίειν (einschliesslich der Komposita und Derivata) und seine hebräisch-aramäischen Äquivalente im Gräzismus des A.T.," *ZAW* 26 (1906), 85–90; " ΛΑΜΒΑΝΕΙΝ (including Compounds and Derivatives) and its Hebrew-Aramaic Equivalents in Old Testament Greek," *AJSL* 22 (1906), 110–119. The first of these three articles, with Margolis' introductory remarks translated from German into English, appears as "Specimen Article for a Revised Edition of the Hebrew-Aramaic Equivalents in the Oxford Concordance to the Septuagint . . ." in Robert A. Kraft, editor, *Septuagint Lexicography*. Sepuagint and Cognate Studies 1 (Society of Biblical Literature, 1972), 52–64. Margolis' other two studies are reprinted on pp. 65–79.

[37] Margolis, "Entwurf," as translated in Kraft.

thoroughly sound; he had attained maturity in this erudite discipline before he dared rush into print.[38]

Sound and well-conceived, this project won the support of major American and European scholars. The record shows that Margolis was in no way exaggerating when he wrote to Mayer Sulzberger that "my proposed plan for a revision of the Hebrew-Aramaic equivalents in the Oxford Concordance to the Septuagint has elicited the praise of the most noted specialists in Europe and in this country."[39] This support and praise were not, however, sufficient to provide Margolis with the opportunity to realize fully his planned revision; fortunately, he continued to publish articles elaborating and illustrating his call for "complete induction" in identifying Greek elements with their Semitic equivalents.[40] Even with all of this, the thought cannot be suppressed that it would be extremely valuable to have in one's possession Margolis' own copy of Hatch-Redpath, into which he had introduced numerous corrections.

By at least the early part of 1905 Margolis had let it be known that he desired to return to Hebrew Union College, "the place where you won the hearts of the students as teacher and guide."[41] Acting on this information, the new president of HUC, Kaufmann Kohler, contacted Margolis in mid-March 1905.[42] Detailed negotiations led to a formal offer

---

[38] Harry M. Orlinsky, "Margolis' Work in the Septuagint," *Max Leopold Margolis: Scholar and Teacher*, (Philadelphis: Dropsie, 1952), 36. Kraft's assessment of Margolis' work in this area is also, on the whole, very favorable (Robert A. Kraft, *Septuagintal Lexicography*, 46–48). He speaks of discovering "methodological gems" in the work of Margolis and concludes that "Margolis has surely described the most fruitful path for researching the material."

[39] Max L. Margolis to Mayer Sulzberger, April 28, 1907 (American Jewish Archives). Among the specialists were Deissmann, Driver, Kautzsch, Nestle, and Strack. Marx (*Proceedings*, 373) records that in 1908 these and other scholars

> issued an appeal to raise a fund to enable Margolis, whom they state to be 'admirably qualified to execute the work,' to devote two years to its execution. After careful examination they enthusiastically endorsed the plan as to be 'of the utmost importance, both for the scientific study of the Old Testament and also for checking the unscientific and hazardous use often made of the Septuagint. It will be a work that can never be antiquated, but will simply be indispensable to every student of the Old Testament.'

Non-specialists like Benjamin Ide Wheeler also endorsed Margolis' plan (Wheeler, in a letter dated September 30, 1905 [University Archives, Berkeley]).

[40] On "complete induction," see chapter 4.

[41] This phrase is found in a letter from Kohler to Margolis, dated March 13, 1905 (American Jewish Archives). That Margolis had been "putting out feelers" is clear from the way in which Kohler began this letter: "I earnestly contemplate a change in our Professorial staff, and having learned . . . that you desire to return to the place where you won the hearts of the students as teacher and guide, I herewith put before you the following questions. . . ."

[42] The letter quoted in the previous fn. gives every indication of being Kohler's initial (formal) contact with Margolis on the question of employment.

of the professorship of Biblical Exegesis for Margolis. He accepted the offer. Even after this acceptance, Berkeley president Wheeler continued to press Margolis to remain, urging him to seek a release from his commitment to HUC. The situation at Berkeley was being made so attractive, Wheeler reasoned, that "I should be surprised if Margolis, after all this, went to Cincinnati. I think his position as a Professor in a large university is out of all comparison with the proposed position at Cincinnati."[43]

What led Margolis to leave the admittedly pleasant atmosphere of Berkeley, where he had come to enjoy the strongest possible support from the University administration and in addition would soon be joined by marriage with the leaders of the local Jewish community?[44] Margolis set forth his reasoning in this straightforward statement addressed to Kohler:

> Nothing but my love for Judaism on the one hand and the unbounded confidence in yourself and the gentlemen constituting the Board of

[43] This phrase is found in a letter from Wheeler to Dr. Jacob Voorsanger, who had been instrumental in efforts to retain Margolis at Berkeley. The Wheeler-to-Voorsanger letter, dated July 14, 1905, is quoted by Margolis in a lengthy communication from him to Charles S. Levi, who was serving in 1907 as president of the Hebrew Union College Alumni (see below on the circumstances that led Margolis to write to Levi). The July 14 letter, as well as two letters from Margolis to Wheeler (dated July 6 and July 21 and found in the Berkeley University Archives), makes it clear that Wheeler, Voorsanger, and others continued working up until the last moment to dissuade Margolis from leaving California.

[44] The answer to this question, as well as to almost every other question that arises from Margolis' two years at HUC (1905–1907), is to some extent controversial. As will be seen below, weighty issues and strong personalities combined in such a way that it is difficult to be certain about causes and motives even when detailed information on the "facts" is available. A good deal has been written about the activities of Margolis, Kohler, and others during these years. Among the most important secondary sources are the discussions found in Naomi Wiener Cohen, "The Reaction of Reform Judaism in America to Political Zionism," *Publications of the American Jewish Historical Society* 40 (1950/51), 361–394; Samuel S. Cohon, "The History of the Hebrew Union College," *Publications of the American Jewish Historical Society* 40 (1950/51), 17–55; Kenneth H. Kudisch, "And Then There Were None," unpublished paper submitted to Jacob R. Marcus, 1969 (American Jewish Archives); Michael A. Meyer, "A Centennial History," *Hebrew Union College-Jewish Institute of Religion at One Hundred Years*, ed. Samuel E. Karff (Cincinnati: Hebrew Union College Press, 1976), 1–284; David Polish, "The Changing and the Constant in the Reform Rabbinate," *American Jewish Archives* 35 (1983), 263–341. In addition, there are hundreds of pages of primary documentation—official records of Hebrew Union College, letters, and newspaper accounts—that relate to Margolis' experiences at Cincinnati. Most of these primary sources, which are particularly abundant for the year 1907, can be consulted at the American Jewish Archives.

Sometime in the future I would like to write a comprehensive article on the myriad of issues and personalities that make up "L'Affaire Margolis." In the present work I have largely limited myself to matters that relate to Margolis as a teacher and scholar of the Bible or that reveal how this period was to prove decisive for the future course of Margolis' academic and scholarly career.

Governors on the other, would induce me to abandon my present position in which I am so firmly rooted and which means to me so much in the future.[45]

Earlier, he had stated that he "would gladly and enthusiastically devote all the time at my disposal to the high task of training men for the Rabbinate imbued with the right *religious* spirit" and "give the College the best that is in me . . . in all that will concern the welfare of the institution and its efficiency as a nursery for learning the fount of Jewish knowledge."[46]

These optimistic sentiments on the part of Margolis would seem to cast serious doubt on Wheeler's credentials as a prophet, for the Berkeley president felt "tolerably certain that he [Margolis] would make a mistake in going [to Cincinnati]."[47] It was unfortunate, on all sides, that events over the next two years confirmed Wheeler's gloomy prognostication.

The source of Margolis' difficulties at Cincinnati has usually been traced to his strong advocacy of Zionism, in opposition to the strident anti-Zionist position taken by Kohler and others at HUC. There is considerable evidence to show that the Zionist controversy was indeed near, if not at, the center of a growing animosity between Margolis and the College's administration. Nevertheless, the bitterness expressed on both sides had multiple roots, several of which we explore in the following paragraphs.

In mid-January 1906, after only a few months back in Cincinnati, Margolis' assessment of the situation was bleak: "I regret to say that my enthusiasm has been considerably chilled by the touch of reality as embodied in a head whose fitness for the position he occupies may seriously be doubted."[48] One cause of this disenchantment was Margolis' sense that Kohler had misled him concerning the scope of his pedagogical responsibilities. While still in California, Margolis repeatedly sought from Kohler a definite statement on what areas of Biblical studies he would teach. Finally in late August 1905, after Margolis had committed himself to leave Berkeley for Cincinnati, Kohler informed him that he could "take charge of the Pentateuch both exegetically and critically, of the Hagiographa and the whole history of the Canon."[49] A

---

[45] Margolis to Kohler, June 5, 1905 (American Jewish Archives).

[46] Margolis to Kohler, April 1905 (American Jewish Archives). In the first quote, Margolis was echoing a phrase from a letter Kohler had previously sent him.

[47] Wheeler to Voorsanger (July 14, 1905). This letter was quoted as part of Margolis' communication to Charles S. Levi (see above and also below).

[48] Max L. Margolis to "my dear friend" (almost certainly Max Heller, an HUC alumnus and reform rabbi in New Orleans), January 14, 1906 (American Jewish Archives).

[49] This quotation, from a letter sent by Kohler to Margolis and dated August 30, 1905, is found in Margolis' communication to Charles S. Levi. This thirteen-page communication, which has already been referred to above, was prepared by Margolis in April 1907, when the situation at

month later, when he arrived at the College, Margolis was shocked to learn that Kohler interpreted this mandate so as to exclude Margolis from teaching the Prophets, which the president was intent upon entrusting to an individual with the rank of instructor. At that time Margolis "succeeded in obtaining full charge of the exegetical instruction in the Collegiate classes."[50]

This victory was only partial, however. Margolis felt that Kohler never provided for "the proper coordination of the Biblical work in the College."[51] Moreover, in the spring of 1907, when the situation had badly deteriorated, Kohler was ready to force Margolis "to relinquish instruction in the Pentateuch, in fact in the major part of the Bible, barring such a book as Ecclesiastes."[52] As can be seen from the 1906 letter quoted above, Margolis allocated the lion's share of blame to Kohler. In reflecting upon his early sparrings with this adversary, Margolis' feelings could not be clearer:

> Had the conditions [upon which Margolis was supposed to teach] been communicated to me in due time, I should never have left Berkeley. In keeping his intentions to himself until such time as I was powerless to reestablish connections with the University, I cannot help thinking that Dr. Kohler acted in bad faith and that he brought me to the College under false pretenses.[53]

Disagreements over academic matters did not stop with the question of what Margolis was to teach, for there was also a marked difference of opinion over how the Bible was to be taught. Robert Gordis has laid out the divergent views on this matter in a clear and very fair manner:

> Margolis was a leader of a minority of the faculty who felt it important to have the rabbinical students read in the original Biblical, Talmudic, or medieval texts, on the theory that however small the amount of material that the students might cover, they would gain a better understanding of Jewish literature by direct contact with the soruces. Dr. Kohler and

---

HUC had deteriorated to the point that Margolis felt compelled to submit a letter of resignation. As stated by Margolis at the beginning of his remarks to Levi, "at your request, I gladly submit to you the following considerations which led to my resignation." Margolis' letter to Levi soon became known to others, and—at the May meeting of the HUC Board of Governors that resulted in the final separation of Margolis from the Institution—Kohler offered a detailed, often impassioned point-by-point rebuttal of Margolis' charges. In introducing this material, I am not contending that Margolis was necessarily correct on each point, but that—correct or not—Margolis was expressing himself frankly on pedagogical and professional, as well as personal, issues that clearly mattered a great deal to him.

[50] Margolis to Levi (see above), April 8, 1907.
[51] *Ibid.*
[52] *Ibid.*
[53] *Ibid.*

> his supporters, on the other hand, doubtless motivated by practical considerations, favored survey courses on such themes as Biblical prophecy. . . .[54]

Although Margolis made no secret of how he intended to teach and had in fact written to Kohler that he "would deem it a privilege to introduce the *Seminar* method at the College," his pedagogical approach in the classroom was, from the Administration's point of view, another irritant in an already souring relationship.[55]

From Margolis' perspective the gravest challenge to his integrity probably involved the area of academic freedom *(Lehrfreiheit)*. Margolis felt that Kohler, before hiring him, was familiar with how he felt on issues such as Zionism and that it should be clear to both men that their disagreements would be hard, if not impossible, to reconcile. With this in mind, Margolis expressed his hope that "as an educated layman" he be permitted to continue his practice of stating, in appropriate contexts, "whatever views I may hold on the problems which agitate the Jewish mind."[56] In turn, Kohler offered firm assurances to Margolis: "I trust that you did not understand my remarks in regard to your theological views as differing from mine as if I would in any way restrain your frank expression of the same on any occasion."[57] Margolis, for his part, records occasions on which Kohler publicly criticized him when the opinion he expressed was at variance with his own, which Margolis interpreted as efforts at the sort of restraint Kohler had earlier disavowed.[58]

Kohler went further still in charging that Margolis used his classroom as a forum to promote a Zionist approach to the Bible. This charge, were it true, would have been an abuse of academic freedom especially in the context of HUC. Margolis emphatically denied Kohler's contention that "as a Zionist I could not be entrusted with the teaching of Biblical

---

[54] Gordis, "Appreciation," *Max Leopold Margolis: Scholar and Teacher,* 7f. Gordis' discussion of this period in Margolis' life (pp. 6–8, with extensive bibliography) is well worth consulting.

[55] The quotation cited in this sentence comes from a letter Margolis wrote outlining "in brief my conception of the character of the instruction in the three divisions of the College, the preparatory, the undergraduate and the graduate." This letter, written in mid-April 1905, was in response to Kohler's "invitation to give you my personal views and suggestions with reference to the subject which is now deservedly engrossing your attention, the building up of graduate work in your institution." (Both Kohler's letter to Margolis, dated April 12, 1905, and Margolis' response are found in the American Jewish Archives.)

The issue of "pedagogical approach" has received very little attention in discussions of Margolis' difficulties at HUC. It may be, however, that this issue, which directly addresses the type of education a seminary should provide, ought to be investigated more closely, both in terms of Kohler's sense of HUC's overall mission and in the context of early twentieth-century educational philosophy and practice.

[56] Margolis to Kohler, June 5, 1905, as quoted in letter to Levi (see above).

[57] Kohler to Margolis, June 11, 1905, as quoted by Margolis in his letter to Levi (see above).

[58] Margolis to Levi, April 8, 1907, 6ff.

Exegesis at the College."⁵⁹ Margolis' self-stated point of view was a Jewish one—in his opinion, at least, consistent with HUC's goals and in no sense partisan: "I maintain that at no time have I introduced the subjects of Zionism or Reform in my class instruction. I have uniformly resisted all attempts by students at drawing me into present-day controversies."⁶⁰ No administration, Zionist or anti-Zionist, would find in Margolis an ally in any attempt to insinuate modern ideologies into the academic study of the classic texts of Judaism:

> Were I to teach in a Zionist College, I should resent all dictation with a view to so teaching my subject as to lead up to Zionism. I should say, if you Zionists wish to know the Bible, you must study it as Bible, and not as a basis for Zionistic discourses or a Zionistic theology.⁶¹

Margolis did not shrink from comparing the current president of Hebrew Union College with his predecessor and the Institution's founder, Isaac Mayer Wise. On the issue of academic freedom, Wise's actions toward Margolis showed him to be the antithesis of Kohler:

> From my own experiences in the years 1892–97 [Margolis writes] I can testify that Dr. Wise never interfered with my arrangement of the curriculum or with my methods of teaching, the entire subject of Biblical Exegesis in the Collegiate classes being committed to my care in the academic year 1896/7, and that our relations were always extremely pleasant.⁶²

With Margolis and his few allies at odds with the HUC Administration on so many points and with both sides sincerely believing in the justness of their positions, it is difficult to imagine that, even under the best of circumstances, they could have arrived at mutually acceptable compromises. The strong personal note in many of Margolis' statements—he felt deceived; his integrity was attacked; Kohler was untrustworthy, disingenuous at best—reveals the considerable, if unmeasurable role played by the clash of personalities in drawing the protagonists in this drama even further apart.⁶³ In Margolis' assessment, personal considerations motivated many of his opponents; writing to Max Heller, a New Orleans rabbi, Margolis singled out several such individuals:

> My impression, however, is thatB[ernard] B[ettmann] is supporting K[ohler] out of sheer fear of [Emil] Hirsch's big stick. . . . I presume

⁵⁹ Margolis to Levi, April 8, 1907, 7.
⁶⁰ Margolis to Levi, April 8, 1907, 8.
⁶¹ Margolis to Levi, April 8, 1907, 9.
⁶² Margolis to Levi, April 8, 1907, 10f.
⁶³ We should, however, heed Gordis' warning not "to interpret the entire controversy in personal terms" ("Appreciation," 6).

you know what is at the bottom of it all. The stand the College is taking against Zionism is dictated by a man who unable to secure the Presidency for himself, is interested in keeping—*you* out of it.[64]

Of Hyman Enelow he writes, "His attack on me was marked by personalities, even the charge of lying being resorted to."[65] Margolis' assessments of personalities and motives may have been unduly harsh; this was sometimes the case on the other side as well.

This combination of personal and professional disagreements bitterly divided the College and also the alumnni and other organizations associated with it. The HUC campus came to resemble the battle-scarred "'ole west" town that wasn't big enough for both of its leading factions. In this case, it was either the Administration and its numerous allies or Margolis and his few supporters. Margolis lost; by late April 1907 he was writing to Mayer Sulzberger in Philadelphia about the possibility of joining the faculty at an institution that was then being founded in that city, the Dropsie College for Hebrew and Cognate Learning.[66] By the first week in May both HUC's Board and Margolis himself had moved toward a final, irreversible separation. While Margolis' long-term prospects were in doubt, he had made definite plans to put considerable distance between himself and this controversy in the near future—he would spend 1907–1908 traveling and researching in Europe.

Before departing, Margolis felt it necessary to combat what was for him a particularly painful legacy of this experience: the charge, from his point of view totally untrue, that he lacked "the power of cooperation with colleagues."[67] When Sulzberger acquainted him with this charge, Margolis spoke up firmly in his own defense:

> I can stand a rebuke when it is deserved, but I am free to say that the present rebuke is wholly undeserved. . . . The difficulties which culminated in my resignation as well as in that of two other members of the Faculty were all on the other side. . . . As to my relations with men in my own department . . . I am confident that my statement will be supported by all those who are familiar with the facts. . . . Both Professor Toy and Professor Moore have expressed their regret that only lack of funds makes it impossible for them to give me a place on the Semitic faculty at Harvard. . . . Their warm and sympathetic letters certainly betray no distrust of my power of cooperation with colleagues.

[64] Margolis to Heller, April 26, 1907 (American Jewish Archives).
[65] *Ibid.*
[66] Margolis to Sulzberger, April 28, 1907 (Dropsie College Archives, Philadelphia).
[67] In a May 3, 1907 letter to Margolis, Sulzberger had written: "Personally I should hope that to your undoubted qualifications for a professorial position you unite the power of cooperation with colleagues." It is this statement that Margolis was quoting in his May 10 response to Sulzberger (see below). (Both letters are found in the Dropsie College Archives).

It was a severe blow to me to realize that my position in the matter was so misunderstood by you.[68]

Unlike the characters in the shoot-outs of the "Wild West," the leading players at Cincinnati did not consistently don black or white hats; heroism and villainy have been variously assessed. The extended narrative of these events serves to demonstrate that Margolis, whether consistently right or not, could be a strong-willed, determined advocate of what he strongly believed in and that he could effectively draw from an extensive arsenal of rhetorical weapons to defend his causes. If, up until this time, he was little known outside of academic circles, that was not to be the case in the future. In the years that followed he apparently sought, even though he never fully achieved, a prominent place in the councils of Jewish leadership. He was to produce a steady stream of articles, as well as public presentations, in which he commented on contemporary affairs. These forays outside of the ivory tower are of a somewhat more ephemeral character than his scholarly work, but they adhere to the same exacting standards and vigorous argumentation.[69]

It was in the midst of these crises that Margolis went back to California to marry Evelyn Aronson.[70] The situation that this newlywed couple

[68] Margolis to Sulzberger, May 10, 1907 (see above).

[69] A survey of Margolis' efforts is this area is found in Joshua Bloch, "Max L. Margolis' Contribution to the History and Philosophy of Judaism," *Max Leopold Margolis; Scholar and Teacher* (Philadelphia: Dropsie College, 1952), 45–59. In the obituary he wrote for *The Jewish Exponent*, David Galter dealt very frankly with Margolis' limited success in achieving a leadership role within the American Jewish community at large:

> A profound student, [Margolis'] mind was carefully attuned to the general needs of the American Jewish community. Not only did he understand these needs: he was also conversant with the numerous obstacles on the road to achievement—the men, the motives, where the currents crossed, where individuals clashed, the pros and cons. He was willing to become a part of this maelstrom. He had the equipment— background, perspective, a sympathetic understanding, a facile pen, which he put to splendid use in the interpretation of Jewish life—everything except a persuasive voice. Somehow, however, he did not achieve in the communal world that distinction, that place of pre-eminence which was his in the realm of Jewish scholarship. Margolis was able to serve both masters, he could have graced both tables, but somehow, for reasons difficult of explanation, he just didn't.
>
> At times this annoyed him, for he felt that to live a full Jewish life one should serve his people in every way. Learning was part of Jewish life, but learning without serving was incomplete.
>
> Occasionally he unburdened himself. There was irony in his remarks. One detected chagrin, at times even an element of hurt. He could not flatter. Sweet words of nothing were not at his command. The gallery did not fascinate him; at no time did he make the slightest attempt to play to it. Pretense was foreign to him. Always he spoke his mind. With the result that even those who should have known better not infrequently overlooked him.

[70] Max Margolis and Evelyn Aronson were married in June 1906. For details see Mrs. Max L. Margolis, *Biographical Appreciation,* 12.

faced in Cincinnati could hardly be termed ideal. At least they were able
to face it together; their relationship may even have become closer
through the sharing of burdens. As Mrs. Margolis recalls, some fifty
years later, other relationships were shattered by the events of these
years:

> Nothing—nothing today in American Jewish circles has ever equalled
> the animus that developed after this action. Lifelong friendships were
> completely, irreparably dissolved. The atmosphere was bitter.[71]

Remarkably, Kohler and Margolis were able to reestablish a working
relationship several years later. His contributing to the Kohler Festschrift,[72] a clear sign that hostilities had at least somewhat abated, was
probably far from Margolis' mind when he wrote wearily of the relocation
necessitated by his impending departure from HUC:

> We are just now breaking up house. We had a three years' lease on the
> house, and we had to dispose of it in view of the uncertainty of this
> situation, at a sacrifice of course. We shall go boarding for the rest of the
> term.[73]

It is not possible to gauge precisely the effect these controversies had
on Margolis' scholarly productivity; it is possible to point to at least two
lengthy studies, on very different topics, that he produced during these
years. He refers to both in a letter to Mayer Sulzberger:

> Professor Marti has just notified me that my first instalment of 'Studies
> in Biblical Greek' (covering seventy type-written pages) will be pub-
> lished in one of the forthcoming numbers of Stade's Zeitschrift to the
> editorship of which the Bern scholar has just succeeded. . . . My aim is
> to carry on research along those lines both in the immediate future and
> later on, and at the same time to contribute to the Bible Commentary in
> English planned by the Jewish Publication Society after the pattern of
> the Micah volume recently handed in by me.[74]

As to the first of these projects, published as "Studien im griechischen
alten Testament,"[75] Harry M. Orlinsky has judged this "an unsurpassed

[71] Mrs. Max L. Margolis, *Biographical Appreciation*, 13.
[72] Max L. Margolis, " των ενδοξων   Josh. 4, 4," *Studies in Jewish Literature, issued
in honor of Professor Kaufmann Kohler, Ph.D.* (Berlin: Georg Reimer, 1913), 204–209. Even
before 1913 Margolis had begun working with Kohler on the Jewish Publication Society's Bible
translation (see chapter 3).
[73] Margolis to Heller, April 26, 1907 (American Jewish Archives).
[74] Margolis to Sulzberger, April 28, 1907 (Dropsie College Archives).
[75] ZAW 27 (1907), 212–270.

study of various aspects of the Septuagint."[76] This article forms the crowning jewel in Margolis' early published efforts at shaping a revised edition of Hatch-Redpath; like the three earlier and briefer articles, it contains numerous "methodological gems" waiting to be rediscovered.[77]

Margolis' *Micah (The Holy Scriptures with Commentary)*, the only commentary he published in English, appeared in 1908 as "the first of a proposed series of Commentaries on the Books of Holy Scriptures which the Jewish Publication Society of America [J.P.S.] has undertaken to prepare."[78] In format, "the book opens with a concise historical-critical introduction and closes with additional notes dealing with special problems." On each page the Biblical "text in English is given above, and a brief factual commentary follows below."[79]

The J.P.S. series was "intended primarily for the teacher, the inquiring pupil, and the general reader, who need help to obtain an understanding of the Scriptures, at once reliable and Jewish."[80] In the judgment of Frank Zimmermann, Margolis' volume met and exceeded these goals:

> The resultant commentary [by Margolis] accomplished what it set out to do in an admirable fashion: for the Jewish reader, it made use of Jewish tradition for exposition. . . . It is remarkable, too, how extensively the comments of the medieval exegetes anticipate modern interpretations: Margolis will whimsically bracket the name of Rashi or Ibn Janah with Wellhausen. At the same time, the modern methodology of comparing the ancient Versions and of utilizing the labors of modern exegetes are

[76] Orlinsky, "Margolis' Work in the Septuagint," *Max Leopold Margolis: Scholar and Teacher*, 36.

[77] See above the remarks of Robert A. Kraft, *Septuagintal Lexicography*, 46–48.

[78] This quotation is taken from the Advertisement to the Series that appears at the beginning of Margolis' commentary on Micah. Gordis ("Appreciation," *Max Leopold Margolis: Scholar and Teacher*, 12) points out that Margolis also wrote brief Hebrew commentaries on the books of Zephaniah and Malachi. In his bibliography of Margolis' works, Joseph Reider ("Bibliography of the Works of Max L. Margolis," *Max Leopold Margolis: Scholar and Teacher* [Philadelphia: Dropsie College, 1952], 76) states that

> these commentaries, written in Hebrew, are rationalistic and factual, strictly grammatical and versional, though based chiefly on Jewish sources and tradition. The exegesis is straightforward, and there is no recoiling from *non possumus*. The standpoint taken is that there is nothing esoteric or supernatural in the Bible and some passages are difficult only because for some reason or another we have lost the proper key to their understanding.

In Harry M. Orlinsky's office I found typescripts of commentaries that Margolis had prepared for all or parts of the books of Isaiah, Amos, Job, and Jeremiah. It is not clear whether Margolis intended any of this material, which I suspect he used in the classroom, for publication.

[79] This description is found in Reider, "Bibliography of the Works of Max L. Margolis," 67 (see above).

[80] Advertisement to the Series (see above).

systematically resorted to; never is a question brought up by the critical school by-passed or slurred over; the reader has the feeling that Margolis honors his intelligence by logic and documentation. It would appear that Margolis tried to do this work at his level best as if occupying a sacred office in interpretating a prophet who spoke in the name of the Holy One. More. With all the unpretentious objective, it is astonishing how much the book instructs the specialist and contrasts surprisingly with works that purport to be written for the technical student. . . .[81]

---

[81] Zimmermann, "The Contributions of M. L. Margolis to the Fields of Bible and Rabbinics," *Max Leopold Margolis: Scholar and Teacher*, 20f. See chapter 5 for further discussion of this commentary.

2. THE PHILADELPHIA YEARS (1907–1932)

In the spring of 1907, Margolis had written to Sulzberger that "I have made up my mind to spend the coming academic year [1907–1908] in a European University town for study and productive research. Our savings which would not carry us very far in this country may last that long abroad."[1] The Margolis' itinerary in Europe is not known in detail, although Mrs. Margolis mentions their attending a Zionist Congress at the Hague and their spending several months in Berlin.[2] Early in their journey, in July 1907, Margolis wrote that "I have spent a delightful few days in Hamburg and several weeks here in Halle. . . . I leave in a few days for travel in Belgium and Holland. Then for the Hague where we are due August 13."[3]

The yearlong stay in Europe afforded Margolis the opportunity to do firsthand research on material unavailable in America. One of his most important works, *A Manual of the Aramaic Language of the Babylonian Talmud. Grammar, Chrestomathy and Glossaries*,[4] is the direct result of his availing himself of just such research opportunities. In the preface to that work Margolis stressed the importance of working with original texts, a procedure he had found impossible to follow in America:

> As far back as 1894, Professor Hermann L. Strack of the University of Berlin, who had favorably noticed my first two publications, both dealing with the textual criticism of the Talmud, suggested to me the writing of a work to all intents and purposes similar to the present one. . . . I actually commenced work. . . . Soon, however, I realized that with the means at my disposal [in America] it was impossible for me to arrive at a satisfactory form of the text. . . .[5] While in the autumn of 1907 I visited

[1] Max L. Margolis to Mayer Sulzberger, April 28, 1907 (Dropsie College Archives).

[2] Mrs. Max L. Margolis, *Biographical Appreciation*, 13.

[3] Max L. Margolis to Max Heller, July 24, 1907 (American Jewish Archives). For further details concerning the year in Europe, see "Dr. Max L. Margolis' Work in Europe," *The American Hebrew* 83 (August 21, 1908), 376. Margolis himself wrote this article.

[4] Munich: Beck, 1910.

[5] Alexander Marx (*Proceedings*, 371), notes that early in his career Margolis

> conceived the ambitious plan of a critical edition of the Talmud 'based [in Margolis' words] not only on the direct evidence of the MSS. but also on secondary sources as the gaonic responsa, Nissim, Hananel, Alfasi, the Aruk, Rashi, and so on.' However, [Margolis] goes on, 'Not only did America prove the wrong place for such an undertaking, but the circumstances were not lacking to lead me away from my proposed plan into entirely different work.'

Germany, Prof. Strack urged me to let go for a while my Septuagint
studies and to resume that long neglected piece of Talmudic work. . . .
I once more realized that unless I secured manuscript evidence at first
hand, my texts as well as the grammar that I had constructed from them
would be unreliable. I therefore proceeded to Munich, where . . . I was
privileged to collate [a number of manuscripts and early printed editions, many of which were sent there from elsewhere].[6]

As a contemporary reviewer noted, the laborious task of collation to
which Margolis committed himself gave to the reader of this volume the
feeling that "he is everywhere treading upon the safe ground of manuscript tradition and of a rich collection of material resulting from an
independent study of the Talmudic texts."[7] When constructing his para-
digms, through which "the author has been successful in realizing the
greatest measure of completeness within the smallest possible compass,"
Margolis chose to incorporate "solely such forms of the most varied origin
as actually occur."[8] All examples "were [in Margolis' own words] marked
by that certainty which comes only from a personal perusal of the
sources."[9]

In Margolis' hands, then, "the paradigm loses its artificial character
and serves in itself as a direct introduction to the living linguistic material
deposited in the texts of the Babylonian Talmud."[10] Margolis never tired
of insisting that scholars rid themselves of the habit of relying on readings
and related data gathered by others. This insistence on going to the
sources themselves is a hallmark of Margolis' scholarship in Biblical as
well as Talmudic studies. It is also an essential component of the legacy
he passed on to his own students. In his work, and in the best of theirs,
the benefits that accrued from this approach are as visible to the careful
reader of today as they were to the reviewer over 70 years ago.

The reviewer cited above found that

a further scientific merit attaches to the manner in which the author
conceived his function as a grammarian in that within the Aramaic texts
of the Babylonian Talmud, he sedulously distinguishes those portions
which exhibit remnants of an *earlier* form of the language from those in
which the common Aramaic vernacular of Babylonian Jewry manifests
itself.[11]

---

[6] *Manual*, "Preface," VIIf.
[7] W. Bacher, "Margolis' 'Manual of Talmudic Aramaic,'" *JQR* n.s. 1 (1910/11), 266.
[8] Bacher, "Margolis'," 267 (see preceding fn.).
[9] *Manual*, "Preface," VIII.
[10] Bacher, "Margolis'," 267 (see above).
[11] Bacher, "Margolis'," 267f (see above).

E. A. Speiser likewise observed approvingly that "the several linguistic strata embodied in Talmudic Aramaic received methodological attention in Margolis' judicious presentation."[12] Speiser's overall judgment of Margolis' *Manual,* including its chrestomathy and glossary, is similarly positive:

> The upshot is that this effort in a virtually virgin area stands up better today [Speiser's remarks were published in 1952] than many a similar work in a field that has been under constant cultivation for centuries.[13]

While it is clear that Margolis accepted Strack's invitation to resume his "long neglected piece of Talmudic work," it is also certain that he did not entirely "let go" of his Septuagint studies. Margolis wrote a large number of significant articles on the Septuagint in the years immediately following his return to America;[14] that extraordinary productivity (he was at the same time engaged in Bible translation and also teaching) was at least partially the result of research conducted in Europe. In addition to conducting academic research, Margolis was also researching academic conduct:

> Whatever my future vocation will be in America, I am gathering useful information and am gaining an insight into academic life such as at a younger time of my life I should not have been able to obtain. I am comparing conditions in both countries [he was then in Germany] and I am glad to be able to state I am full of hope for our own country which is developing her own educational institutions along her own ways, and sanely. There is much to admire here, but it will not do blindly to copy.[15]

Margolis would soon have the chance to put into practice some of the "insight into academic life" he was gaining; in less than two years he was to be appointed to a senior position on the faculty of a new educational institution in Philadelphia.

It was to a Jewish leader in Philadelphia, Mayer Sulzberger, that Margolis had written when it became clear that he would have to leave Cincinnati and seek employment elsewhere. Margolis was then writing to Sulzberger in the latter's role as president of the board of Dropsie College, named for Moses Aaron Dropsie, whose bequest made possible the establishment of this center for Hebrew and cognate learning.

---

[12] Ephraim A. Speiser, "The Contribution of Max Leopold Margolis to Semitic Linguistics," *Max Leopold Margolis: Scholar and Teacher,* 32.

[13] *Ibid.* Speiser cites as "another important contribution to Aramaic linguistics" Margolis' article entitled "The Elephantine Documents," *JQR* n.s. 2 (1911/12), 419–443.

[14] See chapter 4.

[15] Margolis to Heller, July 24, 1907 (American Jewish Archives).

Max and Evelyn Margolis did indeed move to Philadelphia upon their
return from Europe, but this decision was not connected with Dropsie
College. It was, however, connected with Sulzberger, who among other
posts chaired the Publication Committee of the Jewish Publication Society (J.P.S.), which had its headquarters in Philadelphia. Margolis had
already produced a commentary on Micah for J.P.S.; with this and other
accomplishments in mind, Sulzberger and his associates turned to Margolis as the best qualified individual to serve as editor-in-chief of the new
English translation of the Hebrew Bible that J.P.S. was undertaking.
While still in Europe, Margolis had been contacted on this matter; he
wrote to Cyrus Adler, who was to serve as chairman of the Board of
Editors, that

> your kind favor [letter] of April 27 . . ., containing as it does the
> promise of hearty support, more than anything else facilitated my
> determination to waive other plans which had been maturing thanks to
> the efforts of Continental and English friends so as to undertake the
> work suggested by the Jewish Publication Society.[16]

In that same letter to Adler, dated August 7, 1908, and written from
Far Rockaway, New York, Margolis mentions the family's move to Philadelphia in a matter-of-fact manner: "Upon the advice of Judge Sulzberger, I expect to settle before the end of this month in Philadelphia."
Mrs. Margolis' recollection of how Sulzberger imparted this bit of advice
is anything but matter-of-fact:

> Dr. Margolis was invited to become editor-in-chief of the [J.P.S.] pro-
> ject, and in July, 1908, the couple returned to this country. At first, they
> were a little uncertain about where they wanted to live, and in one of
> his interviews with Judge Mayer Sulzberger, chairman of the Society's
> publication committee, the new editor-in-chief casually inquired, 'Does
> it make any difference where we live?' At this point Judge Sulzberger
> pointedly declared, 'I don't care. You may live in Timbuctoo, but the
> Jewish Publication Society is in *Philadelphia!*' From this emphatic
> reply, Mrs. Margolis says, laughing, 'We just assumed that we were
> expected to live in Philadelphia.'[17]

---

[16]Max L. Margolis to Cyrus Adler, August 7, 1908 (Archives of the American Jewish
Historical Society). In his *American Hebrew* article (published on August 21, 1908) cited above,
Margolis wrote that

> Some of my friends in Germany and England urged me to remain abroad and to
> continue my work on the Septuagint. . . . Some very tangible plans had been made
> for the continuation of my work on the Greek Bible, when a tempting offer reached
> me from America, and I decided, for the time being, to postpone that work.

[17]Mrs. Max L. Margolis, *Biographical Appreciation*, 13f.

Margolis' work as editor-in-chief of the J.P.S. Bible translation and secretary of its Board of Editors, a task that was to occupy him for a period of months full time and for a period of years part time, is among his most important and best-known achievements. As such, it forms the subject of chapter three of this book. It is sufficient at this point to note that when Margolis began the J.P.S. project, he did not anticipate that it would lead to permanent employment in the Philadelphia area: "It behooves me to let you know of my present abode, a temporary one, it is true," he writes to a friend in late September 1908. "My days of wandering," he continues, "are by no means over, nor do I see anything ahead of my present position which of course terminates with the work."[18]

Margolis' appraisal was in this case faulty. Within a matter of only a few months he and Cyrus Adler, who had been selected as the first president of Dropsie College, were in the midst of negotiations that would lead to Margolis' appointment to the professorship of Biblical Philology.

Margolis' credentials as an academician and scholar were impressive even before he came to Philadelphia. Added to these were his involvement (albeit sometimes controversial) in contemporary Jewish affairs, his pivotal role in shaping the J.P.S. Bible translation, and his working relationship with influential men such as Sulzberger and Adler.[19] Early on Adler made it clear to Margolis that, from his perspective as the Institution's president, the position he invited Margolis to occupy was a comprehensive one, of the utmost importance for Dropsie:

> I explained to you that it was part of the plan to have a Department devoted to Biblical study. That by this I meant a Department in which the language or rather languages in which the Bible was written should be the primary subject; that whilst Biblical Hebrew being the principal language should have the greatest share of attention devoted to it, there must also be considered the Biblical Aramaic, the old Aramaic versions and the old Greek versions. . . . It was further the idea to include in this Department, the study of the Jewish and Modern Commentaries, Biblical Archaeology, Geography of Palestine, in fact everything that would aid in a thorough understanding of the language, history and condition of the people of Israel during the period in which the Bible was created. . . . I told you that I had, after careful consideration, concluded that you could most worthily fill the position of Professor of this Department, and that I further felt that in an institution of the kind we are about to organize, devoted to post-graduate work and connected with organized research, your general aid would be most valuable. I also told you, and desire especially to repeat this, that it would give me

---

[18] Margolis to Heller, September 21, 1908 (American Jewish Archives).

[19] In his August 7, 1908 letter to Adler, Margolis made reference to their "combined efforts in a previous piece of Biblical work. . . ."

personal satisfaction and pleasure to have you as my colleague, both because I am convinced you know how to work cooperatively, and because of your previous experience, both as a University Professor and in the scholarly world.[20]

In his reply, dated January 17, 1909, Margolis recorded his assent to Adler's general framework and to the role Dropsie's leader envisioned for him:

[After you outlined] in particular your conception of the scope of the Department of Biblical Languages and Literature . . . I said that the manner, candid and friendly, in which you approached me was no less pleasing than the fact itself; that I considered it an honor that my scholarly attainments and my cooperativeness had been found worthy of your confidence, and a distinction that I should be entrusted with the Chair above mentioned, so as to become, to use your own language, your first colleague; that the work appealed to me, especially as it was to be conducted along the lines of post-graduate instruction and research; that both my wife and myself were pleased with the city of Philadelphia and were content to take up there our permanent abode.[21]

On March 28, 1909, Dropsie's Board of Governors, in a unanimous vote, formally elected Margolis a professor. Margolis immediately accepted.[22]

For better or worse, Margolis was to remain on the Dropsie faculty from 1909 until his death in 1932. On the positive side, Robert Gordis could tally up many features that made Dropsie an attractive milieu for Margolis' "talents and interests—a small college dedicated to research and advanced teaching, a limited teaching-schedule allowing time for original research, and a student body containing promising young men, among whom he found enthusiastic disciples."[23] In like manner, Dropsie president Abraham A. Neuman placed emphasis on the advantages his Institution had offered to Margolis:

It was in the Dropsie College that Margolis found ideological peace and freedom of the spirit . . . the Dropsie College, founded in the spirit of academic freedom, was a haven of peace to the agitated soul of the exiled scholar. Here he came in contact with students who met his own high standards. Teaching was no longer a grind but a challenge. The

[20] Adler to Margolis, January 3, 1909 (Dropsie College Archives).

[21] Margolis to Adler, January 17, 1909 (Dropsie College Archives).

[22] Adler's letter, informing Margolis of the decision by the Board of Governors, is dated March 29, 1909. Margolis' acceptance ("with pleasure") was written on March 30. (Both letters are in the Dropsie College Archives.)

[23] Gordis, "Appreciation," *Max Leopold Margolis: Scholar and Teacher*, 10.

courses announced by him in the College Register were basic outlines
and creative works of scholarship.[24]

In addition to these attractions, a full appraisal of Margolis' long career
at Dropsie must also include mention of factors that frustrated him and
limited the scope of his activity. Personal and institutional considerations
mixed to produce these negative features, which may have weighed more
heavily on Margolis in his later years. In any event, the following por-
trayal of Margolis' views, drawn from personal reminiscences of his
former students, represents their master's thinking as they perceived it
in the late 1920s and early '30s.[25] Although Margolis was on the whole
happy in his work, he is portrayed as being frustrated, hemmed in,
straining at the leash. In part, it is felt, this was a result of Dropsie's small
size and limited student body, most of whom weren't interested in
pursuing Margolis' "ideal goals." Among this group were rabbis, for
whom Margolis frequently expressed great disdain. The opinion was
expressed that Margolis would have been much better appreciated at a
school like Harvard or Berkeley (had he remained there). At a great
university every student in the natural sciences would have had the
marvelous opportunity of learning the scientific method from him.

A considerable portion of Margolis' unhappiness stems, it is stated,
from his relationship with Cyrus Adler. At best, their relationship is
described as formal, without any warmth between them. They were of
entirely different temperaments, poles apart in their personalities. Adler
had, on the one hand, tremendous regard for Margolis as a scholar; on
the other, he adopted a sort of standoffish attitude toward him. An
overpowering personality, Adler is portrayed as discouraging his faculty
from seeking public exposure and, in the case of Margolis, as failing to
provide him appropriate support for some of his endeavors. In their
respective attitudes toward each other it is possible to discern a rivalry of
sorts: to Margolis, Adler was the widely influential Jewish leader he
could never become; for Adler, Margolis was the full-time scholar and
researcher that his many other duties kept him from being.

It is clear that, in spite of their differences (which apparently extended
to a rivalry between their wives), they managed to establish a correct, if
not cordial modus vivendi professionally and personally. There was never
the open animosity that characterized the far shorter and stormier period
when Kaufmann Kohler and Margolis had attempted to work together as
president and professor. Cyrus Gordon recounts an incident that cap-
tures well the essence of the Adler-Margolis relationship as it was played

---

[24] Abraham A. Neuman, "Foreward," *Max Leopold Margolis: Scholar and Teacher*, x.
[25] These "personal reminiscences" were shared with the author in a series of oral interviews.

out in everyday events: once Margolis told a new student to go to hell. The student, offended, went to Adler to object. After Adler, in Margolis' phrase "the boss," told him not to continue doing that, Margolis said to Gordon: Don't you think it simply adds to the informality of my class? There was, so Gordon recalls, always the spectre of "the boss."[26]

It is from Margolis' former students, in addition, that we arrive at a full picture of what their mentor was like in the classroom. Remarkably clear images of their teacher remain in the minds of these gentlemen, who frequently recollected vivid details more than half a century after they last sat in the classroom as Margolis' students. It seems, therefore, appropriate to allow each of these individuals to describe in some detail his own experiences with Margolis as a classroom teacher. To do so leads to a certain amount of repetition; to do otherwise, however, runs the greater risk of omitting a possibly significant part of the picture.

Simon Greenberg was the student speaker at the Memorial Meeting that followed Margolis' death in the spring of 1932. In words appropriate to this event, he lovingly recalled his teacher:

> To my mind, Professor Margolis possessed practically all the qualities of a great teacher, especially in graduate school. He was, in the first place, anxious to teach. I never knew him to be late at class nor to leave early. He literally overflowed with knowledge and nothing gave him greater delight than to impart it. . . . One felt that the greatest joy one could give Professor Margolis was to show that you actually followed and understood the particular point he was trying to make. Even at the risk of being considered childish, I would like tonight to recall that full, warm, happy smile of satisfaction that would light up his face when it would seem to him that he had succeeded in getting even me to understand some of the more baffling and intricate phases of Hebrew grammar, a subject of which he was so supreme a master.
>
> One felt that he always prepared himself anew for every hour. He could not tolerate confusion in thought or expression. And I believe he never came into the classroom without having a clear idea of what it was he wanted to teach and how he was going to teach it.
>
> But one must not get the impression that Professor Margolis had a paternalistic attitude towards his students. He did not 'baby' them. Quite the contrary. A new student sitting in his room for the first time would probably get the notion that he had before him a teacher who was hard, aloof and unsympathetic . . . . There were some traits for which [Margolis] had no patience. A new student possessing any such undesirable trait would soon learn the Professor's attitude towards it, and in no uncertain terms, nor in faltering tones. He had no time for the 'know-it-all,' the 'smart,' and the superficial or lazy student. Nor could any man long remain in his class without either losing or suppressing those traits. And when he did, then there was no teacher to respect and

love more readily than Margolis. And the Professor . . . would bring such a student close to him and made him his eternal friend. For the serious, devoted and conscientious student, for the one who had gone through the fire of the first test and had come out chastened and purified, for such a student there was nothing within his power that our beloved teacher would not do.

His classroom added immeasurably to one's factual knowledge. But surpassing that in importance was the training in scientific method of research that any one of his courses afforded. Professor Margolis was not the lecturer type of teacher primarily. He did not desire to be an oracle pouring forth wisdom upon the heads of the young. His chief aim was to take us to those sources from which he himself had drunk so deeply. And what a delight it was to sit in his room in this College, surrounded by his remarkable collection of works in all languages on the Bible and Hebrew grammar and as the discussion progressed to bring one volume after another out of the shelves and pile them high on the table until the meaning of a doubtful word or phrase was finally established or until we felt that we had gathered at least as much information about the subject at hand as our knowledge at the present time or as the sources at our disposal make available. One of his great aims as a teacher was to train us never to use a secondary source for our information if the original source was at all within our reach, and never to tire searching for all the information available on any particular point. Dependence upon secondary sources and resting satisfied with a study of only a part of the available material was literally repugnant to him. He was indefatigable in following this rule in his own work and never lost an opportunity to inculcate that habit of mind and of work in his students.

But it was not merely book-knowledge, wide and deep as it was, that we got from him. Margolis possessed sterling qualities of character that influenced profoundly those who came to know him. . . . He reverenced the Bible as the word of God. . . . And he loved Israel. He was attached to his people by ties of profoundest affection; and though he taught us to try to be exact and honest and scientific in our studies, and beautifully exemplified these qualities in all of his own researches, he was not himself and he did not want his pupils and their studies to be dissociated from the living concerns of his people. Though he was steeped in the study of ancient texts his ultimate concern was to bring glory to his God and his people in the present.

And, finally, he loved his pupils, sought their friendship and companionship and gave them freely of his inexhaustible wealth of knowledge and experence. We went to him not merely with our problems in research. Many of us brought our intimate personal problems to him and he never knew to what an extent and in what a variety of ways he influenced our lives.[27]

[27] Simon Greenberg, "Talk Delivered at Professor Max Leopold Margolis Memorial Meeting." Monday evening, May 9, 1932, at Dropsie College. The remarks quoted above are from pp. 2–6 of a typescript of this address found in the Dropsie College Archives.

Louis L. Kaplan, like Simon Greenberg, spent the year 1924–1925 with Margolis in Palestine (see below). Upon arriving at Dropsie, Kaplan recalled, he quickly became friendly with Margolis. Kaplan was "somewhat shocked" at the method Margolis used in speaking to students, some of whom were rabbis: "He had nothing but contempt for rabbis and begged them to stay out of his classes if possible. If they insisted on writing theses under him, Margolis would volunteer to write it for them if they'd stay home and not bother him." When Kaplan told Margolis that he was shocked by his teacher's rather rough manner of dealing with rabbis, Margolis told Kaplan not to worry: "You need only worry when I don't talk to those people like that, when I don't tell them to go to hell!"

Kaplan recalls that

> Margolis' whole library was in his office and that was where his classes met. In the course of an hour's lesson in, e.g., Bible, probably 60 books would be brought down from their shelves. This was an extremely interesting, stimulating thing. He wanted to teach students method; he wasn't interested in covering ground. He was content with covering 6–8 chapters of a Biblical book during a semester. He was analyzing the versions and teaching students how to use versions, etc. In grammar he had his own unique way: he organized and prepared a table to show, not paradigms like Gesenius, but, e.g., vowel changes. He was very much interested in morphology.[28]

Cyrus Gordon was 18 years old when he began studying with Margolis. The master was "such an inspiring teacher, such a phenomenon that I was hooked on him," Gordon recalls. For four years Gordon took every course Margolis offered, and this while pursuing a Ph.D. degree at the University of Pennsylvania.[29] In his book, *Forgotten Scripts,* Gordon painted a memorable portrait of Margolis, portions of which follow:

> My most effective teacher was a martinet—Max Margolis. He was a thorough craftsman and a master of his subject. He was a biblical philologian, working on the Septuagint. His knowledge of the Old Testament was phenomenal. He expected all his students to recognize any oral quotation from Scripture and identify it by book and chapter. If he fired a three- or four-word Hebrew quotation at a student and the student failed to identify it, he promptly told the student, 'Go to hell!' and went around the room telling each student that failed to recognize the source the same thing, sometimes varying it with 'There is room for you, too.'
>
> After being reviled before the class a number of times for not spotting his Hebrew citations, I asked him how I might improve my familiarity

---

[28] Louis L. Kaplan to Leonard J. Greenspoon. Oral interview.
[29] Cyrus H. Gordon to Leonard J. Greenspoon. Oral interview.

with the Hebrew text. He told me to read as much of the Hebrew Bible as I could make time for each day, starting with Genesis 1:1 and reading straight through to the end of the Old Testament. I did this and noticed how many more citations I was progressively able to locate in class.

When I finished the final chapter of Chronicles, I reported to Professor Margolis to tell him the good news. He replied with a faint smile, 'Now begin over again.' I never forgot the moral; mastery comes only through familiarity with the subject matter. He scorned the kind of scholarship that depended on dictionaries, concordances, and other reference books. There is a place for such books (and his library contained them), but a master has to have the basic knowledge of his field in his head. He used to say, 'When you buy a loaf of bread in the grocery store, you do not tell the clerk that you have money in the bank; you have to lay a coin on the counter. In the same way, no scholar should think that he does not have to know his basic material by heart because he can look it up in concordances and indices. Money in the bank does not take the place of ready cash in the pocket.'

Margolis' classes made an indelible impression. A Bible seminar required the entire apparatus on the large central table. Of course, every student brought his own Hebrew Bible. But on the table were the huge rabbinic Bible, some giant polyglot with the ancient versions, the leading ancient and medieval commentaries, and finally the best modern commentaries. The entire apparatus was scrutinized for each verse read. Naturally it would take a year to cover a couple of chapters, but the student who survived [elsewhere Gordis notes that very few did] a few years of such training got something precious that most students lack.

Margolis would ask each student to take a special assignment, such as a particular version or commentary and be responsible for its evidence. He told me on my first day in class to handle the Syriac version. 'But I don't know Syriac,' I protested. He looked at me sternly and growled, 'Where do you think you are? In a kindergarten? Go home and learn Syriac.'

The subject that I learned better than any other in all of my schooling was Hebrew linguistics under Margolis. He was not interested in the normal forms of the Hebrew language. . . . He taught the underlying principles. . . . Then he would call someone to the board and ask him to write a Hebrew word which happened to be a rare or exotic form. The student would almost invariably botch it and would be called an ignoramus [Gordon noted, on another ocassion, that "ignoramus" was one of Margolis' favorite words; a favorite saying of Margolis' was that ignorance is a curable disease]. Then Margolis would draw out of the student the principles that had been taught and have the student apply them to the form, thus correcting it. Then he would ask the student, 'Does this look right?' The student would be afraid to say 'Yes' or 'No,' whereupon Margolis would tell him to look up such and such a passage, and there the form would be in the classical text. This would teach the student to understand and apply the basic principles. . . . [Gordon and others remember that Margolis had constructed "grammatical charts," on which he put 80% of the way the Hebrew language behaves. In this context Gordon speaks of Margolis' "ability to reduce a subject to the very bone." To Gordon, this was infinitely greater than producing a thousand-page grammar of the Hebrew language.]

Any seasoned Semitist can recognize a familiar Hebrew passage when he sees the consonants. Margolis, of course, could spot any consonantal citation from Scripture by chapter and often by verse. But he had so mastered the structure of Hebrew that he could also spot any biblical verse if confronted with its vocalic skeleton without any indication of the consonants.[30]

Robert Gordis also began studying with Margolis at the age of 18 (see above on Cyrus Gordon). Although "Margolis had a reputation for being very abrasive," he "took a shine" to Gordis and did everything he could to encourage the young scholar. As a result, Gordis began taking all of Margolis' courses every year.[31]

As editor of the Dropsie volume on Margolis, Gordis had occasion to describe some of his experiences in the classroom:

As one instance of his method, we may cite the course on Nahum which he gave one year. He dedicated four hours a week throughout the academic year to this small book of three chapters, and succeeded in covering only the first two chapters, totalling only twenty-eight verses. The students, however, had been given invaluable training in scientific methodology by an unforgettable master. [In a short interview, Mrs. Gordis remembered sitting in on a class when Margolis was teaching Koheleth. They covered only one verse, but—Mrs. Gordis recalls fondly—what they did with that one verse!]

His lectures were enlivened by his epigrammatic wit. 'This room, gentlemen,' he would say, casting his eye about the bookcases that lined his room, 'is dedicated to ignorance, but it is collective ignorance—the things *we* don't know. Make sure not to have your own private ignorance, the things you personally don't know!' Or he would insist: 'If it is

[30]Cyrus H. Gordon, *Forgotten Scripts: How they were deciphered and their impact on contemporary culture* (New York: Basic Books, 1968), 140–143. See now also "Remembering Teachers: Max L. Margolis," an article Gordon wrote in May 1984 for New York University. On the last point made above by Gordon, E. A. Speiser ("The Contribution of Max Leopold Margolis to Semitic Linguistics," *Max Leopold Margolis: Scholar and Teacher*, 28) had similar recollections:

Margolis' mastery of [the Hebrew Bible] may be judged from the fact that, given the vowel points alone, he could supply the pertinent consonants for any verse in the Bible. This was by no means a mere feat of memory; it was rather an indication of his absolute command of the historical structure of Biblical Hebrew as reflected by the received vocalization.

[31]Robert Gordis to Leonard J. Greenspoon. Oral interview.

brilliant, it is not true' and then disprove his own statement by a brilliant aperçu or an illuminating observation.[32]

Harry M. Orlinsky studied with Margolis for only a couple of months, in the fall of 1931, after which illness forced his teacher to spend the remaining months of his life at home (see below).[33] Orlinsky remembers well the nervousness he felt upon entering Margolis' classroom for the first time:

> There were a dozen or so students, most of whom had been there previously. It was not until later that I realized that I was the only 'serious student' among them. A lot of them were rabbis. I was the only one equipped really to study the text of the material being discussed, which was then the Elihu speeches of Job. I was the only one who participated in class; the others were just sitting there. I found the course fascinating, for Margolis was dealing with material that I was handling directly, but which—at that time—I was unable to comprehend and organize methodologically. And that's precisely what I had come to Margolis for.
>
> I also remember the incident that brought Margolis and me close: One day Margolis made a statement about Theodotion in Job. Toward the end of the two-hour session I said, 'That's not correct, Dr. Margolis.' Margolis, losing his temper, yelled to me, 'Go to hell!' At the end of class I said privately to Margolis, 'You can't send me to hell; I'm not a rabbi!' Immediately, Margolis became very friendly, almost affectionate. From my short time with Margolis, I learned that he liked to be answered back to; he didn't object if he thought it was legitimate.
>
> I distincly remember how Margolis conducted a class: It took at least two full sessions (four hours) to cover one verse. After about twenty hours, we didn't get past about verse 5 in Job 32. Margolis would talk about different versions, variant readings, how variant readings came into being—if there was anything of substance to them or were they just mistakes; if they were scribal errors, what was the nature of the error. I was fascinated by this approach and was able to absorb because Margolis didn't go too fast. Margolis said that there's much more merit [e.g. in learning Talmud] to studying one page of the text itself and analyzing it thoroughly than to reading 1,000 pages about the Talmud. And, I have come to believe, Margolis was right. I learned more methodologically from five verses in Elihu than I could have any other way.
>
> We always used a great number of volumes during class. For the few sessions after Margolis and I became friendly, he specifically asked me to get this or that volume. We'd get the volume down and consult it

[32] Gordis, "Appreciation," *Max Leopold Margolis: Scholar and Teacher*, 16.

[33] On this see introductory note to Harry M. Orlinsky, "On the Present State of Proto-Septuagint Studies," *JAOS* 61 (1941), 81. Orlinsky's article, which is found on pp. 81–91 of *JAOS*, was reprinted in Sidney Jellicoe (ed.), *Studies in the Septuagint: Origins, Recensions and Interpretations* (New York: KTAV, 1974), 78–109.

immediately. Margolis wasn't content with giving students references that they'd probably never pursue. Then and there they would examine the material. On occasion, Margolis sent me down to the [main] library to bring back a journal article. From Margolis, I learned to do the same sort of thing in my own work—look at something immediately, don't [just] put down a reference.[34]

It is clear then that, from Margolis' point of view, the environment at Dropsie was not perfect. It was, nonetheless, conducive to some serious teaching and to most of the scholarly and professional activities that were of importance to Margolis. It was at Dropsie, for example, that Margolis continued his service as editor-in-chief of the J.P.S. Bible Translation and pursued his growing interest in textual criticism and the Septuagint. His notable achievements as translator and textual critic are the subjects of individual chapters later in this book. The paragraphs that follow present other aspects of Margolis' career while at Dropsie: he wrote numerous book reviews, edited scholarly journals, served as president of the Society of Biblical Literature, spent a year teaching in Palestine, and was co-author of a comprehensive history of the Jewish people.

Some scholars look upon book reviews as a necessary, but frequently tedious way of making a name for themselves in the academic community. For such individuals the tedium can occasionally be broken up by producing devastating attacks on any unfortunate soul who had the misfortune of authoring a work not to their liking. Max Margolis did not abuse the genre of book review in this way. He had long since made a name for himself when he began writing reviews for the *Jewish Quarterly Review (JQR)*, which was a publication of Dropsie from 1910 on. The number of books Margolis reviewed in *JQR* between 1910 and 1914 (volumes 1–4 in the new series) is staggering: around 200.[35] Most of the reviews were fairly brief; others, running as long as 15 pages, approached what is today termed a review essay.[36] In every case, whether extended essay or simple summary of contents, Margolis got to the essence of the work under review. As Gordis notes, his reviews were never superficial.[37]

Merely to list the titles of some of the books, scholarly and popular,

[34] Harry M. Orlinsky to Leonard J. Greenspoon. Oral interview.

[35] For volume 1 (1910/11), Margolis reviewed approximately 40 books (these reviews are found on pp. 403–418, 547–579); for volume 2 (1911/12), approximately 10 books (pp. 281–284, 591–606); for volume 3 (1912/13), approximately 90 books (pp. 101–165); for volume 4 (1913/14), approximately 60 books (pp. 249–302).

[36] Among the latter is his review of J. H. A. Hart, *Ecclesiasticus. The Greek Text of Codex 248* (*JQR* n.s. 1 [1910/11], 403–418). Earlier (during the years 1897–1902) Margolis published a half dozen reviews in the *American Journal of Semitic Languages and Literatures*. Among his other reviews are two fairly lengthy and very interesting discussions that appeared in *The American Hebrew*: on Hermann Cohen's *Religion* (vol. 81 October 4, 1907, 542–543) and on Eduard Meyer's *Geschichte des Altertums* (vol. 82 January 17, 1908, 286–287).

[37] Robert Gordis to Leonard J. Greenspoon. Oral interview.

that he reviewed gives a sense of the extraordinary range of topics in which Margolis had competence: *A Dictionary of the Bible, Reasonable Bible Criticism, I. Mose 14. Eine historisch-kritische Untersuchung, Egypt and Israel, The Source of the Christian Tradition, Sociological Study of the Bible,* Eliezer Ben-Yehuda's *Thesaurus totius Hebraitatis et veteris et recentioris, The Old Testament in Greek, A Coptic Palimpsest containing Joshua. . ., The Book of the Prophet Isaiah, Jefeth b. Ali's Arabic Commentary on Nahum, The Hebrew Personification of Wisdom, Ein babylonische Quelle für das Buch Job?, Les Psaumes de Salomon, "The Son of Man" or Contributions to the Study of the Thoughts of Jesus, Neutestamentliche Grammatik, An Atlas of Textual Criticism, The Gospel according to St. Luke, The Story of the English Bible.* These titles are representative of the far larger number, almost 90, that Margolis dealt with in one series of reviews: *JQR* n.s. 3 (1912/13), 101–165.

To an extent Margolis used these reviews as a vehicle for expressing his opinions on the direction Biblical scholarship was taking. In particular, he was interested in the newer, critical approaches, which he felt had much to offer when not carried to extremes.[38] In all cases, no matter how completely he disagreed with the thesis or approach of a particular volume, "he did justice to each and every book, you can be sure." This is the judgment of Gordis, who recounts a story that illustrates a related point: Margolis never forgot that behind each book was at least one fellow human, an author like himself. Gordis recalls that Margolis once asked him to review a collection of texts by two well-regarded scholars. Upon reading the work, Gordis found some major problems with it. When Gordis reported this to Margolis, the latter's response was immediate: Don't review the book. If you have to devastate a book, don't review it. Margolis understood, Gordis continues, how much effort went into such a work, and—in spite of what many people thought about Margolis—he had enough regard for the energy these authors put into their work not to want to see it lambasted.[39]

Margolis' sensitivity to the feelings of his fellow scholars (a sensitivity all too often lacking in his classroom) found expression in the spoken, as well as the written word. While he could be "very rough" at scholarly meetings, he did not engage in *ad personam* wrangling nor was he himself the target of such attacks.[40] Margolis seems to have maintained cordial relations with the leading scholars of his day, Jewish and Christian alike. Among his closest associates was James A. Montgomery, who was later to speak of Margolis' "moral as well as scholarly genius."[41]

Not only did Margolis and Montgomery share many scholarly inter-

---

[38] On this see chapter 5, where particular reviews are cited.
[39] Robert Gordis to Leonard J. Greenspoon. Oral interview.
[40] Cyrus H. Gordon and Louis L. Kaplan to Leonard J. Greenspoon. Oral interviews.
[41] James A. Montgomery, "The genius of Professor Margolis." (An address delivered at the

ests, but they also occupied several of the same posts in professional organizations; in particular, both served as editor of the *Journal of Biblical Literature* and as president of the Society of Biblical Literature. Margolis was *JBL* editor from 1914–1921.[42] The annual reports that he issued during his tenure in that position give evidence of the particular difficulties he faced and of the graceful manner in which he sought to alleviate, if not eradicate, such difficulties. Most of the difficulties stemmed from the fact that even during the period of World War I *JBL* continued to be printed by the Leipzig firm of Haag-Drugulin.[43] It was no easy matter to arrange for delivery of the printed volume to America, as Margolis duly noted in his December 1916 report:[44]

> The thirty-fourth volume [for 1915] which the librarians of the country are now eagerly inquiring for has made its appearance, so far as the seat of printing at Leipzig, Germany, is concerned; one copy I understand has reached our Treasurer. Our members and the other subscribers will have to be asked to be patient until the time when the peace for which belligerents and neutrals long shall have been consummated and the seas be permitted to carry an inoffensive scientific publication to the homes of American students. I know the authors of the learned contributions are still more impatient, especially for long-lost reprints not only of the year 1915, but also of the preceding year. In the language of the prophet, 'though they tarry, wait for them; they will surely come!'

To expedite the publication of volume 35 (for 1916), Margolis announced that its printing was

> in the hands of the same New Haven firm which is printing the Journal of the American Oriental Society. The first double number appeared on the first of this month, and considering that things had to be done with a certain measure of haste, the typography calls for commendation. Of course, we cannot expect Drugulin facilities in this country; on the other hand, both authors and editors know how our German friends have wrestled with the English—I mean the language and in particular the script—and how long distance proof reading is not exactly a pleasure.[45]

In spite of the best efforts of most of those involved in the production of *JBL*, there were delays and inconveniences for a number of years, a

---

meeting in memory of Margolis, May 9, 1932. The statement quoted above is from p. 8 of a typescript of this talk found in the Dropsie College Archives.)

[42] For a complete list of the editors of the *Journal*, see Ernest W. Saunders, *Searching the Scriptures: A History of the Society of Biblical Literature, 1880–1980* (Chico, CA: Scholars Press, 1982), 115 (Appendix V).

[43] On this see Saunders, *Searching*, 23.

[44] This report was printed on pp. viif of *JBL* 36 (1917).

[45] *JBL* 36 (1917), viii. See also James A. Montgomery's report on p. vi on the same volume.

difficult situation that "taxed the apologetic skills of the editors [chiefly, Margolis]."[46] During his service as editor, Margolis had not only to rely on his apologetic skills and editorial acumen, but also to display a certain degree of diplomatic tact in dealing with printers and contributors alike. In regard to the latter, Margolis reckoned that "much unnecessary delay is in some cases occasioned by the number of proofs asked for by [unnamed] contributors."[47]

One individual he surely had in mind when making that remark was Paul Haupt, from whom many letters have been preserved that relate to *JBL* business.[48] Haupt had one or more complaint for just about every aspect of *JBL's* handling of his numerous articles: he was not getting a sufficient number of proofs, he was not receiving his reprints, his name was not repeated after each of his "brief communications," titles of "brief communications" were not given on the cover, and so forth.[49] In mid-1916 he offered detailed instructions to Margolis on how the editor should be sending material to Germany: "When you send the proofs to Leipzig, you had better send them as first class matter, registered. . . . Be sure you send everything by Scandinavian steamers."[50] Later that year, and into the following as well, Haupt had anything but commendation for the New Haven firm that had been engaged to print *JBL:*

> The printers are unsatisfactory. . . . It is a waste of time to correct [their] arbitrary departures from 'copy'. . . . My 'copy' was plain. . . . The remarks of the printers on my 'copy' show that they have not much experience in printing Oriental work. My 'copy' has always been praised as superior to most manuscripts handed in. . . . I promised to send you some minor communications, and I have some ready, but I am afraid the 'copy' will not be up to the new standard.[51]

Haupt did "not hold [Margolis] responsible for the printers, but the editor should be the intermediary between the contributors and the printers, looking out for the contributors as much as possible. I have always adhered to this principle in my editorial work."[52]

The overbearing Haupt was not a typical contributor; nevertheless, dealing with even the most modest of scholars was time consuming, as

---

[46] Saunders, *Searching*, 23. Saunders notes that *JBL* did not return to its regular schedule of publication until 1923.

[47] *JBL* 37 (1918), vii.

[48] The letters I saw are in the archives at Dropsie College. Others may well be preserved at the Johns Hopkins University, where Haupt taught.

[49] See, for example, his letters addressed to Margolis on May 25 and August 23, 1915.

[50] Haupt to Margolis, April 7, 1916.

[51] These remarks are contained in letters addressed to Margolis on December 7, 1916, and June 14, 1917.

[52] Haupt to Margolis, June 14, 1917.

were the editing of material and the conducting of business with the printers. Margolis' retrospective assessment was on the whole positive:

> I have derived great pleasure from my labor in editing the volumes and carrying on correspondence, highly edifying in dealing with contributors, somewhat less satisfactory in conveying our wishes to the Printers.[53]

In stepping down as head of *JBL* Margolis was not removing himself from journal editing, for he immediately took up a similar position as an editor of the *Journal of the American Oriental Society*. A member of that society since 1890, Margolis continued as its *Journal* editor until his death.[54]

Margolis' contributions to the Society of Biblical Literature, in addition to his other scholarly achievements, led to his election as SBL president for the year 1923.[55] His presidential address, delivered in New York City on December 27th of that year, was titled "Our Own Future: A Forecast and a Programme."[56] In this paper, which Gordis terms "characteristically brilliant and witty,"[57] Margolis focused on "[in Ernest W. Saunders' words] the need for a self-sufficient American biblical science, calling for more collaborative enterprises of magnitude and less preoccupation with historical trivia."[58]

Many of his words, addressed to his colleagues over sixty years ago, apply equally well to the academy of the '80s:

> A presentation of the Old Testament religion which winds up with the skepticism of Koheleth fails significantly in insight. And, worst of all, neither Jahveh nor his words seem to be able to live down their past. So we have passed on the word to the facile popularizers and through them to the reporters . . . that the Old Testament as seen in the light of today is decidedly not worthwhile. . . . If the Scriptures lack in worthwhileness, why then study them. . . . We have furthermore brought our own work into disrepute by indulging in pseudo-science. On the one hand we are beset by a traditionalism which sits tight on the lid, or else by deftly misinterpreting the evidences of archaeology would prop up untenable positions; and on the other hand by a criticism hardened into a tradition and woefully lacking in self-criticism. All scientific questions may be reopened, and the truer solution is not necessarily the

---

[53] *JBL* 41 (1922), x.

[54] Richard Gottheil *et al*, "The Life and Work of Max Leopold Margolis," *JAOS* 52 (1932), 109: "In 1890 [Margolis] had joined the American Oriental Society and from 1922 until his death he had functioned as the editor of the Semitic part of the JOURNAL published by that Society."

[55] For a complete list of SBL presidents, see Saunders, *Searching*, 117f (Appendix VI).

[56] This address is printed in *JBL* 43 (1924), 1–8.

[57] Gordis, "Appreciation," *Max Leopold Margolis: Scholar and Teacher*, 11.

[58] Saunders, *Searching*, 37.

straight-line account. Neither the church nor the synagogue can long continue Scriptureless. After straying in the byways the ancient paths will once more be trodden.

A self-sufficient American—whose "Biblical science [is] mature, competent, veracious, reverent"—has much to offer:

> We have a distinct outlook upon life, itself formed upon the Scripture. . . . The American conscience will brush away finespun quibblings and, purged from all insinuating motives of the present, apply itself to a renewed apprehension and appraisal of that which abides forever.

To what should scholars, thoroughly grounded in philological and historical methods of inquiry, devote themselves? Not "criticism," which "has been overdone, the higher and the lower. Investigations as to date and composition may lie fallow for a while." Not the rewriting of "ancient documents in such manner that their authors would exclaim, 'Well done, but it is not what we wrote!' Rewriting is not at all our business. We may take it for granted that Isaiah knew his Hebrew quite well. Nor did he consult us as to the arrangement of his thoughts." Rather, "let us concentrate on exegesis. It is so easy to break up a text into atoms. It is far more difficult to discern relevancy, continuity, coherence." In so doing, "we" strive

> to recreate the lost context, not the context of a paragraph or chapter, but the context of pulsating life in which these men stood and from which their hope and their faith emerged, touching that of their contemporaries at every point, and yet transcending it so as to focus itself upon eternity.

How can the scholarly world best achieve such lofty goals?

> Away with the multitude of our little publications in which we frequently repeat ourselves! Let us address ourselves to monumental works which will require the cooperation of a large number of us and provide useful occupations beyond the present generation.[59]

At the time Margolis delivered his presidential address he had not traveled outside of the United States, except for a short trip or two to Canada, since his return from Europe in 1908. Sometime earlier, how-

---

[59] The quotations above are taken from pp. 5–8 of "Our Own Future: A Forecast and a Programme," *JBL* 43 (1924). For more on this presidential address and the material it contains, see chapter 5.

ever, in 1922, he had received, and accepted, two invitations that would take him and his family to Palestine for the academic year 1924-1925: he was to be annual professor at the American School of Oriental Research and one of the first professors on the faculty of the newly founded Hebrew Univeristy.[60] Elsewhere I have written about some of Margolis' adventures in Palestine during a year that was marked by enormous professional success but also deep personal tragedy.[61] Here it is appropriate to mention one of the scholarly projects on which Margolis labored while in Palestine and also to indicate the nature and depth of his personal tragedy.

While still in America, Margolis had begun, with Alexander Marx of the Jewish Theological Seminary, a collaborative effort to produce a one-volume *History of the Jewish People* under the auspices of the Jewish Publication Society. Gordis records that "it was only with the greatest difficulty that he [Margolis] was persuaded" to do so.[62] As Marx states in a straightforward manner, it was understood from the beginning that "Margolis was to carry the main burden of this task."[63] The division of labor in this "eminently happy and successful" collaboration[64] was such that Marx "supplied the notes for the book from the period of the Second Temple until the eighteenth century, Dr. Margolis himself being responsible for the Biblical age, while one of his students, Dr. Louis L. Kaplan, assembled the materials for the modern period" and also prepared the Index.[65] In addition, it felt to Margolis to do all the actual writing, much of it during 1924 and 1925. In the earlier stages of their work, Margolis and Marx were in frequent personal contact; this was of course impossible when Margolis was in Palestine. In connection with Margolis' schedule during this period, Marx remarks that "besides all his other duties, he [Margolis] would generally devote eight hours a day to the History which progressed very rapidly, in spite of the fact that the year he spent in Palestine fell within that period."[66]

In his letters from Palestine to Cyrus Adler, Margolis made frequent reference to his progress on the manuscript. In a letter dated July 7, 1924, only three weeks after his arrival in Jerusalem, Margolis informed

[60]The two invitations are referred to, among other places, in a letter from Adler to Margolis, June 16, 1922 (on the annual professorship), and in a letter from Margolis to Adler, November 8, 1922, and its response, November 10 (on the position at the Hebrew University). (These letters are in the Dropsie College Archives.)

[61]Leonard J. Greenspoon, "Max Leopold Margolis: A Scholar's Scholar (A BA Portrait)," *Biblical Archaeologist* 48 (1985), 103–106.

[62]Gordis, "Appreciation," *Max Leopold Margolis: Scholar and Teacher*, 12.

[63]Marx, *Proceedings*, 377.

[64]This phrase is Gordis' ("Appreciation," *Max Leopold Margolis: Scholar and Teacher*, 12).

[65]The quotation is from Gordis, 12 (see preceding fn.). The specific reference to Kaplan's preparation of the Index is found in the "Preface" to *History*, vi.

[66]Marx, *Proceedings*, 377. See also the "Preface" to *History*, vi.

Adler that he had already "sent off twenty odd pages of History to Dr. Marx and I am forging ahead."[67] Later that month Margolis writes: "My work on the history is progressing and I have sent off to Marx in Berlin three installments since coming here. There are all sorts of interruptions, but on the whole I keep working steadily."[68] By mid-October 1924, Margolis had "carried Franco-German History (including England; Mr. Hyamson lent me his own book and other works on the subject) as far as 1500, and I have now returned to Spain where I have gotten to the time of ibn Adret."[69] From this letter, as from the two earlier ones, it is learned that Margolis "sent Marx transcripts of all my work." Their communication at long distance was but an early step of the process that produced the final, published form of *History:* "The manuscript was gone over repeatedly by the two authors in joint conference, every fact and date and expression was scrutinized."[70]

Few would disagree with Marx's favorable judgment that Margolis made good use of this opportunity "to present his view of biblical history in comprehensive fashion" and that "he showed a thorough acquaintance with the later periods of Jewish history and literature as well. The arrangement of the chronological tables at the end of the volume, placing the events in different countries in parallel columns, gives evidence of his practical and methodological mind."[71] Gordis, calling to mind what a reviewer had said about "the principle of conciseness" in *A Manual of the Aramaic Language,*[72] credits Margolis with "possessing an unusual gift of succinct utterance and clarity of expression."[73] Granting that this one-volume *History* "may lack the easy readability of more leisurely and less factual surveys," Gordis nonetheless concludes that "it remains the classic in its field by virtue of its wealth of information, its philosophic grasp of the subject, its objectivity of treatment and the warm love for Israel which permeates its pages."[74]

When Margolis set sail for Palestine on May 15, 1924,[75] he was accompanied by his wife and three children, daughter Catherine and twin boys Philip and Max Jr. When Margolis returned from Palestine in the spring of 1925, his family was not with him. Several months earlier Evelyn Margolis had gone back to the United States with the children—

[67] Margolis to Adler, July 7, 1924 (Dropsie College Archives).

[68] Margolis to Adler, July 23, 1924 (Dropsie College Archives).

[69] Margolis to Adler, October 17, 1924 (Dropsie College Archives). Solomon ibn Adret at Barcelona appears several times in *History* from pp. 397–444.

[70] From the "Preface" to *History,* vi.

[71] Marx, *Proceedings,* 377.

[72] W. Bacher, "Margolis' 'Manual of Talmudic Aramaic,'" *JQR* n.s. 1 (1910/11), 266.

[73] Gordis, "Appreciation," *Max Leopold Margolis; Scholar and Teacher,* 13.

[74] *Ibid.*

[75] For this date, see Max L. Margolis to Henry Hurwitz (of the Intercollegiate Menorah Association), April 24, 1924 (American Jewish Archives).

Catherine and Philip were alive and well, Max Jr. was dead. During the
winter Max Jr., a nine year old described by W. F. Albright as "a most
promising boy," had died from what "was, in all probability, a chest
condition of some kind."[76] Louis Kaplan, who was studying with Margolis at the time, recalls that his teacher was disconsolate as a result of
this loss. When Mrs. Margolis took the children back to Philadelphia,
where Max Jr. was buried, Kaplan helped ease the burden of grief. He
became, in his own words, almost a surrogate son to Margolis, although
Max Jr. had been much younger than he.[77]

Kaplan characterizes Margolis as "a devoted, almost doting, father."[78]
Margolis' letters from Palestine contain expressions of this parental pride
and devotion; in the fall of 1924, for example, he wrote: "The holidays
have somewhat disarranged the schedule, but last Friday [members of]
the School, my twin boys enrolling themselves as scholars for the day,
were conducted on the first topographical walk clear around the walls
. . . and the boys (Philip and Max) sat on the tomb of Zoheleth."[79] These
letters to Adler also contain expressions, subdued ones, of the pain he felt
because of his son's death: "I went down to Egypt [he wrote on March 6]
but had not the heart to go to Luxor: I just remained in Cairo and saw a
few of the sights."[80]

Margolis' sense of loss was no less acute upon his return to the United
States. If anything, it grew even stronger, as is evident from some very
personal and emotional remarks addressed to Adler after Margolis had
been back in America for several months:

> The children are doing well, but Mrs. Margolis has not been well. She
> was with Philip on his birthday, while I prostrated myself over the
> mound covering my other boy who missed his tenth birthday. I am not
> questioning the ways of Providence, but the wound is as fresh as on the
> day it was inflicted.[81]

[76]Albright's statement is found in his "Report of the Director of the School in Jerusalem [for
the academic year 1924–1925]," *BASOR* 20 (December 1925), 10. Information concerning the
death of Max Jr. was provided to me by Philip Margolis in a letter dated June 28, 1985:

> [Max Jr. had developed a mastoid condition and an] operation was performed in
> Philadelphia, prior to our . . . leaving for Palestine. I cannot say, with any surety, why
> my brother died, except that he had always been a rather sickly child, and while in
> Palestine, his health deteriorated and adequate medical treatment was not then
> available. The sickness was, in all probability, a chest condition of some kind.

[77]Louis L. Kaplan to Leonard J. Greenspoon. Oral interview.
[78]*Ibid.*
[79]Margolis to Adler, October 17, 1924 (Dropsie College Archives).
[80]Margolis to Adler, March 6, 1925 (Dropsie College Archives).
[81]Margolis to Adler, August 20, 1925 (Dropsie College Archives).

At the same time, Margolis recognized that there was some solace in scholarly pursuits: "Of course, I am absorbed in my work, and that helps. . . My own work is progressing; I give it 8 uninterrupted hours of time; and Mr. Kaplan is working the same number of hours."[82]

Those who knew Margolis well, however, recognized, for their part, the limited scope of scholarship's solace: "This misfortune left an indelible scar on the rest of his life," writes Marx; "Once his son died, something died within Margolis" is Kaplan's way of putting it; as Gordis saw it, "the joy of life was beclouded for him [Margolis] by the shadow of his bereavement."[83] Almost every Erev Shabbat Margolis visited his son's grave. Even bad weather—Gordis remembers one particularly cold and rainy Friday—did not keep Margolis from going to the cemetery.[84]

Except for the year he spent in Palestine, Margolis lived in Philadephia from 1908 to his death in 1932. A considerable number of additional details about his life there, especially during the period after he returned from Palestine, are provided by his former students and colleagues. In terms of his physical appearance, all describe Margolis as a short man, so short in fact that Kaplan recalls that Margolis always stood when he typed.[85] To this, Adler adds that Margolis was "rather solidly built."[86] More bluntly, Margolis is described as a homely man, who strove without success to be a charmer.[87] Margolis' efforts to make a favorable first impression on others were also hindered by an unpleasant speaking voice, which Kaplan describes as rather hoarse and raspy. Kaplan admits that Margolis' voice was difficult to listen to "for those who didn't know him and love him" as Kaplan did.[88] In addition, Gordon recalls that Margolis always had a spittoon around, which he frequently used.[89] It is also known that he smoked a pipe.

Margolis' personality was on occasion equally forbidding. "He could not suffer fools gladly. Loving truth, he hated sham and pomposity. When he encountered these less attractive attributes of human nature, his wit became caustic and devastating."[90] In the classroom this was especially the case with rabbis. Outside of the classroom he rarely resorted to *ad personam* attacks; however, it is equally clear that he was

[82] *Ibid.*

[83] Marx, *Proceedings*, 376; Kaplan, oral interview; Gordis, "Appreciation," *Max Leopold Margolis: Scholar and Teacher*, 11.

[84] Gordis, "Appreciation," 11 (see preceding fn.), and oral interview.

[85] Louis L. Kaplan to Leonard J. Greenspoon. Oral interview.

[86] This statement is contained in the material Adler prepared for Margolis' entry in the *Dictionary of American Biography.*

[87] By contrast, his brother Elias, who was a successful Conservative rabbi, is judged to have been the charmer Max Margolis never was.

[88] Louis L. Kaplan to Leonard J. Greenspoon. Oral interview.

[89] Cyrus H. Gordon to Leonard J. Greenspoon. Oral interview.

[90] Gordis, "Appreciation," *Max Leopold Margolis: Scholar and Teacher*, 14.

not accustomed to resorting to the kind of flattering and political gamesmanship that places professional advancement over personal integrity.

Most of those who knew him well grew to love him, in spite of (because of?) the gruff image of himself he projected to the world at large. These students and colleagues feel that they came to understand (in Gordis' words) that Margolis "put up an external kind of facade that he had erected as a protection," for "he was essentially a very sensitive and vulnerable individual."[91] Elaborating on this point, Gordis speaks of "the defensive armor of a deeply sensitive soul, wounded by the all-too-common spectacle of hypocrisy, soulless conformity and ignorance enthroned in the high places." Not many were willing to penetrate this "defensive armor," but "a great reward awaited those" few who "were not afraid to" do so:

> Associates and pupils, Christian and Jewish alike, who knew him well, found him to be a loyal friend and a consecrated teacher, loving his students and bringing them closer to Torah, genuinely interested in their welfare and sympathetic to their problems.[92]

Expanding on his portrait of Margolis as a devoted father, Kaplan remarks that when his teacher loved a student, he loved him like a son—there was nothing Margolis wouldn't do for him. And this interest extended to the (future) families of his students as well. When, for example, Kaplan began dating the woman he was to marry, Margolis insisted upon setting aside several hours a week to teach *her* Hebrew.[93]

Margolis gave freely of his time on behalf of favorite students such as Kaplan, who in retrospect feels that these activities cut into the time Margolis had available for "scholarly" pursuits. There were other factors—as each of his former students, including Kaplan, recognizes—that played far greater roles in preventing Margolis from producing the quantity and breadth of scholarship that all judge him capable of. Gordis seems to speak for all of them when he writes:

> [The complete bibliography of Margolis' work] sets forth his rich output. . . . Yet there is a melancholy feeling in conning this list of his writings, imposing as it is, for it underscores the truth of the Talmudic dictum that 'no man dies with even half his desires fulfilled.'[94]

To a large degree, especially during the latter part of his career, Margolis' self-imposed, single-minded determination to concentrate on

[91] Robert Gordis to Leonard J. Greenspoon. Oral interview.
[92] Gordis, "Appreciation," *Max Leopold Margolis: Scholar and Teacher*, 14f.
[93] Louis L. Kaplan to Leonard J. Greenspoon. Oral interview.
[94] Gordis, "Appreciation," *Max Leopold Margolis: Scholar and Teacher*, 12.

the text of Joshua placed severe limitations on his ability to take up any other large-scale projects.[95] A personal characteristic of Margolis' combined with his professional choices to limit his "rich, imposing output": he was a perfectionist. Gordon, commenting on this aspect of Margolis' personality, recalls that when his teacher finally did publish something, he'd say that there was—even for him—an end to slavishness. Margolis realized that his work was slavishness, but there WAS an end to it. In his own career Gordon has come across some people who are such perfectionists that they never publish anything. Gordon is grateful that Margolis wasn't that bad; nonethless, "if he had been a little less strict with himself, the world would have been a richer place."[96]

One additional consideration, its particular claims often in competition with the attractions of lofty scholarship, carried weight whenever Margolis sought to apportion his time among the numerous activities that presented themselves: the desire to maintain his family in a style that Kaplan describes as comfortable, though not grand. Margolis' professorial salary, which Kaplan calls "a disgrace," was not sufficient.[97] For that reason he was forced to do some "hack work" that he would not otherwise have agreed to. As noted earlier, Margolis genuinely liked to write popular articles on a variety of topics of concern to contemporary American Jews. What is suggested is that financial exigencies forced him to expend more effort on such non-academic endeavors than he really desired. A full appraisal of this "hack work" would surely be critical of the necessarily ephemeral nature of most of it; on the other hand, none of it is unsubstantial or carelessly conceived and executed.[98]

Mrs. Margolis, from whose family the Margolis' probably received financial assistance from time to time, was apparently unhappy that her husband *had* to undertake such assignments. Margolis himself seems to be giving vent to bitter feelings of his own when he wrote—is this not at least partly a self-portrait?—of the plight of the ill-paid, almost neglected American Jewish scholar: In a single piece of work this individual has to deal with tens of thousands of facts. Using only his own resources, he is expected to "collate let us say some sixty manuscripts, catalogue the thousands of variations, do an infinite amount of mechanical labor which any trained amanuensis might do." In addition to teaching, he must also engage in a variety of other pursuits to support himself and his family. For all of his labors, the Jewish scholar now counts as "a nonentity" in his community. Consigned to a position of "semi-mendicancy," the scholar is left "to his small work which rejoices neither himself nor the public."[99]

95 On Margolis as a textual critic and Septuagintal scholar, see chapter 4.
96 Cyrus H. Gordon to Leonard J. Greenspoon. Oral interview.
97 Louis L. Kaplan to Leonard J. Greenspoon. Oral interview.
98 On this, see also chapter 1.
99 The remarks above were taken from "The Future of Jewish Scholarship," an undated typescript found in the office of Harry M. Orlinsky.

Such bitterness was, on occasion, not absent when Margolis reflected in a critical fashion on his life. It should not, in any case, overshadow his very real achievements and successes. The following paragraphs, which bring this chapter to an end, provide access to several additional facets of Margolis' rich professional and personal life.

In addition to the Society of Biblical Literature and the American Oriental Society, Margolis was a member of the American Philosophical Society, the American Jewish Historical Society and its Council, and the Publication Committee of the Jewish Publication Society; he was also a fellow of the American Academy for Jewish Research. Among his other affiliations were the Pharisees, "a unique social and cultural group of Philadelphia business and professional men," [100] and the Oriental Club of Philadelphia, before whom he read several papers. [101]

As is true with many academicians, Margolis had a passion for books. His personal library, most of which he kept in his office at Dropsie, was of legendary proportions. That there was substance to this legend is proved by the report of College librarian Joseph Reider, who conducted a thorough inventory after Margolis' death:

> I went through Doctor Margolis' library and obtained the following statistics: the total number of books and pamphlets amounts to approximately 3916. . . . The collection contains the finest and choicest Biblical apparatus, yet it also has many splendid books in general and Semitic linguistics, and in rabbinic and historical literature. There are many rarities and old prints. The books are all in good condition, mostly well bound. [102]

There is reason to think that Mrs. Margolis was somewhat upset by her husband's habit of spending "all" his money on books. When she speaks of his having made "economic" sacrifices "to uphold the integrity of scholarship," she may have had in mind his expenditures for books, as well as his relatively low salary. [103]

---

[100] This description of the Pharisees comes from Gordis, "Appreciation," *Max Leopold Margolis: Scholar and Teacher*, 11.

[101] At least one of these papers was published during Margolis' lifetime: "How the Song of Songs entered the Canon," *The Song of Songs. A Symposium . . . Before the Oriental Club of Philadelphia*. Wilfred H. Schoff, ed. (Philadelphia, 1924), 9–17. I have edited and published another of these papers as "Ars Scribendi: Max Margolis' Paper 'Preparing Scribe's Copy in the Age of Manuscripts,'" *JQR* 71 (1981), 43–56, and "Ars Scribendi; Pars Reperta," *JQR* 72 (1982), 43f. Margolis delivered the paper entitled "Preparing Scribe's Copy in the Age of Manuscripts" on February 8, 1923.

[102] Joseph Reider, memorandum for Doctor Adler, May 26, 1932 (Dropsie College Archives). In this inventory Reider also noted that "among these books are five manuscripts, three in the handwriting of Doctor Margolis' father and two in that of Doctor Margolis himself." (See chapter 1.)

[103] More fully, Mrs. Margolis wrote:

As noted earlier, Margolis was a devoted Zionist. He was also committed to the practice of Judaism. Kaplan, in describing the Jewishness of Margolis, says that he was not a "ritualist," but he did practice ritual.[104] The Margolis home was kosher, and Margolis attended synagogue every Shabbat. When he lived in Germantown he rode the train to and from his synagogue, which was located near Dropsie, every Saturday morning. He did not ride elsewhere on Shabbat. Both Gordis and Gordon recall that Margolis was in the habit of reading during sermons. When queried on this point by Gordon, Margolis replied that he was reading the book of Isaiah—why listen to a bad sermon when he could read a good one![105]

This last incident supplies a good example of Margolis' sense of humor, what Gordon likes to refer to as Margolis' blitheness. While not one to reach for a joke or to sit around swapping stories, Margolis did have a good sense of humor. As Kaplan put it, "Margolis was not always deadly serious or earnest."[106]

Margolis also seems to have struck a balance—between blitheness and seriousness—in his choice of pastimes. Adler, who observed that Margolis "was not a man of many amusements," provides the fullest picture available of the types of activities Margolis did engage in at various periods of his life:

> He was a rather jolly youth, inclined to be an athlete and even to a little mischief. He swam well, skated in the winter, was a good oarsman and, during his California days, an expert fisherman. . . . In his youth he played chess, but up to the end he retained a remarkable knack in the building of houses of cards which children adored. . . . During the last year or two of his life, when his health was not good and physicians advised a change of mental attitude, he gave somewhat less time to his chosen biblical studies and by way of relaxation read the new astronomical and cosmogonic theories.[107]

It was not only in the last few years of his life that Margolis read widely in a number of areas outside of his academic expertise: "Beyond his erudition in Jewish and Semitic learning [writes Gordis] his interests ranged over the entire human scene. He read Oswald Spengler's *Untergang des*

My husband was a born teacher and he loved to teach. But more than teaching, he reverenced scholarship. No sacrifice was too great, personal or economic, to uphold the integrity of scholarship. These ideals he passed on to you, his pupils.

This paragraph is contained in her "Message" at the beginning of *Max Leopold Margolis: Scholar and Teacher* (Philadelphis: Dropsie, 1952), vii.

[104] Louis L. Kaplan to Leonard J. Greenspoon. Oral interview.

[105] Robert Gordis and Cyrus H. Gordon to Leonard J. Greenspoon. Oral interviews.

[106] Cyrus H. Gordon and Louis L. Kaplan to Leonard J. Greenspoon. Oral interviews.

[107] Adler, *American Jewish Yearbook*, 139, 144.

Abendlandes [*Decline of the West*] long before the rise of Nazism and was an avid reader of works in ancient and modern history, biography, and many other fields."[108] He was also fond of the Greek poets, in particular epigrammatists and idyllists.[109]

As noted above by Adler, Margolis' health noticeably declined during the last year or two of his life. Illness did not keep him from research or the classroom until the last few months, however. Harry M. Orlinsky recalls: "I entered the Dropsie College in October 1931 in order to specialize in biblical studies under Margolis. He was then already a very sick man. In November he was stricken and I never saw him again."[110] Orlinksy, although he had just begun his studies with Margolis, was asked to take over one of the classes of his incapacitated teacher.[111] Marx was corresponding with Margolis at this same time: "Last December [1931], two days before illness compelled him to stop his work which he was never to resume, he wrote to me about the present status of the book [on Joshua] which he hoped to finish in the course of this year."[112]

Margolis' condition continued to deteriorate, but at least into the month of January there was hope for recovery. In that month Mrs. Margolis and Henry Hurwitz, of the Intercollegiate Menorah Association, exchanged letters over a review that Hurwitz had requested Margolis to write for the *Menorah Journal*. On January 7, 1932, Mrs. Margolis indicated that Hurwitz "better get someone else . . . unless you are willing to wait *at least* 3 months."[113] The optimistic view that Margolis might be back to work within three months may have been wishful thinking; at the time she wrote the letter his condition had declined to the point that she couldn't "even consult" him on such matters.[114]

Margolis did remain alive, although unable to return to his work, for almost another three months. He died on April 2, 1932, a Shabbat. It was then only a slight exaggeration when David Galter wrote: "Margolis died in the service, died in harness—a servant of his people and their Book, to his very last day."[115] The news of Margolis' death, and an appreciative account of his life, covered the entire front page of *The Jewish Exponent* for April 8, spilling over to page 8, which also contained expressions of sympathy from Associated Talmud Torahs, Dropsie College Alumni, the

---

[108] Gordis, "Appreciation," *Max Leopold Margolis: Scholar and Teacher*, 16.

[109] Robert Gordis to Leonard J. Greenspoon. Oral interview.

[110] Orlinsky, "On the Present State of Proto-Septuagint Studies," *JAOS* 61 (1941), 81 (introductory note).

[111] Harry M. Orlinsky to Leonard J. Greenspoon. Oral interview.

[112] Marx, *Proceedings*, 379.

[113] Mrs. Max L. Margolis to Henry Hurwitz, January 7, 1932 (American Jewish Archives).

[114] *Ibid.*

[115] David J. Galter, "Max Margolis: Lover of the Book," *B'nai B'rith Magazine* May 1932, 254.

faculty of Dropsie College, the Publication Committee of the Jewish Publication Society, among others.

The funeral took place on April 6; a Memorial Meeting, at which several addresses were delivered, was held at Dropsie on May 9.[116] Simon Greenberg, one of the speakers at the memorial meeting, closed his remarks in this way:

> I feel that I speak not merely for myself, but for all who received instruction from his mouth when in the words of the poet I say:
>
> > Whatever way my days decline
> > I felt and feel, tho' left alone
> > His being working in mine own
> > The footsteps of his life in mine.
>
> May his memory continue to inspire and to bless us. Amen.[117]

[116] In his address at that meeting, Adler explained why friends and associates had waited slightly over a month to "gather together to speak words in his [Margolis'] memory" ("Address of Doctor Adler at the Meeting in Memory of Max L. Margolis," p. 1 of typescript found in the Dropsie College Archives):

> Our colleague and teacher, Max Leopold Margolis, departed this life on the Sabbath, April 2nd, the 25th of Adar Sheni, and again following our custom that there should be no public mourning during the festival month of Nisan, we have awaited its conclusion and now are met here to revere his memory and derive lessons for ourselves from his career.

[117] Simon Greenberg, "Talk Delivered at Professor Max Leopold Margolis Memorial Meeting," p. 6 of typescript found in the Dropsie College Archives.

3. BIBLE TRANSLATION

"No translation in the English tongue can be anything but a revision of the English Bible of 1611 [from Margolis, *The Story of Bible Translations*]"

In the summer of 1907, Max and Evelyn Margolis fled the academic and personal turmoil of Cincinnati for a tranquil year of research, writing, and travel in Europe. Margolis' warm reception by European scholars, in marked contrast to the hostility he had left behind, allowed him to produce or lay the groundwork for several important publications. There was, perhaps, but one discordant note: 1907–1908 was not a sabbatical year, at the end of which he could look forward to returning to a secure academic position. For Margolis, upholding deeply held academic and personal principles had entailed sacrifice of the security he would otherwise have enjoyed.

The circumstances under which Margolis left Hebrew Union College had been widely, if not always impartially, reported in the press. In addition, Margolis had taken pains to present his side of the story to Jewish leaders like Mayer Sulzberger. Margolis, then, had reason to hope that he would not be without suitable employment for long. Before his year abroad was over, these hopes were realized through the receipt of offers in Europe as well as in America. As described in chapter 2, Max and Evelyn Margolis chose to return to the United States and to settle in Philadelphia, where the leadership of the Jewish Publication Society (J.P.S.) had settled upon Max Margolis as the editor-in-chief of its new English translation of the Hebrew Bible.

It was in 1892 that the recently formed J.P.S. (it was founded in 1888) had embarked on a plan to produce a Biblical translation.[1] Up until then, only one English rendering of the entire Hebrew Bible had been com-

---

[1] The information in this and the following two paragraphs is taken in the main from these sources: Max L. Margolis, *The Story of Bible Translations* (Philadelphia: The Jewish Publication Society of America, 1917 [reprinted, 1943]), 94, 99f; Jonathan D. Sarna and Nahum M. Sarna, unpublished manuscript on American Jewish Biblical Scholarship, 24–26 (Jonathan Sarna kindly gave me access to this manuscript—which is scheduled for publication in an SBL volume—when I was in Cincinnati during the summer of 1985. All citations to this work [which will be referred to simply as "Sarna"] are based on the unpublished manuscript. I wish to acknowledge my gratitude to Jonathan Sarna, who is in the midst of writing a centennial history of J.P.S., for his

pleted within the American Jewish community. This version, the work of
Isaac Leeser, appeared in 1853; over the next four decades it gained wide
acceptance in synagogues and Jewish homes throughout the English-
speaking world.[2] In the early 1890s, however, influential Jewish leaders
felt the need to provide their constituency with an up-to-date translation,
for by that time Leeser's original work was almost half a century old. In
addition, the 1880s had witnessed the publication of the Old Testament
portion of the Revised Version (1885), a revision of the King James Bible
on which a group of leading Protestant scholars labored for almost fifteen
years.[3]

Several specific steps were taken to implement the 1892 J.P.S. decision
to produce a Jewish translation that would replace Leeser and merit a
place alongside the best of Christian scholarship. Marcus Jastrow was
eventually named as editor-in-chief of this enterprise, and he also served
as chairman of an editorial committee, which was to assign separate
books of the bible to individual translators and later revise and harmonize
the finished products. Among those involved in this rather complex
project, which—it was hoped—would be completed far more quickly
than the Revised Version, were Kaufmann Kohler, Cyrus Adler, and
Sabato Morais.

Both American and British Jews were invited to contribute translations. Originally conceived as a fairly straightforward revision of Leeser,
this undertaking soon became bogged down as each translator approached his task in a somewhat different manner. By 1903, after more
than ten years of labor, the translation of only one book had appeared in
published form, Kaufmann Kohler's rendering of Psalms. Jastrow, who
died two months before Kohler's Psalms came out, was replaced by
Solomon Schechter, who had recently arrived from England to head the
newly-reorganized Jewish Theological Seminary in New York City. Schechter, a scholar of prodigious achievements, remained with this J.P.S.
project for four years, finally resigning in 1907. The cumbersome process
that resulted in a new version of only one Biblical book had consumed an
enormous amount of time, talent, and money. The worthy goal, a new
Jewish translation of the Hebrew Bible into English, remained; what was
needed was a streamlined and more efficient means of attaining it.

No one could hope to recapture the time and money expended on the
previous project; however, a pool of talented scholars remained, ready to

numerous suggestions and comments); "The New English Translation of the Bible," *American
Jewish Yearbook* 1917, 164–166 (Joseph Reider [p. 106, *Max Leopold Margolis: Scholar and
Teacher*] writes that "it is certain that this article was written by Margolis . . . though not signed
by his name.").

[2] On the Leeser Bible, see now Lance J. Sussman, "Another Look at Isaac Leeser and the
First Jewish Translation of the Bible in the United States," *Modern Judaism* 5 (1985), 159–190.

[3] See below for further details on the Revised Version.

be drawn into service if only the proper organizational scheme could be devised. In particular, it was recognized that the idea of individual translators for each book of the Bible had to be abandoned in favor of a strong board of editors and a single editor-in-chief, whose responsibility it would be to prepare a preliminary translation of the entire text. It was also understood that this enterprise would be more successful, both in execution and in reception, if it involved representatives from a number of major organizations and seats of learning within the American Jewish community. The ultimate success of this project, in comparison with the failure of the earlier one, can be credited to the fact that a carefully chosen mix of dedicated people worked energetically within a well-conceived and closely coordinated framework.

This framework was the result of a decision made by two organizations, the Jewish Publication Society and the Central Conference of American Rabbis (C.C.A.R.), to produce the Bible translation as a joint venture. As stated in an article, "The New English Translation of the Bible," which appeared in the *American Jewish Yearbook* for 1917 (although no author is listed for this article, it is generally agreed that it was written by Margolis):

> In 1908 the Jewish Publication Society of America and the Central Conference of American Rabbis, which had taken up the project of issuing the Revised Version of 1885 in a form suitable for the synagogue, reached an agreement to co-operate in bringing out the new translation upon a revised plan of having the entire work done by a Board of Editors instead of endeavoring to harmonize the translations of individual contributors.[4]

The same wording appears in the Preface to the translation itself, with the exception of the clause "which . . . synagogue" that modifies C.C.A.R.[5] The significance of this omission, which is not accidental, will be discussed below.

As a result of the "agreement to co-operate," of which Cyrus Adler and David Philipson were the principal craftsmen, the following were appointed to the Editorial Committee: Solomon Schechter, Cyrus Adler, Joseph Jacobs, as J.P.S. representatives; Kaufmann Kohler, David Philipson, Samuel Schulman, representing the C.C.A.R.[6] These six scholars were "perfectly balanced so as to span both the Jewish academic world

---

[4] This quotation comes from p. 166 of the article.

[5] This statement is found on p. vi of the Preface. On the C.C.A.R. project, see Sarna, 25f.

[6] Each of the "principal craftsmen" wrote autobiographical accounts that include the period of negotiations leading up to the agreement described above: Cyrus Adler, *I Have Considered the Days* (Philadelphia: Jewish Publication Society of America, 1945), 287f; David Philipson, *My Life as an American Jew: An Autobiography* (Cincinnati: John G. Kidd & Son, 1941), 195–197.

(two each from the Jewish Theological Seminary, Hebrew Union College and Dropsie College) and the spectrum of Jewish observance."[7] As stated in "The New English Translation of the Bible" (p. 166), "by mutual agreement Prof. Max L. Margolis was chosen as the seventh member, and was appointed Editor-in-Chief of the work and Secretary to the Editorial Board, of which Dr. Cyrus Adler was elected Chairman."[8]

It is striking to observe that Margolis was "the only biblical specialist among the seven men on the Editorial Committee."[9] Margolis can easily be viewed as a logical choice for the editorship; somewhat less easy, but with a certain logic, nonetheless, is the selection of the other six men, in preference to scholars with more expertise in the specific field of Biblical studies. Commenting on the Committee's make-up, Jonathan Sarna offers several observations that, while necessarily tentative, provide a solid basis for understanding the motives of those responsible for the appointments:

> Viewed retrospectively, the Bible translation committee, aside from Margolis himself, represented much less than the best that Jewish Bible scholarship in America had to offer. Morris Jastrow, Casper Levias, William Rosenau, Moses Buttenwieser, Julian Morgenstern, Jacob Hoschander, and, most talented of all, Arnold Bogumil Ehrlich, although recognized by their peers as qualified biblical and semitic scholars, were conspicuously absent. . . . Scholarly rabbis representing the C.C.A.R. . . .and wide-ranging scholars representing the J.P.S. were deemed more suitable for the task. Religious politics, personality factors, facility in the English language, and, above all, the desire to move ahead expeditiously without becoming bogged down in scholarly fine points may explain the decision; evidence is lacking.[10]

The published accounts of the Bible translation, one of which was cited above, give the impression that Margolis' appointment was made only after the rest of the Committee was formally constituted. This was, however, not the case: the offer to Margolis came in the spring of 1908; not until the fall of that year, when Margolis was already busy at work, did the Committee reach its full strength of seven members. As noted in chapter 2, Cyrus Adler, with whom Margolis had been corresponding throughout the winter of 1907–1908, pledged his "hearty support" to

[7] Sarna, 29.

[8] See also the similarly worded satement on p. vi of the Preface to the translation.

[9] Harry M. Orlinsky, "Jewish Biblical Scholarship in America," *Essays in Biblical Culture and Bible Translation* (New York: KTAV, 1974), 310. See also Orlinsky's comments in "Wanted: A New English Translation of the Bible for the Jewish People," *Essays in Biblical Culture and Bible Translation* (New York: KTAV, 1974), 354. "Wanted . . ." is a copy of an address Orlinsky delivered in 1953 at the annual meeting of J.P.S.

[10] Sarna, 29f. Several of these points will be taken up below.

Margolis if "you will see your way clear to take up the work in connection with the Bible, suggested by the Jewish Publication Society."[11] In this letter, dated April 27, 1908, Adler expressed his firm conviction that the Bible project was sufficiently valuable for Margolis to put aside for a while other, "more scholarly" pursuits:

> I believe that the work will be of great usefulness, and it is necessary for many reasons that it should now be pushed to a speedy conclusion. While it may interrupt more scholarly work, its practical importance is very great.[12]

Margolis seems to have received the J.P.S. communication some time in the second or third week of April 1908. Since earlier correspondence (including a letter from Margolis dated April 6, 1908) lacks even the briefest reference to the activities of the J.P.S., it is likely that its offer of employment came as something of a surprise to Margolis. The apparent goal of his previous letters to Adler was eventual appointment to the faculty of Dropsie.[13] If Margolis' statements can be taken at face value,[14] he had no idea that the editorship at J.P.S. might in the near future lead to a postion at that College.

It may be that the selection of Margolis as editor-in-chief was connected with an April 5 meeting, at which the C.C.A.R. "accepted an invitation from the Jewish Publication Society to cooperate 'in issuing an English translation of the Bible under Jewish auspices.'"[15] At any rate, it is clear that no decision would have been taken without the approval of leaders such as Mayer Sulzberger, chairman of the J.P.S. Publication Committee; Cyrus Adler, whom Sarna describes as "long the power behind the throne at J.P.S."[16]; and the C.C.A.R.'s David Philipson. The assent of Philipson is noteworthy: just a year earlier he and Margolis had hurled bitter charges at each other in the midst of the controversy that

---

[11] Cyrus Adler to Max L. Margolis (in Munich), April 27, 1908 (Dropsie College Archives).
[12] *Ibid.*
[13] Recall that Margolis, while still in Cincinnati, had written to Mayer Sulzberger on this matter. Adler sensed that Margolis' letters to him were not unconnected with Dropsie, as is evident in a letter from Adler to Sulzberger, dated December 23, 1907 (Dropsie College Archives): "I send you a letter from Dr. Margolis and a copy of my reply. I have no doubt that, although he did not ask for it, he expected some statement concerning Dropsie College, but I did not feel warranted in alluding to the subject." This was even before Adler's formal election as Dropsie's president, for which Margolis offered "sincerest congratulations" as the first item in his April 6, 1908 letter (this letter is found in the Dropsie College Archives).
[14] See, for example, his statement (quoted in chapter 2) to Max Heller, in a letter dated September 21, 1908: "My days of wandering are by no means over, nor do I see anything ahead of my present position which of course terminates with my work."
[15] Sarna, 26.
[16] Sarna, 27.

culminated in Margolis' departure from Cincinnati.[17] This new project would also allow Margolis to reestablish relations with another erstwhile foe, Kaufmann Kohler.

In the pursuit of scholarship, it may be hoped, personal clashes have no place. Margolis himself was not sure that this lofty sentiment could be implemented. In the fall of 1908, with the make-up of the full Committee still to be determined, Margolis addressed the question of "personalities":

> It is needless for me to indicate my own preferences. Schechter, I understand, has accepted a place upon the board; and Kohler's chances are enhanced. The two will hardly be able to work harmoniously together. What a pity that personalities cannot be kept out of this work.[18]

In this instance, Margolis' worst fears did not materialize: personality clashes did not mar the deliberations of the Editorial Committee during its several years of sometimes very intense activity.

Margolis was more hopeful when it came to the prospect of working with Adler, whose elevation to the post of Committee chairman was welcomed by Margolis in a letter of August 7, 1908:

> I am glad to learn from a conversation with the Chairman of the Publication Committee [Sulzberger] that you are contemplated by him as a member of the Board of Editors, indeed as the chairman thereof. . . . I am confident that our joint labors will carry the stupendous task to a speedy and successful termination, and that, with you in the chair, the deliberations on mooted questions cannot be carried on but in a dignified and objective manner.

The record shows that Margolis and Adler did work well on this project; in addition, as suggested above, Adler managed to keep the Committee's attention focused on the scholarly work before it.

[17] In his autobiography, *My Life as an American Jew* (p. 197), Philipson wrote of the discussion between himself and Adler that culminated in the offer to Margolis:

> The task of finding [the] man who was to be the editor-in-chief was entrusted to Dr. Adler . . . and myself . . . . At a meeting between Dr. Adler and myself, we canvassed possibilities for this most important task, possibly the leading literary task in the history of American Jewry. To my mind there was one man in the country best fitted. When I mentioned the name, Dr. Adler was greatly surprised and pleased. He was surprised because of the known differences of opinion between the scholar I mentioned and myself, notably on the subject of Zionism. . . . The man in question was Prof. Max L. Margolis. . . . I told Dr. Adler that I considered Margolis the leading Jewish exegete in the country, and that this was all that counted with me in the present situation.

[18] Max L. Margolis to Max Heller (American Jewish Archives).

Margolis as editor-in-chief first met with the other members of the full Editorial Committee in December 1908.[19] By that time he had completed his draft of a translation of the Pentateuch. Prior to the initial meeting, he had forwarded this draft to each Committee member, along with a statement of the principles that guided him in his work.[20] It is clear, then, that in Margolis the J.P.S. had found not only a preeminent scholar, but also—what was for them of at least equal importance—a speedy one. Margolis' letters throughout the fall of 1908 chronicle the fast pace of translation he set for himself. In a letter written on September 4 and addressed to Stephen S. Wise, Margolis provides evidence for the date upon which he commenced his labors: "the revision of Genesis begun a week ago will be finished to-day."[21] The press of work made it necessary for him "to forego the pleasure of lengthy discussion" with Wise should he wish to visit Margolis at his home.[22] Some three weeks later (on September 21), he wrote to Max Heller in New Orleans that he had begun the translation "with zeal and earnestness."[23] These two attributes undoubtedly served Margolis in good stead as he continued to make rapid progress. Shortly after the letter just quoted, he again wrote to Heller, informing him that "I have just gotten as far as Numbers 16. Without impairing the efficiency of the work, I am instructed to make haste."[24] And "make haste" he did. On November 1, he was able to write

---

[19] Philipson described the mood of this first meeting—which changed, decidedly for the better, as the session progressed:

> The first meeting of this joint board was scheduled to take place in the closing week of December, 1908. Adler and I looked forward with some trepidation to this meeting, owing to the not very warm feeling that existed between Dr. Kohler and Margolis. We arranged that he should sit next to Dr. Margolis at the meeting and I next to Dr. Kohler so that we might pour oil on troubled waters should there be disturbances between the two gentlemen. We knew that this first meeting was crucial. Happily, the session passed off peaceably and the great work was successfully launched.

David Philipson, *My Life as an American Jew*, 197. For his part, Adler recalled that

> The Board met at first in a rather strained atmosphere. Margolis had, a couple of years before, left the Hebrew Union College after a serious difference of opinion between himself, Kohler and most of the Board of Governors, amongst whom Philipson was prominent. This attitude of strain soon relaxed and, in the course of the seven years the Board sat together, clashes became less frequent, and it was in a spirit of thankfulness to God that we completed these labors.

Cyrus Adler, *I Have Considered the Days*, 288.

[20] See Margolis, *Bible Translations*, 102.

[21] Max L. Margolis to Stephen S. Wise, September 4, 1908 (Archives of the American Jewish Historical Society).

[22] *Ibid.*

[23] Margolis to Heller, September 21, 1908 (American Jewish Archives).

[24] Margolis to Heller (American Jewish Archives).

to Stephen Wise that "I have finished the revision of the Pentateuch."[25]

Others may have paused, if only momentarily, after completing—in little more than two months—so ardous a labor as the preparation of a revised Pentateuch. Margolis did not. In fact, he wrote on November 1, not to establish a milestone, but to give Wise one last opportunity to assist him in his rapidly approaching work on the book of Judges: "I can definitely calculate [Margolis states] that I shall need your translation of the Book of Judges not later than Nov. 10. I must be through with the revision of Judges by Nov. 16."[26] Less than a week on Judges! This is just the timetable Margolis had set for himself as far back as September, when he wrote, in an earlier letter to Wise: "I have calculated that I could give the Book of Judges just five days, allowing one day for the Song of Deborah."[27] No wonder that even the writing of letters and the celebration of holidays seemed something of a burden to Margolis: "Pardon the brevity of my answer [he wrote to Max Heller Erev Sukkot 1908], as I am snatching these moments from my busy day, and there have been so many interruptions this month owing to the holidays."[28] As was the case with Wise and Judges, Margolis had to set a firm deadline for Heller also: "[Your] translation of Samuel I shall need towards the end of November of the present year."[29]

By January of 1909, Margolis was giving vent to at least three specific complaints about the conditions under which he toiled: "With the salary I am present receiving for my Bible work, I am living in cramped conditions, and I am giving the work much more time than could reasonably be expected. . . ."[30] The trace of bitterness that can be detected here may be a result of the almost constant pressure under which Margolis was working—by then for more than eighteen weeks. The context in which Margolis made this statement, however, suggests that other factors also came into play: he was writing to Adler about what was, from Margolis' point of view, the inadequate salary being offered him in connection with his professorship at Dropsie.[31] It was to Margolis' advantage to paint a reasonably dark, though not inaccurate picture of his present circumstances, in the hope that Dropsie's Board would be moved

[25] Margolis to Wise, November 1, 1908 (Archives of the American Jewish Historical Society).

[26] *Ibid*.

[27] Margolis to Wise, September 4, 1908 (Archives of the American Jewish Historical Society).

[28] Margolis to Heller (American Jewish Archives).

[29] *Ibid*.

[30] Margolis to Adler, January 17, 1909 (Dropsie College Archives).

[31] See, more fully, the entire six page letter, dated January 17, 1909, that Margolis sent to Adler, and the earlier communication (dated January 3) that Adler had addressed to Margolis. Extensive quotations from both of these letters may be found in the preceding chapter.

by his current plight to compensate him all the more generously as the first faculty member hired at their Institution.

Even if it is agreed that Margolis overstated the difficulty of his situation, it should not be overlooked that the task he set for himself was formidable. Although the Editorial Board had been willing to allow Margolis approximately two years to prepare his draft of a translation of the entire Hebrew Bible, he could earn a bonus by completing his job sooner. This is clear from the continuation of Margolis' remarks in his January 17, 1909 letter to Adler: ". . . and I am giving the work much more time than could reasonably be expected, in order to complete the work in the minimum of time and obtain the bonus which it was promised I should be allowed in proportion to the maximum of time (twenty months)." In that same letter, he estimated that "by September 1 of this year I shall have completed the manuscript of the Bible translation, so far at least as my own part therein is concerned."[32] A revised translation of the Bible in twelve months (he had begun the work on approximately September 1, 1908) would have been a singularly impressive achievement. How much more impressive is the reality: Margolis actually finished his manuscript on August 1, a month earlier than his own estimate.[33]

Margolis had another reason, in addition to monetary considerations, for wanting to be finished by September 1, 1909. As he wrote to Adler:

> I fully coincide with your wish that my duties with the Dropsie College should not begin until I had terminated my work on the Bible Translation, or had at least so far completed it that my duties with Dropsie College would not hinder this Bible Translation. I calculate that by September 1 of this year I shall have completed the manuscript of the Bible Translation . . . I should therefore wish that, should the Board of Governors ratify your recommendation [to hire Margolis], my duties should be made to begin on September 1.[34]

As it was, Margolis did formally assume his duties at Dropsie on Septembr 1, 1909, shortly after completing, ahead of his own schedule, the Bible translation.

It is clear that Margolis proceeded very rapidly in his translation of the Hebrew Bible; it is also clear why he maintained the pace and schedule he did. Still to be discussed is the procedure he adopted in fashioning his revision. It was necessary to consult all potentially useful sources and yet to do so in as expeditious a manner as possible. No one was better

---

[32] Margolis to Adler, January 17, 1909 (Dropsie College Archives).
[33] Margolis, *Bible Translations*, 101.
[34] Margolis to Adler, January 17, 1909 (Dropsie College Archives).

qualified than Margolis to achieve these goals, for he was able confidently to rely upon his thorough acquaintance with ancient languages and scribal practices, with the Jewish exegetical traditions, and with the techniques and results of modern critical scholarship. The task of examining the sources is but part of the process of producing a translation, a process than even Margolis could not have completed in less than a year had it been his and the Committee's intention to create an entirely new rendering, independent of earlier English language versions.

In fact, neither Margolis nor the Committee thought of the J.P.S. translation in terms of *creatio ex nihilo*. On several occasions (see, e.g., his letters quoted above) Margolis referred to his work as a "revision," implying by his usually careful choice of words that he was dependent on an existing text, into which he introduced corrections and improvements in accordance with principles formulated by him and "somewhat modified by the whole Board."[35] Nor can there be any doubt what the existing text was: it was the Revised Version (RV) of 1885.

This translation of the Old Testament came about as a result of a recommendation adopted by the governing bodies of the Church of England in 1870. By that recommendation, the Church put into motion a plan to produce an "official" revision of the King James Version (KJV) that would remain close to KJV's language and cadence and yet reflect the critical scholarship then in vogue. Committees of English scholars and ministers were established to prepare texts of the Old Testament, the New Testament, and the Apocrypha. (The RV of the New Testament appeared in 1881; the volume containing the Apocrypha was published ten years after the Old Testament, in 1895.) American experts also formed translation committees and, following guidelines and procedures similar to their English counterparts, prepared a revision of their own. Some readings suggested by the Americans were accepted into the final text of the RV; others, which the British committees rejected, were printed as an appendix to the editions published by the University presses of Cambridge and Oxford.

In accordance with an agreement reached by the committees in both countries, a new edition of the RV appeared in the United States in 1901. The innovative feature of this version, often known as the American Standard Version, is its incorporation into the text itself of the American

---

[35] Margolis, *Bible Translations*, 102. As Margolis writes, using the third person to describe his own activities:

> When in December 1908 he met his colleagues on the Board . . . , he set forth to them the principles which had guided him in the preparation of the draft, a transcript of which containing the Pentateuch had been forwarded to all of them in advance. The principles were discussed and somewhat modified by the whole Board. . . .

preferences that had been previously relegated to an appendix.[36] Although Margolis made use of this American version as well as of the sixteen pages of corrections prepared by the Jewish Religious Education Board in London,[37] it was the 1885 text itself that was the basis of Margolis' revision.

From Margolis himself come several indications of the extent to which the J.P.S. translation was dependent on the RV. Among the letters cited above are two from Margolis to Stephen S. Wise. Wise, who by 1908 was already a prominent Jewish leader and who was also one of Margolis' oldest friends, had been asked to prepare a translation of the book of Judges for the earlier project headed by Marcus Jastrow. Jastrow's request, initially made in the 1890s, had been renewed in 1905.[38] Wise had agreed, on both occasions, to undertake the translation, but he had apparently submitted nothing to the J.P.S. by the time Margolis took over. Early in September 1908, Wise forwarded to Margolis a description of the Judges translation he envisioned; Wise's plan, which seems to have been fairly elaborate, included "a discussion of divergent opinions of translators."[39]

In response to this plan, Margolis quoted from "the instructions sent to me by authority of the Chairman of the Publication Committee [Mayer Sulzberger]":

It shall be the duty of the Editor-in-Chief to prepare the manuscript of the translation for the press on the following lines:- The text of the Revised Version [the words "of the Revised Version" are underlined twice by Margolis] is to be used as the basis, and the revision of it by our Society shall be primarily of such a nature that it will remove all non-Jewish and anti-Jewish phrases, expressions, renderings, and usages. Into the text of the RV improvements shall be worked in from the following sources: 1:- The marginal notes of the RV; 2:- Changes of the American Committee of Revisers; 3:- Jewish divergent renderings prepared for the Jews of England; 4:- The translations already made for the JPS of America; 5:- Standard commentaries.[40]

[36] On the Revised Version, see Bruce Metzger in *The Word of God: A Guide to English Versions of the Bible*, ed. Lloyd R. Bailey (Atlanta: John Knox, 1982), 30–32; Sakae Kubo and Walter F. Specht, *So Many Versions? 20th Century English Versions of the Bible* (Grand Rapids, Michigan: Zondervan, 1983 [revised and enlarged edition]), 44–48; Margolis, *Bible Translations*, 95–98; Sarna, 24f.

[37] Sarna, p. 25: "The Jewish Religious Education Board in London [published] sixteen pages of corrections titled *Appendix to the Revised Version* (1896)." On Margolis' use of these and other sources, see below.

[38] For this, see the letter of Marcus Jastrow to Stephen S. Wise, dated December 26, 1898, and a communication to Wise from Israel Friedlaender, dated May 24, 1905. (Both of these letters are in the Archives of the American Jewish Historical Society.)

[39] Margolis to Wise, September 4, 1908 (Archives of the American Jewish Historical Society).

[40] *Ibid*. The first part of this statement is also quoted by Sarna (pp. 27f), who notes that it was

It is noteworthy that not only is the RV "the basis" for the J.P.S. text, but also three of the five sources for "improvements" are directly related to the RV.

The Editorial Board did not attempt to hide the fact that Margolis and other Board members made use of the RV in preparing the J.P.S. translation. After all, the Preface to the printed edition of this translation contains a statement similar in content to Margolis' "instructions":

> In preparing the manuscript for consideration by the Board of Editors, Professor Margolis took into account existing English versions, the standard commentaries, ancient and modern, the translations already made for the Jewish Publication Society of America, the divergent renderings from the Revised Version prepared for the Jews of England, the marginal notes of the Revised Version, and the changes of the American Committee of Revisers.[41]

It would, however, be impossible for an outsider, relying on an enumeration such as this, to ascertain that the RV actually served as "*the* [emphasis added] basis" for the translation he was about to read.

The RV's central role in the formation of the J.P.S. translation is further obscured by a lengthy list of other material used by the Editorial Board. In the Preface this listing, in which Jewish sources predominate, follows immediately after the enumeration quoted above:

> Due weight was given to the ancient versions as establishing a tradition of interpretation, notably the Septuagint and the versions of Aquila, Symmachus, and Theodotion, the Targums, the Peshitta, the Vulgate, and the Arabic version of Saadya. Talmudic and midrashic allusions and all available Jewish commentators, both the great mediaeval authorities, like Rashi, Kimhi, and Ibn Ezra, and the moderns S. D. Luzzatto, Malbim, and Ehrlich, as well as all the important non-Jewish commentators, were consulted.[42]

It is hard to imagine that the Editorial Board members were unaware of the favorable impression that the mention of famous Jewish authorities would have on the intended audience to which the Preface (and the translation itself) was addressed.[43]

---

drawn up and approved at the April 5, 1908 meeting of the J.P.S. Publication Committee during which representatives of J.P.S. and C.C.A.R. "agreed on 'the desirability of issuing an English version of the Bible under Jewish auspices.'"

[41] See pp. vi–vii of the Preface.

[42] See p. vii of the Preface.

[43] There is no reason to doubt that all of the sources named above were indeed consulted; what is at issue here is not deception over what was used, but lack of full disclosure—in public pronouncements—concerning the translation's dependence on the RV. Board members, intent

Later in the Preface there occurs a further reference to the RV and other English renderings of the Biblical text:

> We are, it is hardly needful to say, deeply grateful for the works of our non-Jewish predecessors, such as the Authorised Version [KJV] with its admirable diction, which can never be surpassed, as well as for the Revised Version with its ample learning—but they are not ours. The Editors have not only used these famous English versions. . . . Upon doubtful points in style, all English versions have been drawn upon.[44]

Doubtless the editors did consult a variety of English translations produced under the auspices of Protestant and Catholic bodies, but it is also the case that only one of these, the Revised Version of 1885, provided the text into which the Editors introduced "improvements," some of which derived from KJV and other early translations.

When it comes to describing the procedure by which Margolis "worked . . . improvements . . . into the text of the RV," it is not necessary to resort to conjecture. The very workbooks he used as editor-in-chief have been preserved at Dropsie College.[45] From them comes the clearest evidence of how the RV served as the basis for the J.P.S. translation. The workbooks (there are twenty-one in all) contain blank pages, onto which individual pages from a large-print edition of the RV have been pasted. Margolis then inserted the desired changes into the text of the RV itself or placed them in the wide margins formed by the blank pages. It was this procedure, in its early stages, that Margolis described to Wise in his letter of September 4, 1908:

> If you care to be really helpful in my revision work, work out your divergences of the RV after the manner of the enclosed slip, exactly as I am constrained myself to work out similar cases even though I avail myself of all possible literature whether in print or in MS. form.[46]

---

on gaining wide acceptance in the Jewish community for their labors, surely felt justified in following the course they did. It is in this light that we can understand the Preface's omission of any statement about the C.C.A.R.'s earlier plan to issue "the Revised Version of 1885 in a form suitable for the synagogue," a statement found, for example, in the *American Jewish Yearbook*, where it was less likely to draw the attention of numerous readers. An air of secrecy on these matters appears to date from at least as early as the April 5, 1908 meeting between leaders of the J.P.S. and C.C.A.R. At that meeting, during which the decision was reached "to produce the Bible as quickly as possible," both sides also agreed "secretly . . . that the only way to accomplish this feat was 'that the text of the Revised Version be used as the basis'" (Sarna, p. 28).

[44] See p. viii of the Preface. See below on matters of "diction" and "style."

[45] My sincerest thanks go to David M. Goldenberg, Dropsie's current president, for calling my attention to these workbooks and making them available to me. In an oral interview, Harry M. Orlinsky recalls seeing these workbooks, which he refers to as ledgers, on a big desk in Margolis' office at Dropsie. This was in the fall of 1931. (See chapter 2.) After Margolis' death, Orlinsky had the opportunity to look through these ledgers in some detail.

[46] Margolis to Wise, September 4, 1908 (Archives of the American Jewish Historical Society).

Although no researcher has yet compiled a precise statistical analysis of the "divergences of the RV" accepted into the text of the J.P.S. translation, a glance through Margolis' workbooks confirms the general observation of Orlinksy that "in truth, the 1917 Jewish version was essentially but an extremely modest revision of the English Revised Version of 1885, a revision that probably did not exceed more than a very few percent of the whole."[47] At the same time, it is important to recognize, with Sarna, that "more than anyone originally expected, he [Margolis] also proceeded to deviate from the Revised Version, sometimes on scholarly not just religious grounds."[48]

The range of "deviations," both technical and exegetical, as well as their frequency, can be gauged in part by reading through the last portion of the Preface, two sections of "The New English Translation" ('Technical Improvements' and especially 'The Merits of the New Translation'), and the final chapter of *The Story of Bible Translations* (Chapter VIII: "The Difficulties Inherent in All Bible Translations"). These remarks, aimed primarily at Jewish audiences, place emphasis on new features of the J.P.S. translation: "In all externals the new translation is especially adapted for use in synagogue and school," "the changes introduced in passages involving improved exegesis . . . constitute the chief merit of this translation," and so forth.[49]

And yet, in fashioning the text, Margolis took care to acknowledge his debt, not only to the Jewish tradition and the gamut of Biblical scholarship, but also—and this is significant—to the "style" and "diction" of the KJV, which were largely retained in the RV:

> Great care was taken to harmonize the style in every change introduced, and the stately diction of the Elizabethan period was retained throughout the book. The Editors have thus succeeded in clothing new interpretations in the old garb.[50]

For Margolis, this "old garb," dismissed by some of his contemporaries as hopelessly dated and threadbare, supplied the only vestment suitable for rendering the sacred writings of Israel into the English language:

> No translation in the English tongue . . . can be anything but a revision, a revision of the English Bible of 1611 [KJV], itself a revision. All

[47] Harry M. Orlinsky, "The New Jewish Version of the Torah: Toward a New Philosophy of Bible Translation," *Essays in Biblical Culture and Bible Translation* (New York: KTAV), 1974), 399f. The introductory note to this essay states that it is "reprinted—with some slight changes—from *Journal of Biblical Literature* 82 (1963), 249–264."
[48] Sarna, 29.
[49] The two quotations come from pp. 169 and 171 of "The New English Translation."
[50] The New English Translation," 171. See also the statement from the Preface quoted above.

attempts at modernizing the Bible English must necessarily fail. Once and for all time the revisers of 1611 fixed the model for all future undertakings.[51]

These twin themes—the beauty and power of "the stately diction" of the KJV, the utter failure of "all attempts at modernizing the Bible English"—frequently find their way into Margolis' discussion of Bible translations:

> [KJV] has an inimitable charm and rhythm; the coloring of the original is not obliterated, and yet examples abound of idiomatic renditions reproducing the thought in an admirable manner. It ranks as a classic in English literature, and has exercised a potent influence upon writers of English to this day. . . . When modern revisers have changed its matchless diction where no difference of meaning was involved, they have erred in their zeal. Practical as the object of all Bible translations must be, the King James Version, in which so many earlier efforts have deposited their happiest and best, has pointed out the way how with accuracy of rendition there must go elegance of style, and how a translation of the Scriptures must aim at rivalling the stately diction of the original.[52]

> The English Bible is a classic. The best English writers have modeled their productions upon it. Competent scholars assert that the English of the Bible is a great force in the English that is written today. Quaint though it be, it has not ceased to be understood. Many of its expressions have passed into proverbs and live in the mouth of the people. What gives it particular charm is its matchless simplicity. Its rhetoric is not of the cheap sort. There is no straining after effect, no playing on or with words. . . . What imparts to the English Bible its beauty, aye, its simplicity, comes from the [Hebrew] original.[53]

> [Commenting on "a translation into present-day English" of the book of Genesis] As with other attempts in the same direction. . ., the effect is not a pleasing one. I doubt whether the modern man is so far removed from the language of Shakespeare that the English of the Authorized Version [KJV], barring isolated cases, is for him unintelligible. As for style, generations have labored in creating the English biblical diction which alone seems to fit the sacred literature. Somehow the older translators had the right feeling for the simplicity of the original which no modern paraphrase can match.[54]

[51] Margolis, *Bible Translations*, 104f.
[52] Margolis, *Bible Translations*, 78.
[53] Max L. Margolis, "The Tercentenary of the English Bible," *B'nai B'rith News* April 1911, 10.
[54] Max L. Margolis, "Review of F. P. Ramsay, *An Interpretation of Genesis. Including a translation into present-day English*," *JQR* n.s. 3 (1912/13), 134f.

The Revised Version of 1885 appealed to Margolis precisely because it retained, even in its changes, the language of the KJV and because so many of its changes reflected the best of late nineteenth century Biblical scholarship. Margolis, then, had no difficulty in accepting the RV text as the basis for a revision tailored to the needs of Jewish audiences, in accordance with a general framework already established before his assumption of duties as editor-in-chief.

As chronicled above, Margolis plunged into his work, which, despite some misgivings, he completed with dispatch and (for the most part) considerable enthusiasm. Much of this enthusiasm stemmed from his love for language, a love he shared with his wife Evelyn, who served as her husband's secretary for this project:

> Mrs. Margolis . . . was secretary to her husband on the Bible project, drawing the munificent salary of $25 per month. In order to prepare for the work, both she and her husband had re-read Shakespeare, Marlowe, Ben Jonson and every possible Elizabethan author to 'steep ourselves in the language of the times for the full flavor of the period. . . .' Many times, as her husband was considering the translation of a certain phrase or word, Mrs. Margolis remembers, 'he would turn to me and say, "Repeat this phrase. How does it sound? How would you say it?"'[55]

In his address at the memorial service for Margolis, James Montgomery called attention to the remarkable fact that it was the Russian-born Max L. Margolis who, along with another eastern European, Solomon Schechter, had major responsibility for shaping the language of the J.P.S. translation.[56] Other Editorial Board members, such as Adler and Philipson, "were products of the American educational system . . . and had obtained the bulk of their Jewish knowledge in the United States."[57] Yet, on matters of style as well as of interpretation, they regularly deferred to Margolis, who, not so many years earlier, had felt more comfortable composing his Ph.D. dissertation in Latin rather than in English.[58]

When Margolis received his doctorate from Columbia in 1891, he had been in America less than two years. During the three years he was in New York City, he came to know well the difficult conditions in which other recent immigrants lived. Margolis' close ties with Jewish immigrant communities survived the passage of time and changes in his residence. In fact, concern for the welfare of his fellow immigrants can be

[55] Mrs. Max L. Margolis, *Biographical Appreciation*, 14.
[56] James A. Montgomery, "The Genius of Professor Margolis." (An address delivered at the meeting in memory of Margolis, May 9, 1932. Montgomery's observation is found on p. 6 of a typescript of this talk [Dropsie College Archives].)
[57] Sarna, 28.
[58] On this point, see chapter 1.

detected in Margolis' endorsement of the important principle "that the text of the Revised Version be used as the basis" for the J.P.S. translation:[59] Margolis was confidently offering the RV text to immigrant Jews as a model of dignified, formal English worthy of study and emulation. As he wrote:

> The English Bible is a classic. The best English writers have modeled their productions upon it. . . . The English of the Bible is a great force in the English that is written today. . . . As English-speaking Jews, we must be here receivers, not givers. Our children that are educated in the schools of the land get the influence of that great English classic at least indirectly, in every poem they memorize, in every oration they study. We of maturer years who have come to this country will fail of our purpose if we model our English upon the daily newspaper or magazine article. With the ephemeral subject goes the ephemeral diction. Our standards become vitiated, and we measure the dignity of a language by its intelligibility at the hands of the illiterate immigrant, even though his date of arrival may be half a century ago. We Jews of America—and of England—must study the Bible English, read it and re-read it, that we may possess ourselves of an English style which may pass scrutiny on the part of those who know.[60]

Margolis made clear, of course, that he was recommending reliance on the RV's language and style, not on its interpretations and theological perspectives:

> We of this generation . . . welcome assistance from any corner. . . . Scientific method we are glad to acquire from the Christian . . . we are admirers of the beauty of diction in the Anglican Church Versions; but we have a knowledge of the Scriptural language which is at once intimate and full. The stores of Jewish interpretation are to us an open book and we make free use thereof. Would that all Jews could read the Scriptures in the original! The next best thing is to read them in a translation done by Jews for Jews, permeated with the same Jewish spirit which pervades the original.[61]

To Margolis and his co-workers, the J.P.S. translation met and exceeded all of these criteria.

From approximately September 1, 1908 to August 1, 1909, Margolis had devoted his, and his wife's, time and energy to the preparation of a draft of the J.P.S. translation. It was not, however, until 1917 that the

---

[59] See above on this principle; note references to Sarna, 27f.

[60] Max L. Margolis, "The Tercentenary of the English Bible," *B'nai B'rith News* April 1911, 10.

[61] Max L. Margolis, "A Jewish Translation of the Scriptures," *B'nai B'rith News* May 1913, 10.

translation finally appeared in print form. During the intervening years it was the responsibility of Margolis and Adler, both of whom were involved in a myriad of other activities,[62] to keep the Editorial Committee meeting and deliberating at regular intervals and to shepherd the completed manuscript through the series of galley and page proofs that preceded publication. It is not clear that anyone in 1908 or 1909 had an idea of how long the editorial process would take.

In the absence of any criticism of Margolis' and Adler's leadership, it is safe to assume that those involved were satisfied with the rate of progress and the procedures adopted. These procedures, which were similar in many respects to those utilized by the Committees that produced the RV, established an open forum for the airing of divergent points of view, a mechanism for settling differences of opinion in an orderly fashion, and a systematic approach toward proofreading aimed at "placing this book before our readers without blemish":[63]

> A copy of [each section of Margolis'] manuscript was sent in advance to the members of the Board of Editors in order to give them ample time to consider the merits of every improvement proposed by the Editor-in-Chief and to enable them to make new suggestions not included in the draft. Sixteen meetings, each lasting ten days or more, covering a period of seven years (1908—1915), were held, at which the proposals in this manuscript and many additional suggestions by the members of the Board were considered. Each point was thoroughly discussed, and the view of the majority was incorporated into the manuscript. When the Board was evenly divided, the Chairman cast the deciding vote. From time to time sub-committees were at work upon points left open, and their reports, submitted to the Board, were discussed and voted upon. Before being sent to the printer the manuscript was once more examined in order to harmonize, as far as possible, the various suggestions made in the course of seven years. The first proof of the entire work was sent to each member of the Board for revision. The various corrections and suggestions made by the Editors were tabulated, and those which were supported by a majority or by a general rule of the Board were immediately inserted in the proof. There remained about three hundred cases for which the Editor-in-Chief and Chairman did not think it advisable to assume responsibility, and these were referred to the Board for discussion at the final meeting, the seventeenth, which

[62] It was during the latter part of this period, for example, that Margolis served as editor of the *Journal of Biblical Literature*. In addition, throughout this period Adler and Margolis were occupied, on a daily basis, with affairs at Dropsie.

[63] Simon Miller, J.P.S. president, to Margolis, November 26, 1915 (Dropsie College Archives): "I can appreciate the need of the most extreme care in placing this book before our readers without blemish, and therefore heartily concur in your plan [concerning proofreading]."

took place in the autumn of 1915.[64] The printer then prepared another proof which was carefully compared with the first by the Editor-in-Chief and Chairman, who removed slight discrepancies, consulting their colleagues by correspondence on weightier matters. In order to

[64] Looking back at these deliberations some thirty years after their completion, Adler expressed satisfaction that

> in the course of the seven years the Board sat together, clashes became less frequent, and it was in a spirit of thankfulness to God that we completed these labors. Although here and there a rendering crept in, by vote, which I thought was unhappy, on the whole I felt that a distinct contribution had been made to the interpretation of the Scriptures.

Cyrus Adler, *I Have Considered the Days*, 288f.
It was in a similarly positive vein that Philipson recalled these years:

> Three sessions of ten days or two weeks each were held yearly for seven years by the editorial board. These meetings were great and joyous experiences in the lives of all the men. Differences of opinion arose frequently during the deliberations, but all these differences were amicably composed. . . . That seven men of decidedly differing views on many questions could unite in a great common task was an unusual achievement and was so regarded by men of all shades of opinion. . . . Never did seven men of widely differing views work together more harmoniously.

David Philipson, *My Life as an American Jew*, 198–200.
From a different perspective, Jonathan Sarna (pp. 30f) observes that

> despite all good intensions, unforeseen, highly delicate problems continually cropped up. . . . To cite just one example; at the very end of the translation process, a fierce and quite revealing dispute broke out over how best to render Isaiah 9:5 (9:6 in Christian texts). The King James translation exuded Christology. . . . The Revised Version followed suit, with only minor modifications in style. Jewish translators properly insisted that nothing in Isaiah's original referred to the future . . . , but they had trouble with the translation of '*sar shalom.*' Leeser employed the phrase 'prince of peace,' presumably using the lower case to avoid misinterpretation. Samuel Schulman of the J.P.S. translation committee urged his colleagues to follow the same practice, since 'it calls attention to the fact, that we wish to avoid any possible Christological interpretation of the phrase.' Max L. Margolis and Cyrus Adler, by contrast, insisted that using the lower case would imply that the 'prince of peace' was a human being, 'exactly the thing we wished to avoid.' Strongly worded letters flew back and forth. The final translation, clearly more influenced by the desire to instruct Christians and defend Jews than by considerations of scholarship, banished 'prince of peace' altogether.

Harry M. Orlinsky, recalling Margolis' unique scholarly credentials vis-à-vis the other Committee members, paints an insightful, if necessarily speculative picture of what may well have been going on in Margolis' mind during many of the deliberative sessions:

> It must sometimes have been very difficult for Margolis to see a hand raised in opposition to a rendering of his, when the owner of the hand was voting on a linguistic problem involving the '"a'id' construction, or a rendering which revolved about the Coptic and Ethiopic versions, which were Greek to some of the Committee. But that is the penalty which an erudite Bible scholar must be prepared to pay.

Harry M. Orlinsky, "Wanted: A New English Translation of the Bible for the Jewish People," *Essays in Biblical Culture and Bible Translation* (New York: KTAV, 1974), 354.

issue as correct a translation as possible, the various proofs were read by
professional correctors, and each stage of proof was carefully compared
with the Hebrew original. Every measure was taken to make the edition
attractive from all points of view. No labour, no expense was spared.
Even at the final stages of proof, paragraphs were reset to make the
appearance more artistic. No detail, no matter how trivial, was neglected.[65]

Margolis also took upon himself the responsibility of producing two
other works in connection with the J.P.S. translation. The first, titled
Notes on the New Translation of the Holy Scriptures, is described by
Robert Gordis as "a highly valuable conspectus of all the scholarly
evidence upon which his [Margolis'] translation rested. This massive
collection of text-critical and exegetical material was issued, though only
in mimeographed form for private circulation in a tome of 646 pages,
under the title *Notes*. . . ."[66] The second book, which by contrast was
aimed at a popular audience, was *The Story of Bible Translations*.[67] Published in the same year as the J.P.S. translation (1917), it
succeeds in covering an extraordinarily large number of translators and
translations in an extraordinarily small number of pages (135 in all). This
volume, which at the time was well received by the general public, can
still be read with profit today, even by scholars and other specialists.

The J.P.S. translation itself evoked an enthusiastic response from much
of the Jewish community. Its immediate success can be judged by the
fact that "the first impression of 20,000 copies, issued January, 1917, was
disposed of by April, 1917."[68] The forty-second impression, which appeared in May 1959, brought to over 800,000 the number of J.P.S. *Holy
Scriptures* in print. By that year, a new generation of Jewish scholars and
scholarly rabbis had already begun work, again under the aegis of the
J.P.S., on a new translation of the Hebrew Bible. Harry M. Orlinsky, who
was named editor-in-chief of this new Jewish Version (NJV), had spoken
in 1953 of the inevitability and desirability of a "revised Jewish version":

> History [has] begun all over again. Leeser's Bible flourished in
> usefulness for some fifty years, until new conditions brought the JPS
> version into being. The JPS version, on the other hand, could not be

[65] "The New English Translation," 167f. Another, similar description of this nine-year process
appears in Margolis, *Bible Translations*, 102f. Both accounts mention the generosity of Jacob H.
Schiff, whose contribution of $50,000 (the largest amount donated by any single individual)
enabled J.P.S. "to carry out its plans on such a [grand] scale and yet sell the Bible at a very
moderate price" ("The New English Translation," 168).

[66] Gordis, "Appreciation," *Max Leopold Margolis: Scholar and Teacher*, 9.

[67] Frequent references to this work have been made throughout this chapter.

[68] "The New English Translation," 161, fn. 1. When published, the translation bore (and
continues to bear) as its complete title, *The Holy Scriptures, according to the Masoretic Text; a
new translation; with the aid of previous versions and with constant consultation of Jewish
authorities.*

expected to maintain undisputed popularity for so long a period, and for two reasons: firstly, the English language itself has undergone rapid change . . . and secondly, our knowledge of the background and text of the Hebrew Bible had increased since World War I by . . . enormous leaps and bounds. . . . In this respect there is a close parallel that may be drawn between the American Standard Version of 1901 and the Revised Standard Version of 1952, on the one hand, and between the Jewish Publication Society Translation of 1916 and the inevitably forth-coming revised Jewish version, on the other. . . . The basic cause for . . . the ever increasing urgent need for a new Jewish version . . . was precisely that which had brought into being, first Leeser's Bible, and then the Jewish Publication Society's Bible, namely intelligibility and correctness, the accord with the new English style and the latest scholarly truth.[69]

It is difficult to gauge how Margolis would have reacted to the NJV, whose text reflected a "new philosophy of Bible translation."[70] It is not likely that he would have felt that this text met the needs of the largely immigrant Jewish community of his own day. It is equally unlikely that Margolis would have abandoned, without a struggle, his firm conviction that "no translation in the English tongue can be anything but a revision of the English Bible of 1611."[71] However, just as Orlinsky's criticisms of the J.P.S. version are mixed with a sincere respect for its ability to have led several generations of Jews to the Hebrew Bible, so it is probable that Margolis' objections to the now-complete NJV would be tempered by the recognition that the enormous changes of the past few decades justify a new approach that will succeed in making the Bible more accessible to today's Jews. (In making these admittedly conjectural concluding re-marks, I am influenced by two complementary features of Margolis' scholarly personality: his refusal to express an opinion without giving long and careful consideration to all available data and his willingness to modify any opinion in the face of new data. In the interplay between tenacity and flexibilty, it was the latter, I suspect, that won out most often.)

[69] Harry M. Orlinsky, "Wanted: A New English Translation of the Bible for the Jewish People," *Essays in Biblical Culture and Bible Translation*, 355f. As noted above, "Wanted . . ." is a copy of an address Orlinsky delivered in 1953 at the annual meeting of J.P.S. Orlinsky recalls (p. 349) that

> The express purpose of the . . . address was to influence some reluctant members of the Society into agreeing to sponsor a new Jewish translation of the Bible. Shortly thereafter the project was voted into being, and the New Jewish Version was officially launched in 1955. [It was] this address [that] triggered the NJV into being.

[70] This phrase is taken from the title of one of Orlinsky's articles: "The New Jewish Version of the Torah: Toward a New Philosophy of Bible Translation," *Essays in Biblical Culture and Bible Translation* (New York, KTAV, 1974), 396–417.

[71] This phrase, also quoted earlier in this chapter, comes from Margolis, *Bible Translations*, 104.

4. TEXTUAL CRITICISM

"The Text as it appears on the top of the page is the nearest approach to
the Greek original as it left the hands of the translator(s) [from Margolis,
The Book of Joshua in Greek]"

In November 1931, Max Margolis, noticeably weakened by illness, left
his office and classroom at Dropsie College for the last time. At home he
was able to continue his research for a while; however, before the arrival
of the new year he was forced to lay aside, once and for all, the stacks of
papers and piles of books that he had assembled for the project on which
he was then working. That project, the culmination of several decades of
concentrated effort, had already borne fruit in the publication of a
number of articles and the production and partial publication of a text of
the book of Joshua that was "the nearest approach to the Greek original as
it left the hands of the translator(s)."[1] It was the Introduction to this
Greek Joshua that occupied Margolis' last scholarly hours: "The transcription of the text [of the Greek Joshua] had been entirely finished long
ago, and at the time of his death Margolis was engaged in the preparation
of the elaborate prolegomena."[2]

In many ways, it is fitting that at the end of his career Margolis should
be working on the Septuagint, especially the textual history of the Greek
Joshua. Although his earliest publications did not focus directly on this
field, a thorough grounding in classical, as well as Semitic languages did
play a prominent part in his education from Lithuanian village through
German gymnasium. His ability to sort through a mass of data, recognize
and organize the pertinent readings, and chart the intricate relationships
that unite and differientiate various manuscripts—all of which came into
play in the preparation of his mature works on the Septuagint—were
evident as early as his dissertation and 1892 monograph on a Talmudic
manuscript from Columbia's library. By the mid-1890s Margolis was
producing brief notes on selected topics in the Septuagint, by the early
1900s he had commenced his extended program to improve Hatch-

---

[1] The quoted statement comes from the Prefatory Note to the first part of Margolis' *The Book
of Joshua in Greek* (see below for an extensive discussion of this work).

[2] Alexander Marx, "In Memoriam: Prof. Max Leopold Margolis," *Proceedings of the Rabbinical Assembly of America* 4 (1932), 379.

Redpath, and by 1910 he published the first of a long series of articles on the Greek Joshua.[3]

There is no scholarly field with which Margolis is more closely identified, to which he made more significant contributions, or on which he expended more effort. The editorship of the J.P.S. Bible translation, a year in Jerusalem, writing a history of the Jews, and a host of other activities certainly caused Margolis to slacken the pace of his Septuagintal research, but there was never a question of his abandoning it. What occupied his last hours is exactly what had occupied (some would say, preoccupied) him for so long that it can aptly be termed his lifework, and the results of these labors, when combined, form his *Summa*.

When Max Margolis began his work on the Septuagint, there was considerable scholarly interest in Greek and other ancient versions of the Hebrew Bible. As Harry M. Orlinsky describes it, textual critics and others regularly used and abused this material as they sought, with widely varying results, to construct and reconstruct early forms of the Hebrew text. Abuses seem to have predominated:

> When Margolis began in the Nineties to do serious work in the lower criticism of the Hebrew Bible, it was already very fashionable for scholars to use the ancient versions, especially the Septuagint, rather indiscriminately to support emendations of the standardized (Masoretic) text. . . . Duhm and Marti and Ehrlich and many other lesser critics never made it a practice to study any of the primary versions (not even the Septuagint) *per se;* they 'used' these versions indiscriminately only when they thought they might be of some use to them in the emendation of the present Hebrew text—a most unscientific procedure![4]

In marked contrast were those scholars characterized by "their discriminate and keen use of the old translations, both the primary and the secondary, of the Bible in the attempt to understand and reconstruct its original Hebrew text."[5] Unfortunately, they were fewer in number than the legions of the indiscriminate:

> There were not very many scholars who emulated 'the monograph of Julius Wellhausen on "The Text of the Books of Samuel" [1871] . . . in the strictness with which it emphasizes the *discriminating* use of the Ancient Versions for the purposes of textual criticism,' or the model philological commentary by Driver on Samuel, or the serious commen-

---

[3] See chapter 1 for details on many of these works.

[4] Harry M. Orlinsky, "Margolis' Work in the Septuagint," *Max Leopold Margolis: Scholar and Teacher* (Philadelphia: Dropsie College, 1952), 35f.

[5] Orlinsky, "Margolis' Work in the Septuagint," 35.

taries of Cornill on *Ezechiel* (1886) and of the erudite G. F. Moore on *Judges* (1895).[6]

Needless to say, Max Margolis is to be counted among the discriminate; in fact, he was "preeminent" among them.[7]

As suggested in the previous paragraph, most scholars of Max Margolis' day were not interested in the Septuagint for its own sake or as an end in itself, but instead saw it as a means of arriving at a correct understanding of the underlying Hebrew, which may or may not have been preserved in our Masoretic Text. On a number of occasions, Margolis demonstrated his ability to utilize the Septuagint in that way:

> More than most textual critics of the Old Testament, Margolis used the Septuagint for the correct understanding and even the emendation of the Hebrew text; cf. this pithy statement, '. . . The "tradition which our fathers have handed down to us" is, alas, often but a scribe's subjective reasoning coupled with a blurred vision.'[8] His efforts in this direction were generally recognized by his contemporaries as models for scholars to follow.[9]

These efforts will be discussed in the following chapter.

In the present chapter emphasis falls on the numerous works in which Margolis studied the Septuagint *per se* (cf. Orlinsky's characterization [cited above] of the indiscriminate majority):

> But even while exploiting the Septuagint in the interests of the Hebrew, Margolis was pondering over a more fundamental and all-embracing question; namely, how could one be certain that he had before him the original text of the Greek translation as it left the hands of the translators? After all, there were several Greek manuscripts of the entire Hebrew Bible, and several hundred Greek manuscripts of various divisions and books of the Bible. These manuscripts differed from each other to a greater or lesser extent. Moreover, the Septuagint itself had been translated in various periods into other languages. . . . And a third source of the Septuagint are the quotations made from it in the commentaries and writings of Church Fathers and other writers (e.g., Philo and Josephus).[10]

[6] Orlinsky, "Margolis' Work in the Septuagint," 35f.

[7] Orlinsky, "Margolis' Work in the Septuagint," 35.

[8] Margolis used this "pithy statement" to conclude an article he wrote on a textual problem in the book of Joshua: "Ai or the City? Joshua 8. 12, 16," *JQR* n.s. 7 (1916/17), 497.

[9] Orlinsky, "Margolis' Work in the Septuagint," 37; Orlinsky continues by referring to several of Margolis' "efforts," from which readers will "readily" discern "the reason for this favorable attitude."

[10] Orlinsky, "Margolis' Work in the Septuagint," 37f.

Only a systematic approach to the mass of long-available and newly-discovered data could produce the sorts of results that would be useful to scholars who took seriously the quest for the original (sometimes called Proto- or Ur-) Septuagint text. It was fortunate for Margolis, a serious quester if there ever was one, that a productive systematic approach had been laid out and tested in the period just prior to the awakening of his own interests in the Septuagint. That approach, which served as a basic guide for Margolis and others, was developed in the middle to late 1800s by Paul Anton de Lagarde, "the first scholar to have outlined an approach . . . which would lead to the recovery of the Proto-Septuagint. . . ."[11] Orlinsky provides a succinct outline of Lagarde's approach to the manifold problems in this area:

> He [Lagarde] argued that all the preserved manuscripts of the Old Greek translation of the Bible . . . , as well as all the manuscripts of the translations made directly or indirectly from the Septuagint, such as the Old Latin, Ethiopic, Coptic, go back to the *trifaria varietas* of the Septuagint, which, according to St. Jerome, was made in the third-fourth centuries A.D. in Egypt, Palestine, and Syria by Hesychius, Origen, and Lucian respectively.[12] These three varieties, or recensions, in turn go back to the original Septuagint translation. Furthermore, it is possible to identify the Septuagint manuscripts as belonging to the one or the other recension with the aid of patristic citations and some of the daughter versions. . . . When [for example] the text of a group of Greek manuscripts coincides overwhelmingly with the Greek text underlying Theodoret of Antioch (fifth century), then the group of manuscripts may be designated as belonging to the Syrian (Lucianic) recension. . . . Once the basic text within each recension has been attained, with the proper use of textual criticism, then the texts of the three recensions, again with the application of the principles of the textual criticism peculiar to the Hebrew-Greek, are reduced to a basic text which is, in the words of Margolis, 'the nearest approach to the Greek original as it left the hands of the translator(s).'[13]

[11] Orlinsky, "Margolis' Work in the Septuagint," 38.

[12] On the *trifaria varietas* or "threefold variety of text," see Sidney Jellicoe, *The Septuagint and Modern Study* (Oxford: University Press, 1968 [reprinted in 1978 by Eisenbrauns]), chapter VI (pp. 134–171) and elsewhere. Jellicoe (p. 134) provides a translation of the relevant passage from Jerome:

> Alexandria and Egypt attribute the authorship of their Greek Old Testament to Hesychius. From Constantinople as far as to Antioch the rendering of Lucian the Martyr holds the field; while the Palestinian provinces in between these adopt those codices which, themselves the production of Origen, were promulgated by Eusebius and Pamphilus. And so the whole world is in conflict with itself over this threefold variety of text.

[13] Harry M. Orlinsky, "On the Present State of Proto-Septuagint Studies," *JAOS* 61 (1941), 82.

Orlinsky speaks of Margolis as the scholar "who carried out the Lagardian idea most completely and successfully to its logical conclusion." At the same time, Orlinsky wishes to refute the "prevalant idea that Margolis was simply carrying out Lagarde's *a priori* reasoning." In working out textual difficulties, Margolis was "guided it is true by Lagarde's hypothesis, but basically, like the careful and methodical scholar that he was, [he followed] the road indicated by the material itself, using the inductive method throughout."[14]

The decision to concentrate his efforts on the book of Joshua is a fine example of Margolis' use of the inductive method within the framework established by Lagarde: as early as 1909 Margolis clearly saw that the grouping of manuscripts, an indispensible step in achieving Lagarde's program, was facilitated in Joshua, as in no other Biblical book, by the occurence of numerous place names and geographical terms, which frequently gave rise to distinctive transliterations or translations that seemed to link certain manuscripts with each other. This "criterion of transliteration," which had been of no particular significance to Lagarde, was central to Margolis in the early stages of his research into the textual history of the Greek Joshua:

> While engaged in a study of the transliterations occurring in the Greek Old Testament . . ., I deemed it advisable to include geographical terms (like 'Ashedoth,' 'Gai,' 'Emek,' 'Negeb,' etc.) and names of places for which a perspicuous etymology is available (comp. 'Bethaven,' 'Bethel,' 'Beth-hammarcaboth,' etc.), especially as in some of these cases translation alternates with transliteration. This additional material being particularly abundant in the Book of Joshua, my attention was caught by the frequently recurring collocation of certain sigla in the apparatus of Holmes-Parsons. In one instance where an entire verse had to be investigated, the grouping was unmistakable. With the key found, I set about working up chapters 15 and 19 which are replete with place-names, but also other passages, covering in all one half of the book. My key proved to work. . . . [For example], in the middle part of the book there is a remarkable agreement between Lucian (= 19.108.Compl.) and Hexapla (G for instance), even if the points of difference which are constant (comp. the Greek for 'south') are had in mind.[15]

---

[14] Orlinsky, "Proto-Septuagint Studies," 82f. See also, Orlinsky, "Margolis' Work in the Septuagint," 38f.

[15] Max L. Margolis, "The Grouping of the Codices in the Greek Joshua: A Preliminary Notice," *JQR* n.s. 1 (1910/11), 259f. Margolis' study of transliterations (to which he makes reference at the beginning of the passage quoted above) had resulted in "The Pronunciation of the שׂוֹא according to New Hexaplaric Material," *AJSL* 26 (1909), 62–72.

Margolis' "preliminary" results revealed six manuscript groups: the Complutensian, the Aldine, the Oxford, the Hesychian, the Catenae, and the Sixtine.[16] Transliteration proved indispensible in discerning these groups and continued to be relied on at the next stage of investigation:

> When we come to arrange these six groups (Lagarde's 'manipuli') into larger divisions (Lagarde's 'legiones'), the test of Hexaplaric additions or omissions proves of less value than the criterion of transliteration. . . . Thus, from the point of view of transliteration and its close approach in consonants and vowels to the received Hebrew text, there practically result two main divisions which group themselves respectively about the Vatican (B) and Alexandrine (A).[17]

Margolis was no more enslaved to his own insights than he was to those of Lagarde, for he recognized that results obtained through application of the "criterion of transliteration" needed to be supplemented, if not corrected, on the basis of data gathered through other methods of evaluating textual affiliations. Nevertheless, in 1910, when he published his "preliminary notice," Margolis seemed confident that the foundations he had laid would support the weight of further, expanded research into the text of Joshua: "My key [the use of transliterations] proved to work; of course, as my range of observation widened, slight rearrangements in detail ensued which, however, left the general grouping intact."[18] Such rearrangements were sure to occur again ("My results [are] at present naturally only tentative");[19] however, major revelations, such as the recovery of a third main division, did not seem likely as Margolis viewed his future work on the book of Joshua:

> A critical edition of the Greek text of the book of Joshua thus becomes a matter of realization within sight. For with a knowlege of the grouping as above outlined, the process of collation is reduced to utmost simplicity. . . . New material . . . may be found to fall in with the groups recognized or, as the case may be, serve to reveal new groups, though hardly a new main division. The text should be printed in two columns corresponding to the two forms which it assumed in Palestine and Syria on the one hand and in Egypt on the other.[20]

Margolis' confidence was in many respects well placed, but it was not long before he was to realize that two columns were inadequate to

---

[16] Margolis, "Grouping," 260f.
[17] Margolis, "Grouping," 261.
[18] Margolis, "Grouping," 259.
[19] Margolis, "Grouping," 260.
[20] Margolis, "Grouping," 261f.

contain the data produced by a process of collation that defied reduction to "utmost simplicity." "Much," Margolis wrote, "will become more accurate as the complete induction becomes ready for tabulation."[21] More accurate, yes—also more complex and more time consuming than Margolis likely envisioned in these early stages of the series of Joshua studies that would remain unfinished and only partially published at his death more than two decades later.

It is important to remember that by 1910, when Margolis brought out his first study devoted exclusively to the Greek Joshua, he had already published close to a dozen articles dealing more generally with textual and lexical problems of the Septuagint.[22] Among those not mentioned earlier are a detailed study of "The Character of the Anonymous Greek Version of Habakkuk, Chapter 3" in the William Rainey Harper *Festschrift* of 1908 and four articles that appeared during 1908 and 1909 in volumes 25 and 26 of the *American Journal of Semitic Languages and Literatures:* "Short Notes on the Greek Old Testament," "The Particle ἤ in Old Testament Greek," "The Greek Preverb and its Hebrew-Aramaic Equivalent," and "The Pronunciation of the שָׂוְא according to New Hexaplaric Material."[23] These four studies reveal the breadth and depth of research Margolis had been conducting in the preceding years. In these articles material is drawn from a number of sources and subjected to the sort of minute analysis that Margolis had earlier displayed in, for example, his dissertation and monograph on the Talmud. It was while working on material for "Pronunciation," Margolis tells us (as quoted above), that he began to consider the value of transliterations for the grouping of manuscripts.[24]

---

[21] Margolis, "Grouping," 262.

[22] See chapter 1 for details.

[23] Max L. Margolis, "The Character of the Anonymous Greek Version of Habakkuk, Chapter 3," *Old Testament and Semitic Studies in Memory of William Rainey Harper* 1 (1908), 133–142; "Short Notes on the Greek Old Testament. I: Gen. 3:16; II: Gen. 49:21," *AJSL* 25 (1908), 174; "The Particle ἤ in Old Testament Greek," *AJSL* 25 (1909), 257–275; "The Greek Preverb and its Hebrew-Aramaic Equivalent," *AJSL* 26 (1909), 33–61; "The Pronunciation of the שָׂוְא according to New Hexaplaric Material," *AJSL* 26 (1909), 62–72.

[24] Margolis returned to the question of translation/transliteration in "Transliterations in the Greek Old Testament," *JQR* n.s. 16 (1925/26), 117–125. Among the topics he treated in that article was "the problem of transliteration in the Septuagint, where the words should have been translated, or where the transliteration occurs by the side of the translation (p. 124)." In opposition to Franz Wutz, who believed "that these transliterations are left over from the transliterated text which served the translator for a basis (p. 124)," Margolis ventured to guess "that the transliterated words originally stood in the margin of the translation as it issued from the hands of the translators and were subsequently dragged into the text by copyists either beside or in place of the translated words (pp. 124f.)." Certain types of transliteration, it is now generally agreed, are helpful in identifying the *kaige* recension. (On this see Leonard J. Greenspoon, *Textual Studies in the Book of Joshua* [Chico, CA: Scholars Press, 1983], 332–337.)

Notice should be taken of two other works, of even broader compass, that also appeared in 1910. The first, which is over 30 pages long, is titled "The Scope and Methodology of Biblical Philology."[25] This survey, which "deals with the problem of interpretation of the biblical text from every possible angle,"[26] has to a large extent retained its value. Because its expansive coverage goes far beyond questions of the Septuagint itself, "Scope and Methodology" will be discussed in the following chapter, where (among other matters) Margolis' exegetical attitude will be explored.

The second article, shorter in number of pages (12) though not in length of title ("Complete Induction for the Identification of the Vocabulary in the Greek Versions of the Old Testament with its Semitic Equivalents: Its necessity and the Means of obtaining it"),[27] begins with a reference to the first of Lagarde's canons for those who aim to recover "the original text of the Greek translation of the Old Testament": "a 'knowledge of the style of the individual translators,' with which is coupled a 'faculty of referring variant readings to their Semitic original, or else of recognizing them as inner-Greek corruptions.'" [28] While readily admitting to the value of Lagarde's goal and his general approach toward attaining it, Margolis did have certain reservations: for example, "It is obvious that Lagarde has reference merely to the material side of the task and ignores the formal questions of orthography and grammar altogether."[29] And again: Although Lagarde was aware of the need to take cognizance of the style of individual translators, he himself on occasion fell into the trap of mechanical retroversion, a result of his neglect of precisely those factors that distinguish one translator from another.[30] Among the factors Margolis lists as illustrations are the historical present (today deemed valuable in identifying members of the *kaige* recension), subordination in the place of coordination, the generic singular, and relative clauses in the place of participles.[31]

More so than any earlier researcher, however, Margolis came to the recognition that even the most detailed analysis of the style of any single translator was inadequate to the task at hand:

[25] Max L. Margolis, "The Scope and Methodology of Biblical Philology," *JQR* n.s. 1 (1910/11), 5–41.
[26] Joseph Reider, "Bibliography of the Works of Max L. Margolis," *Max Leopold Margolis: Scholar and Teacher,* 69.
[27] Max L. Margolis, "Complete Induction . . . ," *JAOS* 30 (1910), 301–312; reprinted in Robert A. Kraft, editor, *Septuagintal Lexicography.* Septuagint and Cognate Studies 1 (Society of Biblical Literature, 1972), 80–91. (See also chapter 1.)
[28] Margolis, "Complete Induction," 301.
[29] *Ibid.*
[30] Margolis, "Complete Induction," 302.
[31] Margolis, "Complete Induction," 304f.

In order . . . to discover the total sum of criteria, the student must obviously collect his data from the *whole* of the Greek Old Testament, whereupon he may proceed to distribute them among the various groups of translators brought to light. The right method would be first to ascertain the attitude of the general sum of translators towards all of the phenomena which go to make up a translator's style; on the basis of similarity or dissimilarity of 'reaction,' the idiosyncracies of the individual translators will reveal themselves. For a translator's style is the total sum of 'reactions,' of the ways in which the original is handled by him in the various provinces of grammar, rhetoric, semantics, and exegesis.[32]

This "right method" was ignored by all too many subsequent researchers, who ended up individualizing what was general, guessing at identifications, and failing to recognize the numerous inner-Greek corruptions that litter the text of all extant witnesses.[33] What was, and continues to be, needed is "complete induction":

[When] the student of the Septuagint aims at restoring the Greek original as it left the translator's hands . . . he is always face to face with problems of identification. . . . All those facts which are general, conditioned by causes which may occur again and again, must be formulated as rules, and as such be placed at the service of students. The complete induction of the sum total of general, typical facts can be secured only by two methods of procedure which can be easily combined. On the one hand, each article in the Concordance . . . must be gone through for the purposes of establishing all *lexical* equations. . . . On the other hand, the text of the versions must be investigated with a view to *grammatical* equations. I use the two terms, *lexical* and *grammatical,* in their widest connotations. . . . Complete induction, at all events, can be had only by means of the two lines of investigation, the lexical and the grammatical. It is a stupendous work, but it must be done; it is of utmost importance not only for purposes of textual criticism, but equally for a study of the oldest exegesis of Scriptures.[34]

Even a partial outline of Margolis' publication in 1908–1911 (see below for other articles on Greek Joshua for the year 1911) gives evidence of enormous productivity in the period immediately following his return from Europe. In the space of less than four years he brought to comple-

---

[32] Margolis, "Complete Induction," 304.

[33] See Margolis, "Complete Induction," 306–310.

[34] Margolis, "Complete Induction," 310–312. In "Complete Induction," Margolis was not interested solely in the Greek traditions; he applied his insights with equal acuity to the individual Hebrew writers and the *Vorlagen* they provided for Septuagint translators. It is also worth remembering that the "stupendous" work Margolis envisioned—and largely carried out, in the case of Joshua—was far more "stupendous" in pre-computer days, when material was collated by hand, than it is today. (See the references below to Margolis' system of file cards.)

tion a large number of projects begun while he was employed at HUC and even earlier at Berkeley. Even if he initiated no new research in his first year or two in Philadelphia, it is still remarkable that he was able to see so many projects through to publication in such a short period of time. This is all the more remarkable when we remember that he was working day and night on the J.P.S. translation for eleven months in 1908 and 1909, that he had an important and time consuming role to play as senior faculty member at Dropsie, and that he contributed to the first volume of the new series of *JQR* not only two articles, but approximately 40 book reviews covering more than 30 pages.[35]

Due to the increasingly complex nature of the scholarly work he undertook, the high level of his participation in professional organizations, the varied pedagogical program he conducted at Dropsie, and the perceived need to supplement his professorial salary with a steady trickle (if not stream) of popular articles and books, Margolis did not maintain this rate of publication much beyond 1913. By then, he had begun to devote more and more time to his *Greek Joshua* and to another detailed, full-length study—of Andreas Masius (see below). Even those relatively few scholars who take the time to look at Margolis' later publications generally ignore the earlier ones. The short discussion provided above can only hint at the wealth of data and insights such modern scholars have, in their haste, deprived themselves of.[36]

Since Margolis intended his "Grouping" article to serve as an introduction to a series of textual studies in the Greek Joshua, it is appropriate that he concluded this article not with a summary of what he had achieved, but with a prospectus of both short- and long-term research goals in this area. As for the latter, the "ultimate" goal was clearly fixed in Margolis' mind: "Ultimately, I expect to print a critical edition of the Book of Joshua in Greek. . . ."[37] No less clear was Margolis on the direction of his research for the period immediately after "Grouping":

[35] On these and other book reviews, see chapter 2.

[36] At this point it is appropriate to recall Robert Kraft's favorable comments on the early articles by Margolis that Kraft reprinted in *Septuagintal Lexicography*. These articles, Kraft judges, contain "methodological gems." In particular, Kraft has nothing but praise for Margolis' insistence upon "complete induction":

> On the whole . . . the general task to which Margolis addressed himself and the way in which he pursued it ('complete induction') seem to me basic for dealing with the Jewish Greek translation materials in a manner that justifies the effort. To stop short of the concept of 'complete induction' is to leave many of the most basic questions unresolved—it is to build a lexicon (or grammar) without an adequate foundation. The problems of exactly how to present the findings of such research . . . require further testing and discussion, but Margolis has surely described the most fruitful path for researching the material.

Robert A. Kraft, *Septuagintal Lexicography*, 46–48. (See also chapter 1.)

[37] Margolis, "Grouping," 263.

A part of my future will be devoted to an edition of the group h [earlier
in "Grouping," Margolis had written that "according to Hautsch, . . .
the Lucianic (Antiochene) rescension is related to group h"][38] on the
basis of all nine or ten manuscripts constituting it . . . photographs of
which have been made available to me by the authorities of the Dropsie
College. . . .[39]

Margolis never did manage to publish a separate edition of group h, but
he did take a significant step toward that particular short-term goal with
the publication, in October 1911, of a 55-page article entitled "The K
Text of Joshua."[40]

At the time Margolis was undertaking his research, there was considerable discussion of Lucian and the manuscripts that could properly be
classed as witnesses to his work, that is as "Lucianic." Given Margolis'
interest in Lagarde's program (described above), it would be natural to
assume that Margolis' primary interest in studying group h was in con-
firming or denying the "Lucianic" epithet that had been attached to
these manuscripts by Ernst Hautsch and others (see above). Moreover, it
was the Lucianic recension that had formed the subject of Lagarde's "first
and only publication of any LXX text extending beyond a single book."[41]

In his article on the K text (a codex discovered by Tischendorf in the
1840s), however, Margolis devoted almost no space to the "Lucianic"
question (although he promised to do so in the final edition), contenting
himself with the statement that K and related manuscripts do constitute a
recension, "but whether Lucian's or not" he was not sure.[42] Moreover, in
the "Grouping" article, Margolis had displaced Lucian from the "unsci-
entific" tripartite division mentioned by Jerome and favored by Lagarde,
preferring instead a bifurcation on the basis of the designations post-
Christian and pre-Christian.[43] Later, Margolis was to restore Lucian to
his familiar status and to go Jerome-Lagarde one better by the discovery
of a fourth recension.

What Margolis did was to present the extant K text (this uncial, found
on palimpsest leaves, is preserved for only the central part of the book of

---

[38] Margolis, "Grouping," 260.

[39] Margolis, "Grouping," 262f. Drafts of letters prepared by Margolis for Cyrus Adler, in
which requests are made for photographs of manuscripts, have been preserved in the Dropsie
College Archives. Of greater importance is the fact that the photographs themselves, supplied
from collections throughout the world, have also been preserved at Dropsie College.

[40] Max L. Margolis, "The K Text of Joshua," *AJSL* 28 (1911), 1–55.

[41] Sidney Jellicoe, *The Septuagint and Modern Study*, 7. This publication is Lagarde's famous
Librorum Veteris Testamenti Canonicorum Pars Prior Graece, which appeared in 1883.
Roundly—and largely properly—condemned for its results, this work deserves both praise and
attention for the method Lagarde employed throughout. (See Jellicoe, 7f.)

[42] Margolis, "K Text," 2. He was, however, sure that the recension "is not Origen's (p. 2)."

[43] Margolis, "Grouping," 262.

Joshua and even there has several lacunae), against which he collated a large number of other manuscripts and also versions. In so doing, he corrected earlier researchers by discerning that "of the group of cursives signalized by Tischendorf it is the smaller group (54. 75. 118 [the first two equal B-McL's g and n]) with which the affinity of K is most marked and among the three it is 54 that must be singled out in particular."[44] Margolis' collation also convinced him that the Old Latin ($Ł$) shared a close affinity with these Greek manuscripts.[45] On the basis of research conducted later, Margolis was to designate these manuscripts S_a and make the claim that, for Joshua, they represent the work of Lucian.[46] At this point, he simply noted, without making any further identification, that "the recensional character of K.54 is obliterated in the larger group . . . into which matter from the cognate, yet distinct recension of Origen has been admitted."[47]

In presenting his data, Margolis constructed three sets of notes, which he placed below the running (and on occasion reconstructed) text of K: (1) containing variants from manuscripts, mentioned above, that were most closely affiliated with K and that later formed Margolis' S_a; (2) containing variants from manuscripts, including d, p, and t, that were related, though not as closely, to K; these textual witnesses were to make up Margolis' S_b; (3) containing variants from a large number of other sources, including the great uncials and material in Syriac and Ethiopic.

Margolis proudly announced his reliance on "first-hand sources throughout."[48] His insistence on going to the sources themselves, thereby avoiding the reproduction of errors in standard editions such as Swete and Brooke-McLean (for the latter, see Margolis' *JBL* article mentioned below), remained a hallmark of Margolis' research and formed a significant part of the scholarly legacy he bequeathed to his students.

Below these sets of notes, impressive enough in themselves, is a continuous textual commentary, often a half page or more in length, drawing together a wealth of material—not restricted to issues raised by the K text—which Margolis handled in what was becoming his typically erudite and detailed manner. Margolis envisioned this article as an opportunity to "take [his] bearings" prior to publication of a complete "edition of the Greek Joshua according to the text of the cursives with which Tischendorf's uncial stands in affinity";[49] inasmuch as that complete edition never appeared, we lack the numerous observations of a

---

[44] Margolis, "K Text," 3.
[45] Margolis, "K Text," 2f.
[46] On this, see below.
[47] Margolis, "K Text," 3. See below also.
[48] Margolis, "K Text," 3.
[49] Margolis, "K Text," 2f.

more general nature that Margolis planned to include there. Nevertheless, Margolis did return to these manuscripts in later studies, where it is possible to observe very definite changes in his evaluation of them (see above and below).

In 1911 Margolis also published another series of short notes in *Zeitschrift für die alttestamentliche Wissenschaft* (an earlier series appeared in 1905), utilizing the Septuagint to help solve a variety of textual problems in Genesis, Ezekiel, Nahum, and Psalms.[50] More substantive, however, was a short article that appeared the same year[51] and that, like "The K Text of Joshua," had its origins in the careful study of a newly-discovered uncial manuscript. In the case of this second manuscript, Codex Washingtonianus I (designated Θ in B-McL and in most scholarly discussions), the discovery was very recent, in that it had been purchased only five years earlier by an American, Charles Lang Freer.[52]

The text of this manuscript is extant for almost all of the books of Deuteronomy and Joshua. In terms of its affinities, Henry A. Sanders, who first edited the manuscript, stated that in Joshua "Θ (= Washington MS.) and A (= Codex Alexandrinus) stand closer together than in Deuteronomy. . . ."[53] Margolis, who applauded the accuracy of Sanders' work (in contrast to Swete's), made his own "fresh collation," on the basis of which he concluded: "the relationship of Θ and A as members of one and the same group is unmistakable. Certain omissions in Θ are intelligible, i.e. explainable as having arisen through homoioteleuton, only when the text of A is compared."[54]

In arriving at this conclusion, Margolis again laid great emphasis on transliterations and especially the handling of proper names: "The disagreements between Θ and A in the proper names are, generally speaking, of a nature to substantiate rather than to invalidate the affinity of the two uncials, the divergence between them being trifling, when their common deviation from B is compared."[55] Near the end of this article, Margolis returned to the topic of proper names, creating an image that all weary textual critics will appreciate:

> On our steep road to the earliest form of the Septuagint, we need resting places, points of vantage; such are the groups, narrower and wider, into which the extant texts may be divided. The proper names in

---

[50] Max L. Margolis, "Hes 27 4," ZAW 31 (1911), 313f; " $\dot{\eta}\nu\dot{\iota}\alpha, \chi\alpha\lambda\iota\nu\dot{o}\varsigma$ " (on Nahum 2:4), ZAW 31 (1911), 314; "Ps 69 11," ZAW 31 (1911), 314; "Ps 74 3," ZAW 31 (1911), 315; "Ps 85 9," ZAW 31 (1911), 315; "Gen 6 3," ZAW 31 (1911), 315.

[51] "The Washington MS. of Joshua," *JAOS* 31 (1911), 365–367.

[52] For details, see Sidney Jellicoe, *The Septuagint and Modern Study*, 211f.

[53] See Margolis, "Washington MS.," 365.

[54] *Ibid.*

[55] Margolis, "Washington MS.," 365f.

the Book of Joshua are the milestones which guide the investigator in finding his way to texts held together by group affinity.[56]

In 1911 Margolis continued to operate within the framework, established in "Grouping," of the six smaller groups and two main divisions into which he had fit all extant witnesses to the text of Joshua. Uncials Θ and A, along with "N, possibly M, and a number of cursives," were placed in the Oxford (Grabian) Group, which in turn was one of the three groups that made up the Palestino-Syrian division—of post-Christian origin.[57] That terminology would not be retained, for in his later writings Margolis came to regard these manuscripts as representatives of a fourth recension, which he designated C and located at Constantinople.[58] The uncovering of a fourth recension is generally credited as a major achievement on the part of Margolis.[59]

If, in 1911, Margolis was still some distance from his more mature formulation of manuscript groupings, he had nonetheless already arrived at what was to remain his view of manuscript A's place in the textual history of Greek Joshua:

> Both Θ and A are excerpts from the Septuagint column in Origen's work which have been adjusted to a   κοινή   text. Following the well-known prescription of Jerome, obelized passages were on the whole retained, while asterisked passages were omitted. Yet the redactors of the two texts in question did not always coincide in the amount excised.[60]

Margolis had referred to the same phenomenon, with particular reference to A, in "Grouping": "The Alexandrine codex reveals itself as the Palestino-Syrian text minus the Hexaplaric additions."[61]

---

[56] Margolis, "Washington MS.," 367.

[57] Margolis, "Washington MS.," 365, and "Grouping," 260.

[58] In 1927 Margolis wrote:

> C is a recension which was at home in Constantinople and Asia Minor. We are helped in localizing the recension by the aid of the Armenian version. . . . Whether the recension had any relationship to the fifty copies ordered by Constantine from Eusebius . . . must remain a matter of conjecture. Jerome says nothing of a fourth recension; but then he is by no means exact, or the recension was at his time just in the process of formation.

Max L. Margolis, "Specimen of a New Edition of the Greek Joshua," *Jewish Studies in Memory of Israel Abrahams* (New York, 1927), 309f. "Specimen . . .," an important article found on pp. 307–323 of the *Israel Abrahams'* volume, was reprinted in Sidney Jellicoe (ed.), *Studies in the Septuagint: Origins, Recensions and Interpretations* (New York: KTAV, 1974), 434–450.

[59] See Jellicoe, *The Septuagint and Modern Study*, 344f.

[60] Margolis, "Washington MS.," 366f. Margolis quotes Jerome's "only too well known . . . prescription" in Max L. Margolis, "Hexapla and Hexaplaric," *AJSL* 32 (1916), 137.

[61] Margolis, "Grouping," 261, where this entire sentence is printed in italics.

When Margolis spoke of Hexaplaric additions and asterisked passages, he had reference to the work of Origen, who in the third century A.D. prepared the Hexapla (and perhaps also a separate work, the Tetrapla; see below), in the fifth column of which he placed his "Septuagint." In constructing that text, Origen compared the Greek text commonly used in his day with a Hebrew (written in both Semitic script and Greek transcription) that he considered to contain the original and authoritative version of the divine word. Whenever he came across something in his Greek that did not have an equivalent in the Hebrew column, he retained it but marked the material as additional (vis-à-vis the Hebrew) with what is called an obelisk (   ).

Origen also provided translations for Hebrew words and phrases lacking an equivalent in his Greek. These "Hexaplaric additions," which Origen took from earlier revisers—in Joshua, especially from Theodotion, but possibly also from Aquila and Symmachus—or devised on his own, were marked with an asterisk (   ), to indicate that Origen had not found them in the common text *(koine)* that lay before him.[62] In the course of time, as Origen's "Septuagint" was extracted from the surrounding columns and repeatedly copied, the two sigla were frequently confused with each other, placed in other than the proper location, or dispensed with altogether.

Codex A presents a text that is characterized to a large extent by the absence of the asterisked material (and to a lesser extent by the presence of passages Origen marked with the obelisk). While Margolis argued that such a text was the result of conscious post-Origenic scribal activity aimed at restoring the Greek to its pristine, pre-Origenic state, the argument might also be made that A's text is in fact the pre-Origenic *koine,* a Greek that takes us behind Origen to perhaps the earliest recoverable form of the Septuagint. This latter argument was put forward, with considerable erudition, by a German scholar, Otto Pretzl, whose work on this topic was not published until the late 1920s although it seems to have been known earlier.[63]

After analyzing selected readings of codex A and related manuscripts, Pretzl concluded that their text type was free of any influence, direct or indirect, from Origen. Thus, he did not list these manuscripts in either of the large categories he designated "Hss., welche im wesentlichen die Bearbeitung des Origenes bieten" and "Von Origenes beeinflusste Hss."[64] For Pretzl, this lack of Origenic influence was attributable to the

[62] On Origen's procedure in Joshua, see Greenspoon, *Textual Studies,* especially 353-356.

[63] Otto Pretzl, "Die griechischen Handschriftengruppen im Buche Josue untersucht nach ihrer Eigenart und ihrem Verhältnis zueinander," *Biblica* 9 (1928), 377-427. There are no references to Pretzl in Margolis' published work; however, Pretzl is cited in Margolis' unpublished work on Masius (see below).

[64] Pretzl, 394ff.

fact that the text displayed by A was earlier than Origen and used by him as the basis for his own further activity as described above.[65]

To counter such a view, Margolis saw that it was necessary to go beyond a simple counting of excluded asterisked passages or included obelized ones. When Origen inserted asterisked material, to fill in a perceived lacuna in his *koine*, he often made slight changes in the surrounding Greek to bring grammatical or stylistic harmony to the new passage he was creating. An unobservant scribe, who came along later with the purpose of simply eradicating asterisked additions, would leave intact the changes outside of the asterisk, in turn creating ungrammatical or stylistically inept constructions that were not part of the older, pre-Origenic Greek. By isolating some of these passages, Margolis demonstrated that codex A, which Pretzl and others took as an unrevised text (and indeed it had that appearance), was in reality the result of extensive, if mechanical revision of Origen.

In a 1916 article, "Hexapla and Hexaplaric," Margolis cited "a flagrant case" of scribal "betrayal" through mechanical handling of Origen's carefully-crafted work:

> The process of excising asterisked passages began early. Jerome's prescription is only too well known. . . . A scribe following the prescription might produce a manuscript which on the surface would look like an unrevised text. Yet he will betray himself occasionally. A flagrant case I have met with in Josh. 15:9.[66]

In order to accomodate new material to the existing text of that verse, Origen had changed an accusative into the genitive. In producing his asterisk-free reading, the "archetypal scribe [of C] mechanically skipped the asterisked words and calmly left the surrounding text intact. . . . with [Origen's] genitive hanging in the air!"[67] Margolis' exhaustive study of a number of such passages served to confirm what he had said as early as 1910 with regard to the position of codex A. He restated his position in another early article, "'Man by Man' Joshua 7, 17" (*JQR* 3 [1912/13]):

> When all the evidence derived from a critical study of AΘ throughout the book of Joshua is brought to bear upon the problem the inference is unavoidable that the two uncials have made use of Origen and not the reverse.[68]

[65] Pretzl, 412ff.

[66] Margolis, "Hexapla and Hexaplaric," 137f.

[67] The first part of this quotation comes from Margolis, "Hexapla and Hexaplaric," 138; the second, from "Specimen," 310. For a discussion of Joshua 15:9, see Greenspoon, *Textual Studies*, 76ff.

[68] Max L. Margolis, "'Man by Man,' Joshua 7, 17," *JQR* n.s. 3 (1912/13), 327. See also Greenspoon, *Textual Studies*, 217f.

If the text presented by Codex A and related manuscripts was nothing more than the result of a mechanical reworking of Origen, in what sense did Margolis speak of a C "recension"? In his years of research on these manuscripts, Margolis came to recognize that they represented far more than a revised Origen, for the author/scribe whose efforts formed the basis of C

> commanded still other resources beyond common text and Hexapla-Tetrapla. Herein consists the [most important] point . . ., which gives the recension rank beside the three principal recensions. In a number of instances, the place-names appear in a form which must have been the original antecedent to the corruptions in the common text such as lay before Origen. . . . Perhaps we may suppose that C made use of the common text prevalent in Palestine, which naturally remained freer from corruptions in the geographical names.[69]

Once again, place names, which had provided Margolis with his indispensible starting point in the grouping of manuscripts, proved invaluable for the study of the Greek traditions in the book of Joshua.

Margolis' research during the 1910s led him to modify some of his views on manuscript groupings even as he retained others. While it had been clear to him from an early date that certain manuscripts clustered around uncials K and A, it was only gradually (as noted above) that Margolis recognized in these groupings a Lucianic and Constantinopolitan recension. Margolis knew, however, that the oldest form of the Greek translation of Joshua was not to be found, as a rule, in those manuscripts. As early as 1910, he had spoken of a main division that grouped itself about Codex Vaticanus (B), and he termed this division Egyptian (E) and pre-Christian.[70] As for Codex Vaticanus itself, Margolis judged that it "represents the purest text, so far as Hexaplaric additions are concerned, but is exceedingly corrupt in its proper names."[71] Having undergone "judicious correction on the basis of its satellites . . ., the Vatican should be made the foundation . . . for the Egyptian division which alone leads the way to the original Septuagint."[72]

Margolis never deviated from this initial judgment on the primacy of

---

[69] Margolis, "Specimen," 310f. Margolis (p. 311) went on to posit a close relationship between the Palestinian common text and Theodotion: "This Palestinian koine was only slightly touched up by Theodotion—Urtheodotion would accordingly be nothing but this Palestinian koine." On the significance of this suggestion, with particular reference to later research on the whole question of Theodotion and Ur-Theodotion, see Jellicoe, The Septuagint and Modern Study, 344f.

[70] Margolis, "Grouping," 261, 262.

[71] Margolis, "Grouping," 261.

[72] Margolis, "Grouping," 262.

recension *E,* in particular Codex Vaticanus, in the reconstruction of the original text of Greek Joshua. In his 1927 article, "Specimen of a New Edition of the Greek Joshua," portions of which were quoted above, he spoke in largely the same terms he had almost 20 years before:

> The road to the original text of *G* leads across the common, unrevised text. In order to get at the latter, we must abstract from the recensional manipulations. . . . Ultimately we must operate with *E,* but not without taking into account the residue of the common text imbedded elsewhere. The scant representatives of *E* in a relatively pure form, virtually the ancester of B β[= B-McL r], will have had singularities of their own which must be brushed aside. A study of the translator's mannerism of rendition becomes imperative. The proper names are, of course, vitiated by all sorts of scribal errors, but on the whole the rectification is possible.[73]

By the time he wrote "Specimen," Margolis had come to see the role to be played by manuscripts of the *C* recension in the process of "rectification."

For Margolis, codex Vaticanus was not only the surest guide to the Old Greek of Joshua, but it also represented more closely than any other extant witness the Greek *koine* with which Origen worked: "The text which Origen made the basis of his revision is none other than the famous Vaticanus (B) or a text closely related to it."[74] In taking this position, Margolis put himself in opposition to those, e.g., Pretzl, who "argued that AΘ constitute the text which Origen made the basis of his revision."[75] In this case, as in many others, subsequent research has borne out Margolis' judgment.[76]

With respect to Margolis' judgments on the Greek texts themselves (as distinct from the question of the Hebrew *Vorlage* of the Old Greek), there is only one major area in which his views have not gained general scholarly acceptance: his division of manuscripts of the *P* or Palestinian recension into two subgroups, one representing Origen's Hexapla and the other the Tetrapla. In "Grouping," Margolis made only passing reference to Origen's work, which Jerome had spoken of in his description of the *trifaria varietas*: "the Palestinian provinces . . . adopt those codices which, themselves the production of Origen, were promulgated

[73] Margolis, "Specimen," 315f.

[74] Margolis, "Man by Man," 327.

[75] Margolis, "Man by Man," 327: "On the basis of the present case it might be argued that AΘ constitute the text which Origen made the basis of his revision. . . . But when all the evidence . . . is brought to bear . . . the inference is unavoidable that the two uncials have made use of Origen and not the reverse."

[76] See Leonard J. Greenspoon, "Theodotion, Aquila, Symmachus, and the Old Greek of Joshua," *Eretz-Israel* 16 (1982: H. M. Orlinsky Volume), 82–91.

by Eusebius and Pamphilus."[77] By 1916, when he published "Hexapla and Hexaplaric," Margolis had given considerable thought to the criteria by which a text could be designated hexaplaric:

> If we bear in mind the three sides to Origen's recension, namely (a) supplying gaps *sub asterisco*, (b) marking additions as spurious by means of the obelus, and (c) transposing elements of the text and introducing tacit changes—the proper names in particular were submitted to correction—the extant manuscripts one and all will have to be characterized with a view to these three points. Origenic additions will be found in all our codices; it is simply a question of degree. . . . The decisive point is the third: the form of the text outside of the asterisked and obelized elements. Accordingly I would define as a pure Hexaplaric text one that contains the greatest number of additions and at the same time conforms elsewhere to the tacit changes introduced by Origen. Next in order those MSS will still be entitled to Hexplaric denomination which, though habitually thrusting out asterisked additions, conform otherwise to the Origenic text as found in the pure codices.[78]

Among those manuscripts that qualified for the Hexaplaric designation were G, b (from the middle of 2:18 on), c, x, and the Syrohexaplar ($).[79] In addition, Margolis made reference to the Greek text in the Complutensian Polyglot.[80]

At this point (in 1916), Margolis had no doubt that the designation hexaplaric or non-hexplaric could be applied in a meaningful way to particular manuscripts. He also had no doubt that the general terms hexapla and hexaplaric were actually describing not one, but in fact two editions of Origen's work—the Hexapla and the Tetrapla. Margolis, as usual, offered his own carefully reasoned arguments to support this view, "which has been well nigh universally held and which is categorically repeated in the standard works."[81] The authority of ancient authors, such as Eusebius and Epiphanius, and of modern scholars, such as Swete and Ottley, was invoked by some. Margolis preferred to buttress his case by a characteristically thorough firsthand examination of the evidence, from which he concluded that in the Hexapla Origen tended to employ asterisks and obeli, but in the Tetrapla—which Margolis came to date as the later of the two—he operated with transposition. Thus, Origen

---

[77] See fn. 12 above.

[78] Margolis, "Hexapla and Hexaplaric," 136f.

[79] *Ibid.* For the Syrohexaplar, see further below.

[80] On this, see Leonard J. Greenspoon, "Max L. Margolis on the Complutensian Text of Joshua," *Bulletin of the International Organization for Septuagint and Cognate Studies* 12 (1979), 43–56.

[81] Sidney Jellicoe, *The Septuagint and Modern Study*, 113.

produced two editions that differed markedly in the method employed to produce conformity with the Hebrew standard.[82]

In 1916, Margolis was still uncertain on one point: his ability to subdivide "hexaplaric" manuscripts on the basis of their exhibiting predominantly a hexaplaric or a tetraplaric text. By 1927, Margolis no longer had any uncertainty on this point, for in the "Specimen" article he was able to divide into two subgroups the "few representatives" that exhibited "in a (relatively) pure form . . . the Septuagint column in Origen's Hexapla-Tetrapla": P_1, containing Gbc (among others), on the whole represents the Hexapla; P_2, made up of x$ (among others), generally represents the Tetrapla.[83]

It might be thought that the scholarly criticism of this division alluded to above would have centered on the placement of this or that manuscript, the chronological priority of hexapla over tetrapla, and/or the identification of a particular method with each edition. It turns out, however, that the criticism has not been on specific points made by Margolis; in fact, the criticism has not been directed specifically at Margolis. What has emerged, especially since the publication in 1947 of an article by Harry M. Orlinsky titled "Origen's Tetrapla—a Scholarly Fiction?,"[84] is a growing consensus that "the Tetrapla was not a separate four-column work but only another term for the many-columned 'Hexapla' in which the four Greek columns of Aquila, Symmachus, Origen's revision of the LXX, and Theodotion were the all important ones."[85] If it is correct that the Tetrapla is just another name for the Hexapla, then Margolis' subdivisions cannot be sustained. (This is no way affects the validity of Margolis' placement of manuscripts in the larger P recension.)

It would, however, be premature to consign Margolis' subdivisions, and the arguments adduced in their favor, to even an honored place among the detritus of yesterday's scholarship. After all, no one has subjected Margolis' evidence to a point-by-point analysis. This lack of analysis is understandable when it is recognized that the more than one hundred pages of Margolis' discussion on the Hexapla-Tetrapla remains as yet unpublished. When it finally appears (albeit in an abbreviated form

---

[82] See "Hexapla and Hexplaric." Margolis' most complete discussion of this issue has not yet been published (see below).

[83] Margolis, "Specimen," 308.

[84] Harry M. Orlinsky, "Origen's Tetrapla—a Scholarly Fiction?," *Proceedings of the First World Congress of Jewish Studies. 1947*, vol. 1 (Jerusalem, 1952), 173–182; reprinted in Sidney Jellicoe, ed., *Studies in the Septuagint: Origins, Recensions, and Interpretations* (New York: KTAV, 1974), 382–391.

[85] Harry M. Orlinsky, "The Septuagint—its Use in Textual Criticism," *Biblical Archaeologist* 9 (1946), 27 fn. 10. In the opinion of Jellicoe, who provides a fine summary of Orlinsky's arguments (*The Septuagint and Modern Study*, 114–118), "Professor Orlinsky has made out a strong case for the rejection of the Tetrapla as a separate work (p. 116)." At the same time, Jellicoe raises a few questions "on some subsidiary points."

[see below]), someone should take it upon himself to look beyond the "nebulous character" of terminology employed, in order to investigate the substance of Margolis' contentions concerning the nature of Origen's important, and in many ways pivotal, work.[86]

Between 1912 and 1920, as Margolis was defining his four major recensions (E, P, S, C) and investigating ever more closely the complex relationships among the individual manuscripts that made them up, he produced a steady stream (though not the torrent of the previous period) of publications that addressed specific questions in the Greek Joshua or more general issues in the study of the Septuagint. Two of the most interesting ("Man by Man" and "Hexapla and Hexaplaric") have already been cited.

Among the more significant of his other articles during these years are "The Mode of Expressing the Hebrew 'Ā'ID in the Greek Hexateuch," "Additions to Field from the Lyons Codex of the Old Latin," "Ai or the City? Joshua 8. 12, 16," and "The Aldina as a Source of the Sixtina."[87] In the first of these, Margolis made use of a particular construction (where "a relative pronoun or adverb is resumed by a demonstrative pronoun or adverb")[88] to make some more general observations on the nature of Septuagint Greek in the Pentateuch and Joshua. Typical of the care with which Margolis addressed any issue is the fact that of this article's 24 pages, 17 are taken up entirely with over 100 footnotes that draw together material from many hundreds of passages in the Hexateuch. In "Additions to Field," which grew out of Margolis' interest in the K Text of Joshua, he uncovered "Hexaplaric elements in the Old Latin of the first nine chapters of the book of Joshua . . . hitherto unknown and therefore constituting additions to Field's monumental work."[89] Not content with providing a mere listing of these elements, Margolis constructed an accompanying commentary that—as was usual with Margolis—covered a range of issues far broader than the specific topic at hand. The remaining articles from this period were similarly fruitful in matters of methodology and textual analysis.

Margolis' scholarly endeavors during these years went far beyond his research on Greek Joshua and other topics related to the Septuagint. Through 1914, he published dozens of book reviews a year in *JQR*. (On this see chapter 2.) During the period from 1914 to 1921, Margolis edited

---

[86] For the phrase "nebulous character," see Jellicoe, *The Septuagint and Modern Study*, 114.

[87] Max L. Margolis, "The Mode of Expressing the Hebrew 'Ā'ID in the Greek Hexateuch," *AJSL* 29 (1913), 237–260; "Additions to Field from the Lyons Codex of the Old Latin," *JAOS* 33 (1913), 254–258; "Ai or the City? Joshua 8. 12, 16," *JQR* n.s. 7 (1916/17), 491–497; "The Aldina as a Source of the Sixtina," *JBL* 38 (1919), 51f.

[88] Margolis, "Mode of Expressing . . . ," 237. "In Arabic grammar," Margolis notes (p. 237), "the retrospective pronoun is known as the 'ā'id."

[89] Margolis, "Additions," 254.

JBL; in this position, he was forced to deal with a new firm of printers, difficult authors, and myriad other problems (see chapter 2). Margolis' responsibilities as an editor were not limited to *JBL*. Even after he stopped writing large numbers of reviews for *JQR*, he continued to function as an editor of that journal. Although Cyrus Adler formally headed this Dropsie publication, he relied very heavily on Margolis' advice concerning everything from acceptance of articles to decisions on style and format.[90]

In addition, Margolis was editor-in-chief of the J.P.S. Bible translation, which did not appear until 1917. Prior to that time, Margolis was meeting regularly with the Editorial Committee and preparing both his *Notes on the New Translation* and *The Story of Bible Translations*. (See chapter 3.) When Margolis' other activities are taken into account—he published several articles apart from those on the Septuagint, he offered a variety of courses at Dropsie (few professors today could match his pedagogical versatility), he frequently addressed scholarly and popular audiences, and (by no means least important) he became the father of three children—it is difficult to imagine that he had very much "free" time.

During the 1920s, Margolis' publications grew fewer in number. In the early part of the decade he produced an important popular work, *The Hebrew Scriptures in the Making* (to be discussed in the following chapter),[91] and during much of the middle portion of this decade (including the year he spent in Jerusalem) he and Alexander Marx were putting together their *History of the Jewish People*. (See chapter 2.)

The chief reason, however, why Margolis produced fewer studies in this period was his deep involvement in two projects of extraordinary complexity—complex in the subject matter being treated, in the form Margolis devised for organizing his material, and in the mechanical processes required for publication of the complicated texts that resulted. These two projects led to *Andreas Masius and his Commentary on the Book of Joshua* and *The Book of Joshua in Greek*.

Joseph Reider summarized in a succinct manner the circumstances that had led Margolis to write a monograph-length study of Masius' commentary on Joshua:

---

[90] Preserved in the Dropsie College Archives are dozens of letters from Adler to Margolis concerning the preparation and publication of *JQR*. From a later date (June 13, 1932) comes this statement from Adler, in a letter to Chaim Weizmann: "I have had a hard winter and through the loss of one of my colleagues, Professor [Max L.] Margolis, about which you may have read, I had an extra amount of work, which I must see through personally, principally in connection with the [*Jewish*] *Quarterly Review*. . . ." This letter is printed in Ira Robinson (ed.), *Cyrus Adler: Selected Letters*, vol. 2 (Philadelphia/New York: The Jewish Publication Society of America and the Jewish Theological Seminary of America, 1985), 243f. (The sentence quoted above is found on p. 244.)

[91] Max L. Margolis, *The Hebrew Scriptures in the Making* (Philadelphia: The Jewish Publication Society of America, 1922 [reprinted, 1943]).

In his work on the Greek text of the Book of Joshua Margolis had
occasion to use the commentary on the Book of Joshua by the Belgian
scholar Andreas Masius (Andrew Du Maes, 1515–1573). This great
commentary, containing the Greek version with an accompanying Latin
translation and copious exegetical notes, was published at Antwerp in
1574 and was subsequently excerpted in the *Critici Sacri* (Francofurti
ad Moenum 1695 ff.). Its importance stems from the fact that Masius
used the famous Syriac manuscript written in 606, which . . . preseved
the readings of Joshua as given by Origen in his Hexapla. Margolis was
so impressed by it that he decided to write a monograph on it, in which
the manner of the construction of the Greek text was most minutely
discussed. . . .[92]

The manuscript used by Masius is now lost, but what is in all probability
the second part of this Syriac text is still available in the Codex Ambrosianus, dated to the eighth century C.E. What this Codex contains, and
what was seen by Masius, was a copy of the Syro-Hexaplar, a Syriac
rendering of Origen's fifth column that was produced by Paul of Tella in
the early 7th century.[93] As noted by Sidney Jellicoe, "the particular
value" of the Syro-Hexaplar (and the early copy of it found in the Codex
Ambrosianus) "is the incorporation of Origen's critical symbols, which
have survived in Greek only in the codices Colberto-Sarravianus (G) and
the Chigi manuscript 88."[94]

In his introduction to *Andreas Masius*, Margolis discussed the importance of the Syro-Hexaplar from the perspective of his overall program for
Joshua:

> The recovery of the the principal recensions of the Septuagint, which in
> Lagarde's programme is the necessary preliminary to a reconstruction of
> the text in its ultimate form, is facilitated in the Book of Joshua through
> the great number of proper names which afford the means for segregat-
> ing the smaller and larger groups and their reduction to a few well-
> defined main types. The proper names furnish just the starting-point;
> the findings are then verified when carried into the remainder of the
> text. For the purposes of identifying the types we fall back on the
> patristic citations and the secondary versions. . . . The Syriac transla-
> tion of Paul of Tella, executed in Alexandria in 616–7, is linked, by the
> direct evidence of its subscription, to the Palestinian recension *(P)*, i.e.
> the hexaplaric-tetraplaric revision as it was worked out by Origen and
> then passed through the hands of Eusebius. . . . The Syrohexaplar
> version of Joshua (𝔖) is extant in the British museum manuscript. . .

[92] Joseph Reider, "Bibliography of the Works of Max L. Margolis," *Max Leopold Margolis: Scholar and Teacher*, 77.
[93] Sidney Jellicoe, *The Septuagint and Modern Study*, 124–127.
[94] Jellicoe, 125.

edited by Lagarde in *Biliothecae Syriacae. . . quae ad philologiam sacram pertinent,* Göttingen 1892 ($\mathfrak{S}$L). . . . A parallel manuscript, now lost, in which only the first six verses of the third chapter were illegible, was in the hands of Andreas Masius, who made it the basis of his critical edition in the work *Iosuae imperatoris historia illustrata atque explicata,* posthumously published Antwerp 1574 ($\mathfrak{S}$M). . . . In external appearance, the lost manuscript resembled very much the one published by Lagarde. It had the critical signs (asteriscus, obelus, lemniscus, metobelus) and was equipped with marginal notes (renderings by the later translators, readings from other sources, scholia). The text was dotted with accent (interpunctuation) points.[95]

Masius' work on this manuscript—which, while parallel to Lagarde's, differed from it in hundreds upon hundreds of details (Margolis covers all of these in the monograph)—was seen by Margolis as indispensible for a proper understanding not only of the Syro-Hexaplar, but of the P recension as a whole:

It is regrettable that Masius forbore to edit his Syriac text. For one thing, the present study [i.e. Margolis' monograph] would have been superfluous. . . . Mas chose rather to issue a continuous Greek text which is accompanied by a Latin translation and followed by a series of notes, Annotationes, in which considerable portions of the text are critically discussed; and an elaborate commentary. . . . Although Mas meant to express in Greek what he found in the Syriac, he really aimed higher. He rightly considered the Syriac a guide to the Origenic-Eusebian recension, and that he proceeded to restore.[96]

The monograph *Andreas Masius,* to which Margolis made frequent reference in his *Book of Joshua in Greek* and elsewhere, was not published during Margolis' lifetime or in the years that followed: "The work was accepted by the Harvard Theological Studies for publication, but for some unknown reason it has not yet been published."[97] The full story of Margolis' difficulties in preparing this lengthy text (it runs over 600 pages in typescript) for publication will be told elsewhere.[98] What follows here is a summary of the delays and frustrations experienced by Margolis in this enterprise.

[95] Max L. Margolis, *Andreas Masius and his Commentary on the Book of Joshua* (unpublished manuscript), 1–5.

[96] Margolis, *Andreas Masius,* 32f. For further reference to Masius—and the historical and theological context in which he worked—see S. L. Greenslade (ed.), *The Cambridge History of the Bible: The West from the Reformation to the Present Day* (Cambridge: University Press, 1963).

[97] Joseph Reider, writing in 1952 ("Bibliography of the Works of Max L. Margolis," *Max Leopold Margolis: Scholar and Teacher,* 77).

[98] See below.

In the fall of 1922, Margolis was in the midst of work on the monograph and in contact with George Foote Moore at Harvard, who assured him that "you are on our books . . . and when you complete the manuscript I think there is no doubt we can go with it without serious delay."[99] In July of the following year, Moore wrote: "Your letter and manuscript are in my hands. I congratulate you on the completion of the important and laborious work. . . . In a few days [I] shall take the first opportunity to look over your manuscript and consult my colleagues about ways and means of publication."[100] In was three years later, in April 1926, before Moore was able to inform Margolis that "the editors of the Harvard Theological Studies have after considerable inquiry found printers from whom we have got estimates on your volume on 'The Syriac Joshua of Masius,' which look as if they would be within the limits of our present resources, and we should like to get the work started without making the long delay any longer."[101] In this same letter Moore began to raise questions about type fonts and potential difficulties in getting some of the more technical matter, which Margolis had placed in a lengthy apparatus, set. Over the next two years, there is more correspondence with Moore and Robert P. Blake, also of Harvard.[102] Finally, Harvard's James H. Ropes sent to Margolis proofs of the first 54 pages of the "Masius" text.[103] In response, Margolis wrote to Ropes, in April 1928, that he was not happy having to forego so "many typographical contrivances for which the Belgian printers do not appear to have facilities."[104] No later correspondence, to or from Margolis, that mentions Masius has been uncovered.

Shortly after Margolis' death in 1932, a search was undertaken for any copy of the Masius manuscript that might be found among Margolis' papers. None was. Some five years later—at the request of Mrs. Margolis, Cyrus Adler, and Harry M. Orlinsky—Harry Wolfson looked into this matter.[105] He in turn got in touch with Robert P. Blake, who wrote to Adler: "I remember very well the various peripeties of Profesor Margolis's MS., but do not recall the final disposition of it. Ropes's long illness

[99] George Foote Moore to Max L. Margolis, quoted in a letter from Cyrus Adler to Harry A. Wolfson, dated May 31, 1937 (on the circumstances of this 1937 letter, see below) (Dropsie College Archives).

[100] Moore to Margolis, July 28, 1923 (Dropsie College Archives).

[101] Moore to Margolis, April 26, 1926 (Dropsie College Archives).

[102] See, for example, two letters preserved in the Dropsie College Archives: Robert P. Blake to Max L. Margolis, July 3, 1926, and Moore to Margolis, November 7, 1927.

[103] See the letter of James H. Ropes to Max L. Margolis, February 26, 1928 (Dropsie College Archives).

[104] Margolis to Ropes, April 13, 1928 (Dropsie College Archives).

[105] See, among others, a letter from Orlinsky to Adler, dated March 31, 1937, a letter from Adler to Mrs. Margolis, also dated March 31, 1937, and the letter from Adler to Wolfson (dated May 31, 1937) cited above. (All of this correspondence is preserved in the Dropsie College Archives.)

brought about towards the end of his life a distinct relaxation of that meticulous attention to detail which had previously characterized him."[106] Neither Blake's search then, nor Arthur D. Nock's later, turned up the manuscript upon which Margolis and others had labored for so long. Subsequent searches at Harvard were equally fruitless.

In 1982 the author of this biography located a copy of *Masius* in a private collection in New York City. In the summer of 1984, the process of editing this manuscript began, with funding provided by a grant-in-aid from the American Council of Learned Societies. When the edited version of this manuscript appears, specialists will finally have access—some sixty years later than originally intended—to one of the most meticulously prepared pieces of modern Biblical scholarship.

As Margolis himself recognized, the *Masius* manuscript, and indeed all of his research on the Septuagint, was in a sense preparatory to the "critical edition of the Book of Joshua in Greek" that had been Margolis' ultimate goal since at least 1910.[107] At that early date Margolis had envisioned that "the text should be printed in two columns correspond-ing to the two forms it assumed in Palestine and Syria on the one hand and in Egypt on the other."[108] Somewhat later, when Margolis had come to recognize the Palestinian and Syrian texts as separate recensions, he

> prepared a working copy of the text of the three major recensions of the LXX, viz., the Egyptian, Syrian, and Palestinian recensions. The text of the central representatives of these three recensions was printed in parallel columns, with the counterpart of the MT printed adjacent to the Greek text. . . . Margolis may have intended to publish his text of Joshua as a three-column edition, but at a later stage he recognized the complexity of the textual transmission. In his final edition, therefore, he reckoned with four different recensions (the three mentioned above, plus *C*). In that edition, Margolis did not publish the text of the recensions as running texts but quoted individual readings from the reconstructed recensions in the first apparatus whenever they differed from the reconstructed original translation.[109]

Margolis experimented with these different formats throughout the 1910s and into the early 1920s. It is not known when, precisely, he hit upon the format finally adopted and briefly described above; however, by April 1927, he was able to write to George Kohut, whose Alexander

---

[106] Blake to Adler, June 3, 1937 (Dropsie College Archives).

[107] See Margolis, "Grouping," 263.

[108] Margolis, "Grouping," 261f.

[109] Emanuel Tov, "The Discovery of the Missing Part of Margolis' Edition of Joshua," *Bulletin of the International Organization for Septuagint and Cognate Studies* 14 (1981), 18f. See also Greenspoon, "Max L. Margolis on the Complutensian Text of Joshua," 54.

Kohut Memorial Foundation was to publish *Joshua*, that "in the matter of the Joshua, I have ready for the Printer fully one half of the Text. Before long I ought to be through with the entire job."[110] Margolis then asked of Kohut whether he had "come to any understanding with the Publisher."[111] According to all accounts, it was this publisher, Geuthner of Paris, who was largely responsible for the numerous delays in publication that Margolis and others were to experience in the following years, delays that did not cease with Margolis' death.

In January 1928, Margolis sent to Geuthner the first 30 pages of his revised *Joshua*. With the remainder of the manuscript awaiting revision, prospects were bright for a speedy publication of this massive work.[112] That same month Kohut thought it prudent to warn Margolis to set "a time limit for the publication of your work, as otherwise we shall be grievously disappointed as we have been in the case of the other work already six months delayed."[113] Sometime in the year 1928 or the early part of 1929, on the evidence of a letter dated in March 1929, a decision was made to reproduce Margolis' handwritten manuscript by photography rather than have it set in type, as had been done so beautifully with the small portion of text included in "Specimen."[114] Margolis does not seem happy about this decision, but acceded to it, probably because it offered the best hope for expediting the entire process, which was then at a standstill. Geuthner, that "slippery and difficult fellow" (in the words of Alexander Marx),[115] managed to thwart any hope that the entire *Joshua* would soon be available to the scholarly world. In fact, it was not until October 1931 that American scholars saw the first part of this text and that was the only part that appeared while Margolis was still alive. Three of the remaining four parts slowly appeared in the years that followed. Even direct appeals from the American ambassador to France, Jesse Isidore Straus, did not persuade Geuthner to publish *Joshua* more speedily.[116]

In 1938, the fourth part appeared; Geuthner never did publish the

[110] Max L. Margolis to George Alexander Kohut, April 29, 1927 (Archives of the American Jewish Historical Society).

[111] *Ibid.*

[112] See Margolis to Kohut, January 10, 1928 (Archives of the American Jewish Historical Society).

[113] Kohut to Margolis, January 18, 1928 (Archives of the American Jewish Historical Society).

[114] See Margolis to Kohut, March 8, 1929 (Archives of the American Jewish Historical Society). The comparison with "Specimen" comes from Sidney Jellicoe, *The Septuagint and Modern Study*, 279 fn. 4: "The 'Specimen,' however, the work of Adolf Holzhausen's successors, Printers to the University of Vienna, is set up in type and is beautifully clear."

[115] Marx to Kohut, October 9, 1931 (Archives of the American Jewish Historical Society).

[116] Alexander Marx refers to interventions by Straus and others in a letter to Adler dated February 18, 1935 (Dropsie College Archives). In this letter Marx succinctly stated his opinion that "Geuthner . . . certainly did not act honorably."

fifth, and final, part. This material, held hostage throughout the '30s to Geuthner's machinations, was later to be numbered "among the literary casualties of the Second World War since repeated inquiries have failed to elicit any trace of it in Paris and it must be presumed to have been irretrievably lost or destroyed."[117] It is extremely fortunate that the missing fifth part was found by an Israeli scholar, Emanuel Tov, in the archives of Dropsie University. As Tov writes,

> to be sure, the recently discovered manuscript does not represent the original manuscript which was probably lost, but an excellent copy which—with the aid of photography—can now be published according to Margolis' original plan. Since photocopy machines did not yet exist in Margolis' day, he—or the publisher—had a fine copy made in negative on hard photographic paper. Dropsie's archives contains such a set of photographs of the complete edition, including the part which has never been published.[118]

Tov is to publish the fifth part, along with an introduction "describing Margolis' system."[119] When it appears, another one of Margolis' major achievements will be fully available for the use of interested scholars.[120]
      In his Prefatory Note to the first part of *The Book of Joshua in*

----

[117]The quoted material is taken from Sidney Jellicoe (*The Septuagint and Modern Study*, 278), who "owes this information to Dr. Orlinsky (p. 278 fn. 3)."

[118]Tov, "Discovery of Margolis' Edition," 20f.

[119]Tov, "Discovery of Margolis' Edition," 21. For this introduction, see now Emanuel Tov, "The Fifth Fascicle of Margolis' *The Book of Joshua in Greek*," *JQR* 74 (1984), 397–407.

[120]In a letter to Felix M. Warburg, dated February 8, 1929, Cyrus Adler made reference to the difficulties Margolis was experiencing in connection with both *Joshua* and *Andreas Masius*. Adler was appealing to Warburg for funds to aid scholars in the publication of their works and, in this context, made use of Margolis' experiences to illustrate his observation that "the whole question of the publication of the works of scholars is a tragedy":

> Only this morning Professor [Max L.] Margolis came to my office and told me of the difficulties that he was having in connection with the publication of his scientific work. He had worked for years on a critical edition of the Book of Joshua in Greek, which was accepted four years ago by the Harvard Press, but which has not yet appeared, probably owing to lack of funds. And another book which George Kohut undertook to publish from the Kohut Foundation, which is being printed in Vienna for the sake of cheapness and he gets eight pages at a time, being sent back and forth across the Ocean. He calculated that it will be five years before the book can be published on this basis.

It must be noted—in spite of the worthiness of his appeal—that Adler has not furnished a completely accurate account of Margolis' attempts to get these two works published (see above). He was, no doubt, relying on his memory of the earlier conversation with Margolis. This letter is printed in Ira Robinson (ed.), *Cyrus Adler: Selected Letters*, vol. 2 (Philadelphia/New York: The Jewish Publication Society of America and the Jewish Theological Seminary of America, 1985), 165.

Greek,[121] Margolis explained the arrangement of Text and Apparatus (see above for references to earlier formats he eventually rejected):

> The Text as it appears on the top of the page is the nearest approach to the Greek original as it left the hands of the translator(s). It has been arrived at after a comparison of the remainders in the principal rescensions, when once the recensional peculiarities in each have been subtracted, and an ascertainment of the form of the text to which the recensions lead and which must be purified of the corruptions antecedent to them all. A comparison of our most ancient manuscript (the Codex Vaticanus) with the text here presented will show right in this first part [a number of] conjectural emendations.
>
> Below the Text is printed the Apparatus. It consists of (1) the variants of the principal recensions: *E S P C (M)*; (2) under the head of each of these the evidence for its readings in the purer members and the defalcations on the part of those given to mixture (impure members); (3) the variants within the basic form of any recension; (4) marginal readings in the manuscripts principally touching the later Greek translators and other data concerning them in so far as they have not found a place above. Lastly, brief notes explanatory of the relation of the Greek to the Hebrew original and of variants, recensional or intrarecensional, of the more difficult sort.

Margolis also used the Prefatory Note to explain the sigla with which he designated recensions, manuscripts, secondary versions, and printed texts. These sigla are different from those found, e.g., in B-McL or H-P.

The four principal recensions have already been discussed. In the Prefatory Note Margolis also made use of an *M*, which he placed in parenthesis to indicate that it is not exactly a recension. In "Specimen" he explained that

> there remain a number of MSS., which may be classed together as *M*, i.e. mixed texts. Mixture is the general characteristic, the elements coming from the four principal recensions in diverse processes of contamination. Perhaps it may be said that the ground work is the *C* type, but not quite wholly so. Certain groups [do] emerge.[122]

In the absence of his Introduction to *The Book of Joshua in Greek*, on which Margolis was working at his death (see the beginning of this chapter), the 1927 article "Specimen of a New Edition of the Greek Joshua" serves as the best "introduction" to Margolis' matured thoughts

---

[121] The complete title of the work is *The Book of Joshua in Greek. According to the Critically Restored Text with an Apparatus Containing the Variants of the Principal Recensions and of the Individual Witnesses.*

[122] Margolis, "Specimen," 314.

on the issues he had addressed, in a host of separate publications, over the span of two decades.[123] Vintage Margolis is also on display in three other articles that appeared in the latter part of his scholarly career. In "ΧΩΡΙΣ," Margolis helpfully observed that the Greek word in question, "which is met with on the margin of certain manuscripts in the Septuagint," can signify *addunt* or *omittunt*, according to the context.[124] In "Textual Criticism of the Greek Old Testament," Margolis subjected a relatively insignificant manuscript, codex p, to a characteristically detailed analysis, in order to make some salient points about singular readings (readings that are found in just one witness "to the exclusion of all others"):

> Singular readings [which, according to Margolis, are found in all manuscripts "recent or ancient"] answer to one of two tendencies marking the course of textual transmission. It is the tendency to alteration. In the singular readings are revealed the habits and idiosyncracies of scribes, their physical and mental failings, and even their moral delinquencies, as when in sheer haste they pass over portions of the text or wilfully indulge in contraction. Generally speaking, singular readings are so much refuse which must needs be swept up and constitute the subtrahend in the operation thrust upon the student who is always far more interested in the antecedent copy, now lost, than in the extant transcript. . . . There are singular readings which are extremely valuable, but in one case only, namely when the manuscript in which they occur happens to be the sole representative of a recension.[125]

An "archetypal" singular reading is a different matter:

> Readings which are common to a number of manuscripts may represent a singular reading of the archetype from which they all descend. This is the other tendency in the history of textual transmission, the tendency to follow copy by which its imperfections are perpetuated. Accordingly such community readings restricted to a definite number of manuscripts furnish the key to establish their common descent.[126]

The third of these articles, which is also the last one he published on the Septuagint (in 1930), records his 900 or so "Corrections in the

---

[123] Note the references to this article above.

[124] Max L. Margolis, "ΧΩΡΙΣ," *Oriental Studies published in Commemoration of the Fortieth Anniversary of Paul Haupt as Director of the Oriental Seminary of the Johns Hopkins University* (Baltimore: The Johns Hopkins University Press, 1927), 84–92. (The quoted phrase is found on p. 84.)

[125] Max L. Margolis, "Textual Criticism of the Greek Old Testament," *Proceedings of the American Philosophical Society* 67 (1928), 187f, 193.

[126] Margolis, "Textual Criticism," 194.

Apparatus of the Book of Joshua in the Larger Cambridge Septuagint."[127] It is hard to imagine a more fitting finale than this report of "a number of rectifications I have been able to make in the Cambridge [i.e. B-McL] apparatus."[128] In many instances these rectifications "concern data cited by the editors from Holmes-Parsons."[129] It was readily acknowledged by the editors of the Cambridge Septuagint that they cited variant readings from certain manuscripts solely on the authority of Holmes-Parsons, without making any independent inquiry as to the correctness of such citations.[130] Margolis' independent inquiry into the manuscripts themselves cleared up many dozens of mistakes from Holmes-Parsons that B-McL had perpetuated in this manner. Far be it from Margolis to rely on secondhand evidence! His insistence on going to the original source had once again richly paid off.

As Harry M. Orlinsky has noted, "there are not many scholars who have devoted themselves sufficiently to Septuagint studies to appreciate the character and value of Margolis' work on the Greek Joshua."[131] Reviewing Margolis' work on Joshua, Orlinsky expressed his own favorable opinion ("I accept his argument and method as correct") and made reference to the equally favorable judgment of James A. Montgomery: "Moreover, and this is of decisive importance in view of the nature of the problem, Prof. Montgomery, working quite independently on another type of book altogether, found the facts and interpretations in Joshua to hold true by and large in the case of the text of Daniel also."[132] Orlinsky went on to list other eminent scholars who have also "accepted the view represented by Margolis." Among them are Gehman, Albright, Marcus, P. Katz, and Bleddyn J. Roberts.[133]

Orlinsky is aware that not all scholars have been so appreciative. In an article entitled "On the Present State of Proto-Septuagint Studies," he "dealt in some detail with the somewhat meager and negative criticism directed at Margolis' approach to the recovery of the original text of the Septuagint."[134] The source of this "meager and negative criticism" was Alexander Sperber, who only incidentally mentioned Margolis in the context of a fullscale assault on the entire Lagardian program, which he

---

[127] Max L. Margolis, "Corrections in the Apparatus of the Book of Joshua in the Larger Cambridge Septuagint," *JBL* 49 (1930), 234–264.

[128] Margolis, "Corrections," 234.

[129] *Ibid.*

[130] See, for example, pp. i–ii of the "Prefatory Note to Genesis" in B-McL.

[131] Orlinsky, "Margolis' Work in the Septuagint," *Max Leopold Margolis: Scholar and Teacher*, 43.

[132] Orlinsky, "On the Present State of Proto-Septuagint Studies," 84, cited in "Margolis' Work in the Septuagint," 43.

[133] Orlinsky, "Margolis' Work in the Septuagint," 43.

[134] This characterization of the "criticism" comes from Orlinsky, "Margolis' Work in the Septuagint," 43 fn. 29.

sought to displace in favor of a theory developed by his teacher, Paul
Kahle.[135]

Milder, more constructive criticism has come from scholars who accept
Margolis' overall approach, but find fault with specific points, such as his
advocacy of a separate Tetrapla (see above), or his method of presenting
material in, for example, *The Book of Joshua in Greek*. Jellicoe, who
praised *Joshua* as a "truly monumental achievement," nevertheless felt
that "it suffers from two disadvantages in presentation: owing to the
impracticability of type-setting, the work is reproduced photographically
from the author's manuscript; and the multiple *apparatus criticus* might
with advantage be coordinated."[136]

Margolis' goal had been to prepare a text that was "the nearest approach to the Greek original as it left the hands of the translator(s)."[137]
This text, as Margolis constructed it, was on the whole shorter than our
Received text or MT. There are basically two explanations for the often
pronounced differences between the Old Greek and the MT of Joshua:
either the Old Greek translator accurately reflected his Hebrew text,
which was itself shorter than the MT, or the Old Greek translator
regularly curtailed a Hebrew *Vorlage* that was essentially the same as our
MT. In Margolis' opinion, the second view correctly characterizes the
Old Greek translator's handling of his Hebrew *Vorlage:*

> On the whole [this translator] handled his Hebrew freely, repeatedly
> curtailing the text. . . . While here and there the translator read a
> slightly different Hebrew text compared with the received Hebrew,
> substantially the Hebrew and Greek . . . do tally.[138]

Or, as he succinctly put it in "Specimen": "A few comments on the
translator's manner of operation. He was apparently given to curtail-
ments."[139]

In a 1969 article, Harry M. Orlinsky pointed to the fact that Margolis'
general views on this matter were frequently reflected in his comments
on specific passages:

> In the notes that are found at the bottom of the page in this edition of
> the Greek Joshua, Margolis observed time and again that 'G
> om(its). . . ,' that is to say, whenever the LXX lacks a correspondent for

---

[135] See Orlinsky, "On the Present State of Proto-Septuagint Studies," 86ff.

[136] Sidney Jellicoe, *The Septuagint and Modern Study,* 279.

[137] As stated, for example, in the Prefatory Note to the first part of *The Book of Joshua in
Greek*.

[138] Margolis, "Textual Criticism," 196.

[139] Margolis, "Specimen," 318.

the Hebrew, it is because the translator omitted the Hebrew word or phrase in question.[140]

Orlinsky writes:

> As I first saw the problem, I kept asking myself: On what basis does one assert 'G omits' instead of, say, 'H lacks.' In conjunction with Rabbis Chesman and Soffer, I studied minutely a dozen or so words and phrases throughout the book of Joshua, e.g., מֹשֶׁה עֶבֶד יהוה . . . . It soon became apparent that in every instance that a clear-cut decision could be reached—and this constituted all but a couple of instances—it was not the LXX translator who was guilty of omission but his Hebrew *Vorlage* that was lacking the word or phrase in question; put specifically, if the LXX read Μωυσῆς, as against מֹשֶׁה עֶבֶד יהוה in our preserved Hebrew text, it was because the LXX *Vorlage* read מֹשֶׁה without יהוה עֶבֶד. [141]

Subsequent research by other scholars has confirmed Orlinsky in his overall assessment that the Old Greek translator of Joshua "was most faithful" to his Hebrew *Vorlage*.[142] It is significant, and no doubt a tribute to Margolis himself, that it was one of his own students, Orlinsky, who—carefully following the methodology perfected by his teacher—proved the master wrong in this one case.

In Orlinsky's view it is not likely that there will again be raised up for us a scholar like Margolis from among our brethren:

> The kind of work done by Margolis will probably never be done again. Social circumstances have changed too radically for that. Even the would-be scholar does not any more acquire Latin and Greek before entering College, nor does he master French, German, Hebrew, Arabic, Aramaic, Syriac, Ethiopic, and the like before leaving it. He does not really master the Hebrew text and Versions of the Bible, and the vast and complex Post-Biblical Hebrew and Aramaic and Arabic material pertaining to it (the Talmud, Saadia, the extensive and important Medieval Hebrew-Arabic philology and exegesis, etc.). In a generation of biblical scholarship which was characterized by erudition and meticulousness, Margolis was probably preeminent.[143]

---

[140] Harry M. Orlinsky, "The Hebrew *Vorlage* of the Septuagint of the Book of Joshua," *Supplements to Vetus Testamentum* 17 (Leiden, 1969 [Congress Volume; Rome 1968]), 191.

[141] Orlinsky, "Hebrew *Vorlage*," 192f.

[142] The quoted phrase comes from Orlinsky, "Hebrew *Vorlage*," 195. On subsequent research, see references in Greenspoon, "Theodotion, Aquila, Symmachus, and the Old Greek of Joshua."

[143] Orlinsky, "Margolis' Work in the Septuagint," 44.

The last word, however, belongs to Margolis, and it is a decidedly
ambiguous word. Robert Gordis captured well one side of this "mixture
of affection and rebelliousness":

> So arduous and complex was this undertaking [the preparation of his
> *Joshua*] that in increasing measure, Dr. Margolis abstained from writing
> papers on other themes during the last two decades of his life, con-
> centrating every moment of his working existence upon what he called
> with a mixture of affection and rebelliousness, 'My damned Joshua.' I
> remember once discussing his total absorption in the Greek *Joshua* to
> the exclusion of less recondite subjects and summoning the courage to
> say to him, 'Professor, where will you find twenty or thirty scholars of
> your eminence to do for the other books of the Bible what you have
> done for Joshua?' He made no reply, for none was possible. Such a
> group of scholars does not exist.[144]

It was a source of regret to Margolis' students that their teacher, chained
to his "damned Joshua" out of a sense of what Gordis calls "scientific
bondage," was unable to complete so many other tasks he had set for
himself.[145] But there was also another component in the "mixture,"
namely "affection." And there is no doubt that Margolis felt tremendous
pride, even as he experienced frustration, in the concentration of effort
that produced his magnum opus. Margolis may have given less frequent
expression to these warmer feelings, but they do show forth, for example,
when, in a 1930 letter to George Kohut, he described his daughter as
"the contemporary of my work on Joshua."[146]

In a sense, Margolis' last word as a Septuagintal scholar has yet to be
spoken. When, in late 1931, Margolis ceased his work, he was preparing
a grand Introduction to his Greek Joshua. Immediately after his death,
there was some talk of engaging another scholar to complete and edit this
Introduction.[147] Nothing came of that idea, nor was any program undertaken to provide a means for publishing those sections of the Introduction
Margolis had written. The author of this biography has come across a
number of Margolis' unpublished writings; in his opinion, many of them
were textual studies destined for inclusion in the Introduction. Plans
have been made to publish the most important of these studies. When
they—and *Andreas Masius* and the remaining part of *Joshua*—appear, all
of Margolis' major works will finally be available, as Margolis himself had
intended. And then, at long last, Margolis will have had his full say.

[144] Gordis, "The Life of Professor Max Leopold Margolis: An Appreciation," *Max Leopold Margolis: Scholar and Teacher*, 14.
[145] For the phrase "scientific bondage," Robert Gordis to Leonard J. Greenspoon. Oral interview.
[146] Margolis to Kohut, August 26, 1930 (Archives of the American Jewish Historical Society).
[147] Several letters preserved in the Dropsie College Archives make reference to this.

5. EXEGESIS AND THEOLOGY

"The truth is that Bible exposition requires a training and preparation which few are willing to undergo [from Margolis, "The Jewish Defense of the Bible"]"

In the early part of 1905, Max Margolis and Kaufmann Kohler entered into negotiations that would lead to Margolis' return, after an absence of eight years, to Hebrew Union College in Cincinnati. In one of the letters Margolis wrote to Kohler at that time, he spoke of his "exegetical attitude":

If Christian scholars, like Kittel and Budde, bluntly assert that their exegesis of the OT is and must be Christian, well then—and I have never repudiated it before my University classes—my understanding of the OT is and must be Jewish.[1]

More than once, Margolis recalled, this "Jewish point of view" had been appreciatively received by non-Jewish colleagues and students:

At the request of Dean Van Kirk of the Berkeley Bible Seminary (Disciples), I taught for two successive years the Synoptic Gospels in Greek, and gave a course on the Semitic Original of the Gospels. It is needless to say that I never denied my Jewish point of view. But it is exactly that point of view which interested my Christian students.[2]

And again:

The President of the Pacific Theological Seminary (Congregational) wrote . . .: 'Our class in the elements of Hebrew had joined the Semitic department of the University, and is enjoying the instruction of Professor Margolis, a Hebrew of fine culture and an admirable teacher. . . . Our students commend Professor Margolis' work as very profitable and full of interest.'[3]

---

[1] Max L. Margolis to Kaufmann Kohler, April 1905 (American Jewish Archives), also quoted by Margolis in his April 8, 1907 letter to Rabbi Charles S. Levi (see chapter 1).
[2] Max L. Margolis to Charles S. Levi, April 8, 1907 (see above).
[3] *Ibid.*

In his letter to Kohler, Margolis did not define more closely what a Jewish "understanding" or "point of view" entails. Nor does he do so elsewhere. He remained, nonetheless, convinced that Jewish scholars were capable of making unique contributions to the study of Biblical material:

> Only a Jew who knows himself at one with the Bible religion can adequately interpret the Scriptures. Surely a poet is the poet's best interpreter, and a philosopher the philosopher's. In the same manner it requires a religious mind to understand psalmist and prophet, and only he that is nurtured by Jewish thought, itself rooted in the Scriptures, may hope to master the Scriptural Word in its fullest and deepest import. Only a Jew can say on approaching Holy Writ: This is the flesh of my flesh, and bone of my bones. He must possess himself, it is true, of the philological method and of the completest apparatus; but he alone can add thereto that which ensures fullest comprehension: the love for his own, for the thought that makes his innermost soul to throb, which still lives in him albeit faintly, so that his understanding of the Scriptures, mediated though it be by philological effort, becomes to a considerable extent immediate, just as the language of Scriptures is to him in a large measure a living tongue.[4]

It is worth observing that Margolis included these comments, which he himself compared to certain statements by Samuel David Luzzatto,[5] in a very far-reaching scholarly article, "The Scope and Methodology of Biblical Philology," which he wrote for the inaugural issue of *JQR*'s new series in 1910. It is as if he thought that no discussion of so important a topic as Biblical philology would be complete without reference to, and acknowledgement of, the exegetical stance of the philologist.

Two years earlier (in 1908), Margolis had published a commentary on the book of Micah that aimed, in the words of the Advertisement to the Series, to be "at once reliable and Jewish."[6] In achieving the latter goal—and thereby enhancing, not diminishing, the former—Margolis had already provided a "flesh and bones" example of "that which . . . only a Jew . . . can add [to] the philological method":

---

[4] Max L. Margolis, "The Scope and Methodology of Biblical Philology," *JQR* n.s. 1 (1910/11), 32f. It is interesting to note that Margolis strongly supported the efforts, initiated by Eliezer Ben-Yehuda, to revive the Hebrew language as a "living tongue." Note also that, in discussing Bible translations, Margolis felt that Jews were uniquely well qualified to make substantial advances in preparing English or other modern-language versions. (On this, see chapter 3.)

[5] Margolis, "Scope," 32 fn. 106 (The fn. itself is found on p. 41). On Adler's assessment that Margolis "felt himself, in a way, a sort of successor to Samuel David Luzzatto," see chapter 1.

[6] Max L. Margolis, *Micah (The Holy Scriptures with Commentary)* (Philadelphia: The Jewish Publication Society of America, 1908).

The resultant commentary accomplished what it set out to do in an admirable fashion: for the Jewish reader, it made much use of Jewish traditions for exposition: the evidence of the Targums, the classic commentaries of Rashi, Ibn Ezra, Kimhi; less accessible material from Ibn Janah, Abrabanel, pertinent suggestions from rabbinic sources, tannaitic and amoraic, are skilfully utilized. Interesting for the Jewish reader is the demonstration of how much rabbinic, midrashic and liturgical material ascends to Micah (Scripture). It is remarkable, too, how extensively the comments of the mediaeval exegetes anticipate modern interpretations. . . . At the same time, the modern methodology of comparing the ancient Versions and of utilizing the labors of modern exegetes are systematically resorted to.[7]

As the remarks just cited make clear, this sustained emphasis on traditional Jewish sources is not pious adornment; rather, this rich exegetical tradition enables readers (Jews and non-Jews alike) to reach back to the Biblical text itself and forward to the best critical scholarship then current.

In reading Margolis' programmatic statement on the Jewish contribution to Biblical studies and the Advertisement to the Series of which Micah was the first volume, it is difficult not to detect a note of defensiveness, to which may be attributed the extravagance of expression that surfaces here and there in these remarks. In his strong support for a Jewish presence in Biblical studies, Margolis was in fact taking cognizance of opposition to this presence from two very different, but also very powerful, quarters.

In the first instance, there was an unmistakably anti-Jewish tone to much of the critical scholarship being produced and studied in Margolis' time and in the two or three generations that preceded him. As Margolis wrote in a popular article for the *B'nai B'rith News* of June 1915:

> The German exposition of the Hebrew Scriptures has been characterized for a century by a spirit of avowed hostility to Jews and Judaism. . . . Wrong[s have been] perpetrated by the anti-Semitic writers from Schleiermacher on in vilifying Judaism and Jewish literature. Blinded by an arrogance of the most blatant kind, steeped in prejudices which though decked up in the trappings of the latest philosophy are as old as the beginnings of the Christian era, they operate on the presumption that Judaism represents an inferior religion and the Hebrew Scriptures a point of view outdistanced by the Christian Bible.[8]

[7] Frank Zimmermann, "The Contributions of M. L. Margolis to the Fields of Bible and Rabbinics," *Max Leopold Margolis: Scholar and Teacher*, 20. At the end of chapter 1 above, the format of this commentary is described, other Biblical commentaries written by Margolis are mentioned, and Zimmermann's comments are continued. See below for further discussion of Margolis' commentary on Micah.

[8] Max L. Margolis, "The Jewish Defense of the Bible," *B'nai B'rith News* June 1915, 10.

A defense of the Jewish Bible was needed, and, as Margolis saw it, that defense must come from Jews, from Jews trained in all aspects of Biblical scholarship:

> In the pioneer days of twenty-five years ago [Margolis wrote, again in 1915] it used to be believed that you might take a Jew and put a humesh in his hand and thereby ordain him a teacher of the Bible. We live in the era of specialization. . . . If we are to defend the Jewish Bible we must be able to cope with the non-Jew. We must know the things he knows and do the things he does as well and a good deal better. . . . We cannot demolish criticism by ignoring it. Entrenched in hatred and prejudice, the critic will not be dislodged unless we assail him by his own weapons. Lagarde, the arch anti-Semite, long ago said that no man can interpret the Pentateuch without a knowledge of the halakah. But a mere knowledge of the halakah will not constitute a Bible commentator. . . . Know the rabbinic expositions we must, but at the same time know how to discriminate between imputed meanings and the original purport. For all of which we need discernment, the discernment which comes from long and laborious preparation. We must show that we know language and grammar better than the Christian. We must prove that we also can consult authorities at first hand in regions not explored in heder. The Jewish expounder of the Bible must be at home in patristic literature as well as in Mishnah and Talmud and Midrash. . . . There is not a verse, there is not a word in the Bible that has not a long history of interpretation behind it which one must know, and know at once for immediate use.[9]

When Margolis had declared five years earlier that "only a Jew . . . can adequately interpret the Scriptures,"[10] this is the sort of Jewish scholar he had in mind—one well supplied from the arsenal of religious and secular education, ready to stand his ground against the onslaughts of the "learned" and to best his "erudite" opponents on their own turf and with their own weapons.

Were there many such scholar-warriors or was there, at least, a large pool of recruits from whom Margolis could call forth potential defenders? The answer to both questions, Margolis knew well, was no. The organized Jewish community of Margolis' day did not encourage its brightest students, even those with a particular interest in religion, to pursue a career in the field of Bible. Margolis felt compelled to oppose this internal lack of support every bit as much—though in different ways—as he combatted the external threat posed by the anti-Semites.

The attitude current among the Jews of Margolis' day was nothing new. After all, it was a tradition, centuries old in observance, that the most

[9] *Ibid.*
[10] Margolis, "Scope," 32 (see above).

gifted of Jewish youth were to prepare themselves for lifelong immersion in the sea of the Talmud. It was to this group (whose numbers, Margolis averred, had sharply declined by 1915) that Isaac M. Wise referred, when he said to Margolis in 1892: "We have plenty of Talmud teachers . . . among us Jews."[11]

More recent trends within Judaism had only served to accentuate this traditional feeling:

> The nineteenth century witnessed the rise of the newer Jewish learning which is characterized by explorations in the whole range of Jewish antiquity along historical and critical lines [, but] the trend of the labors of the whole of [this] 'historical school' . . . was to steer clear of the Scriptures.[12]

Robert Gordis recalls that Margolis "was wont to comment with a wry smile [that] he differed from his contemporaries in teaching a 'non-Jewish subject,' the Bible, which nineteenth century *Juedische Wissenschaft* had tended to neglect, or more accurately, to side-step, for reasons both sentimental and ideological."[13] It is not hard to imagine that, occasionally at least, Margolis spoke of these difficult matters with something other than a smile on his face.

Concerns of a traditional and historical nature did not, however, entirely fill the broadening spectrum of internal opposition to intensive Biblical study among Jews. In an article published in the January 1910 *B'nai B'rith News*, Margolis observed that:

> We have come to such a pass in American Jewish life that it is no longer possible to deny that we are a divided household. . . . There are those among us to whom the Bible is a record of the past, not only of a history that is of the past, but also of a past and antiquated religion. It is true that they have not as yet severed all connection with that past; but then it is only the roots of their own religion that they believe to find in the Bible, roots but not branches. . . . These gentleman tell us that at all times the written word was modified by the unwritten explanation which grew around it and which was the product of a progressive, enlightened religious consciousness. A master mind of the movement . . . long ago composed a bulky volume to prove how in the various

---

[11] Margolis related this anecdote in "Jewish Defense," 10. Of the decline in Talmud teachers, Margolis wrote: "The truth is that even Talmud scholars are nowadays [in 1915] rare. The majority of Jewish students have been impregnated with a distaste for Talmud and Talmudic literature."

[12] Max L. Margolis, *The Hebrew Scriptures in the Making* (Philadelphia: The Jewish Publication Society of America, 1922), 50f.

[13] Gordis, "Appreciation," *Max Leopold Margolis: Scholar and Teacher*, 2. See also the references listed in fn. 16 of chapter 1.

translations and commentaries each age sought to impose its own notions concerning religious and moral matters upon the Bible, how even at an earlier period the very word of Scriptures was without scruple changed to remove from the text what was objectionable to an advanced generation. Our own age, it is reasoned further, has its own contributions to make to that unfoldment of the Scriptural meaning, and its own modifications to impose upon Biblical law or legend that it may be brought into consonance with twentieth century conditions and ideas. It is in this manner alone, it is claimed, that the Bible may still be said to be of importance to this latter generation, to wit, to the extent that the natural meaning which an unsophisticated reader will carry away with him must be replaced by the superimposed meaning which only the learned can construct. In other words, we have gotten, so far as the progressive wing of Jewry is concerned, there where the Catholic Church has ever been: we must restrict Bible reading on the part of the unlearned, and insist that they seek information concerning religion at the hands of the clergy only who will serve them with a 'prepared foodstuff,' whereas if they follow their own lights they will procure nought but the 'raw material'. . . . Hence the Bible must not be read except under ecclesiastical, clerical supervision, that all . . . passages may be duly 'modified' in accordance with the spirit of the age. Once you have arrived at this 'progressive' conception of Judaism, it is perfectly clear and rational that the Bible will be dangerous to your spiritual peace.[14]

Beyond these groups, Margolis could point to the "bulk of Jewish scholars" (or, we might say, scholars who happen to be Jewish), whose "publications . . . deal for the most part with scraps in which the Jewish soul is least manifest. And the Torah, she is consigned to oblivion in a corner."[15] Among these scholars were some who had acquired their knowledge of the Bible during their college years and who

follow only too willingly the Christian writers, whose estimate of the Hebrew Scriptures and of the Hebrew religion is that they are both inferior and have been superseded by the New Testament Scriptures and the New Testament religion. You may hear [such] scholars repeat the Christian boast that the study of the Bible along scientific lines is conducted mainly by Christians.[16]

And finally, there were those who would wish to perpetuate the primitive standards of "the pioneer days." Also known as "the man in the street," individuals of this group felt that Bible exposition—to the limited extent

---

[14] Max L. Margolis, "The Bible as a Text Book," *B'nai B'rith News* January 1910, 9.
[15] Margolis, "Jewish Defense," 10.
[16] Max L. Margolis, "Bible Study and Bible Reading," *B'nai B'rith News* January 1913, 10.

that it was needed at all—was something "that anybody and everybody may try his hand at . . . over night as it were, a Bible teacher may be created."[17]

To each of these groups, Margolis pointed out what were to him the deficiencies and unauthentic features of their respective positions (see above). As a corrective, Margolis commended those relatively few Jewish and non-Jewish scholars who evinced a positive attitude toward Judaism and toward the place of the Bible in Jewish life. As he strove to advance the cause of "sound Jewish education, [which] he regarded . . . as the strongest weapon against the disintegrating effect of anti-Jewish sentiments upon the temper and morale of Jews,"[18] it was the works of these individuals for whom Margolis reserved his highest praise.[19] In the judgment of others, many of Margolis' own popular, non-technical works are deserving of this same high praise, for through them he contributed "to the advancement of Jewish learning":

> Dr. Margolis always insisted upon the importance of maintaining Jewish self-respect. . . . Accepting the idea of Saadia Gaon that the Jews constitute a nation by virtue of their loyalty to the Torah, Dr. Margolis . . . endeavored to bridge over the gap between the written and the spoken word in Jewish Bible study. In other words, he ventured to indicate directly or indirectly, the inseparable bond between Hebrew Scripture and Jewish tradition. The continuity and unity of Jewish literature and tradition are points to which he turns again and again.[20]

In the letter to Kohler cited at the beginning of this chapter, Margolis spoke of his "exegetical attitude" and "understanding of the Bible" as Jewish. In the paragraphs that followed citations from the Kohler letter, we explored aspects of Margolis' "Jewish point of view." This exploration proceeded on the basis of scattered remarks preserved largely in his popular articles. These remarks, when brought together, revealed quite clearly Margolis' thinking on at least three basic questions: the role of the Bible within the Jewish community, the role of the Biblical scholar within Judaism, and the role of the Jewish scholar within Biblical studies. In the discussion above, this third role was approached with an emphasis on the word "Jewish"; thus, Margolis' commentary on Micah became an example of "that which . . . only a Jew . . . can add. . . ." Another, complementary approach suggests itself, one that places emphasis on the word "scholar." When Margolis' career is looked at from this perspective, one

---

[17] Margolis, "Jewish Defense," 10.

[18] Joshua Bloch, "Max L. Margolis' Contribution to the History and Philosophy of Judaism," *Max Leopold Margolis: Scholar and Teacher*, 56.

[19] See, for example, his numerous book reviews in the first four volumes of *JQR*.

[20] Bloch, "Margolis' Contribution," 46, 56, 52f.

basic question arises: How did he react to the critical scholarship that increasingly dominated the academic study of the Bible at his time?

To an extent, the outline of an answer can be fashioned on the basis of the quotations brought together above, for many of them contain statements indicating that on the whole Margolis welcomed and encouraged this critical scholarship. For example, before the Jewish scholar can make his unique contribution, "he must possess himself . . . of the philological method and of the completest apparatus."[21] In envisioning a commentary "at once reliable and Jewish," the editors of the Series to which Margolis contributed his *Micah* had recognized "the progress of Biblical studies in modern times, rendered possible chiefly by the discovery of ancient monuments and lost languages."[22] Margolis, who may have had a hand in shaping the goals of the Series, was comfortable with this formulation: "Margolis . . . systematically resorted to . . . the modern methodology of comparing the ancient Versions and of utilizing the labors of modern exegetes . . . never is a question brought up by the critical school by-passed or slurred over."[23] For reasons of self-interest, if for no other, the Jewish scholar had to be an expert in language and grammar and had to prove that he "also can consult authorities at first hand in regions not explored in heder."[24]

In his openness to at least some facets of the higher criticism of his day, Margolis was in step with what was becoming a general trend among many non-Orthodox Jewish scholars at institutions such as Hebrew Union College, Jewish Theological Seminary, and later Dropsie College. Kaufmann Kohler, for example,

> wholly approved the methods of biblical criticism. . . . He denied that the label 'Higher Anti-Semitism' given to Higher Criticism [by Solomon Schechter, among others] could stand the test of scrutiny . . . and went on to point out the achievements of the science. Once the insights are attained, 'the whole Bible presents to the inquirer a gradual evolution of the God idea,' and 'what geology did for us in laying bare the different strata of the earth telling of the various epochs of creation, Higher Criticism does in disclosing the various stages of growth of the truth of the divine revelation.'[25]

---

[21] Margolis, "Scope," 32. It is to the "scope and methodology" of this Biblical philology that Margolis devoted his long article in the first issue of *JQR*.

[22] As stated in the Advertisement to the Series.

[23] Frank Zimmermann, "The Contributions of M. L. Margolis to the Fields of Bible and Rabbinics," *Max Leopold Margolis: Scholar and Teacher*, 20.

[24] Margolis, "Jewish Defense," 10.

[25] Sheldon H. Blank, "Bible," *Hebrew Union College-Jewish Institute of Religion at One Hundred Years*, ed. Samuel E. Karff (Cincinnati: Hebrew Union College Press, 1976), 291.

"Entertaining such an attitude toward the Bible, Kohler in no wise limited the freedom of his Bible faculty to engage in scientific inquiry."[26] Thus it was that Kohler reacted favorably when Margolis, in addition to highlighting his "Jewish understanding of the OT," termed this "attitude" historical and analytical:

> My exegetical attitude, it is needless to announce to you, is historical both in its narrower sense, that is, with reference to the time conditions in which the author of a biblical document wrote—that is only half the work done—and in the wider sense, that is, with reference to the larger meaning about which Christian and Jew will naturally differ. . . . The Jewish student of the Scriptures must, if for no other reason than that he is a cultured man, learn to understand the biblical documents analytically, in their historical setting. . . .[27]

In like manner, Margolis would have encountered no opposition had he, at a later date, accepted Stephen S. Wise's invitation to join the faculty of the newly created Jewish Institute of Religion—to Wise, who "characteristically" expressed himself in an "outspoken manner," "the higher criticism was not only timely but saving."[28]

Margolis never did work for Stephen S. Wise, but he did for another Wise, Isaac Mayer. It was, as described in the first chapter, this Wise who deflected Margolis from his career as a Talmudist and guided him into the academic discipline of Biblical studies. To Isaac M. Wise, however, Biblical studies meant something quite different than it did to Kohler or Stephen S. Wise, and this is reflected in his completely negative attitude toward higher criticism: "[In] the battle . . . for 'the authenticity of the Mosaic records,' the foe was 'the science commonly called Modern Biblical Criticism, actually Negative Criticism.'"[29] In a work titled *Pronaos*, Wise bitterly attacked the historico-critical method, or rather (in Sheldon Blank's phrase) he attacked "a parody, a caricature of the method."[30] All modern Biblical Criticism, as judged by Wise,

> maintains, on the strength of unscientific methods, that the Pentateuch is not composed of original Mosaic material, no Psalms are Davidian, no

---

[26] Blank, "Bible," 292.

[27] Margolis to Kohler, April 1905 (American Jewish Archives).

[28] Blank, "Bible," 293.

[29] Blank, "Bible," 288.

[30] *Ibid.* Cf. Israel Abrahams' judgment that *Pronaos* was "among the earliest of the reasoned replies to the *Higher Criticism.*" Abrahams is quoted by Lou M. Silberman, "Theology and Philosophy," *Hebrew Union College-Jewish Institute of Religion at One Hundred Years,* ed. Samuel E. Karff (Cincinnati: Hebrew Union College Press, 1976), 386.

Proverbs Solomonic, the historical books are unhistorical, the prophecies are written *post festum*, there was no revelation, inspiration or
prophecy. [As a result, this Criticism] must also maintain that the Bible
is a compendium of frauds, willful deceptions, unscrupulous misrepre-
sentation.[31]

As founder and first president of HUC, Wise's views were bound to be
reflected in the curricular offerings: "With the president taking so firm a
stand, the first generation of instructors in Bible at the College would
hardly present the Bible after the manner of Wellhausen."[32] During the
Wise regime, as Sheldon Blank points out, the word *exegesis* (as in
Margolis' academic title, Preceptor in *Exegesis* and Talmud . . .)[33] "was
not a synonym for biblical criticism," but "simply means Bible with
Targum, Ibn Ezra, Rashi, or Rashbam."[34] By contrast, Kaufmann Kohler,
within three years after assuming the presidency, was speaking of a Bible
exegesis that followed the "purely scientific methods of our age," while at
the same time maintaining "its historical continuity with the past by the
consultation of the medieval commentators and the ancient interpretations."[35]

How well did Margolis fare under Wise? From all indications, very
well. Margolis seems to have taken an immediate liking to Wise; after just
a few weeks in Cincinnati (in mid-September 1892), he wrote a friend:
"Dr. Wise is very friendly, and is no doubt an original man."[36] It is likely
that Margolis' feelings were reciprocated on the part of Wise. In the
midst of his controversies with Kohler, Margolis fondly recalled the Wise
years as a period when his relations with the College president "were
always extremely pleasant."[37] On the professional level, Margolis could
"testify that Dr. Wise never interfered with my arrangement of the
curriculum or with my method of teaching, the entire subject of Biblical
Exegesis in the Collegiate classes being committed to my care in the
academic year 1896/7." So highly did Wise regard Margolis as a scholar
and teacher that "scarcely three months after I had left the institution in
1897. . ., he wrote me: 'I will make arrangements with the Board of
Governors to appoint you Professor of (Biblical) Exegesis, with a satisfac-
tory salary; and you know that this is a life position.'" And this occurred
"notwithstanding my views on the Pentateuchal question which I then

[31] Wise, quoted by Blank, "Bible," 288.
[32] *Ibid.*
[33] On this title, see the letter from Margolis to Dick, September 19, 1892 (chapter 1).
[34] Blank, "Bible," 288.
[35] Quoted in Blank, "Bible," 293.
[36] Margolis to Dick, September 19, 1892 (see above).
[37] This and the following quotes come from the letter of Margolis to Charles S. Levi, dated
April 8, 1907, and referred to above (in chapter 1 and earlier in this chapter).

entertained" and "after the clash between him and myself over the question of the personal Messiah at the Montreal Conference."

But, after all, Margolis was no radical, nor was Wise arbitrary in the exercise of his power. As will be seen below, Margolis came to condemn as excesses of higher criticism many of the same practices that Wise saw as instrinsic to the method. They started from very different positions—to Margolis, higher criticism was flawed but redeemable; for Wise, only its abandonment could bring redemption—but their views frequently converged, and, in an atmosphere of cordiality, they managed to effect practical compromises.[38]

Carefully crafted compromise is evident in Margolis' report of the courses he taught in his last year under Wise, 1896–1897. (This report was published in the 1897–1898 Catalogue.)[39] In the lower division (Grade A), a class on the book of Deuteronomy read Driver's commentary and considered points of archaeology, in addition to consulting Jewish exegetes (Rashi, Ibn Ezra, Nahmani) and going through the ancient versions and medieval Jewish commentaries of chapter 33, "with a view of determining the value of 'traditional' interpretation." In a course on Proverbs, the "ethico-religious side" of the book's interpretation "was duly emphasized," but, in addition, students gained an acquaintance with "the elementary problems of biblical exegesis, textual lexical and purely exegetical (literary)." At the collegiate level, a course on Amos and Hosea provided students with particular training "in making use of the Rabbinical commentators and the Targum." At the same time, sources such as Cheyne, Robertson Smith, and Smend were utilized. Margolis explicitly states that Hosea 7 affords an excellent "specimen of an extremely difficult passage which modern exegesis and criticism have done much to elucidate." The combination of all of this secondary material "assured . . . a good knowledge of the religious significance of Hosea . . . in the short time that was available." In shaping this curriculum, Margolis did not seek to undermine Wise's basic understanding of *exegesis;* rather, through the judicious introduction of what he considered to be moderate and responsible exemplars of the critical method, Margolis felt that he was providing his students—and Wise—with a supplement that was as authentic as it was useful.[40]

[38] Wise reacted very differently when he thought that such compromise was unlikely. When Margolis left for Berkeley, "Wise rejected the suggestion that Louis Ginzberg be appointed, on the ground that his attitude toward biblical criticism was unsatisfactory. Instead he appointed Moses Buttenwieser, who—according to an oral tradition—assured him that his attitude was constructive." (The quoted material comes from Silberman, "Theology and Philosophy," 388.)

[39] The quotations in this paragraph are drawn from Margolis' report, contained on pp. 32–35 of Hebrew Union College's 1897–1898 Catalogue.

[40] When Margolis first arrived on the campus of HUC, in September 1892, he had observed, "The College lacks a scientific spirit," and promised, "So far as I am concerned it is going to get

A quarter of a century later, in December 1923, Margolis took the podium at the annual meeting of the Society of Biblical Literature, to deliver his presidential address to the assembled members.[41] In the context of "forecasting" the "future" of Biblical studies, Margolis had a great many things to say about the discipline's present and immediate past. He felt strongly about a number of issues, but on none did he express himself more forcefully than on the current state of Biblical criticism. Scattered as they were (for the most part) in book reviews and popular works, his views on modern critical approaches were probably not well known to his colleagues. In effect, then, this address afforded Margolis the opportunity to sum up several decades of thinking, writing, and teaching on Biblical criticism.

Margolis tended to group the critics around two poles: on the one hand, there existed an "advanced" or "radical" school; on the other, a "conservative," "cautious," "sane," "more moderate" approach.[42] One characteristic of those who adhere to the former is the tendency to

> go on rewriting the ancient documents in such manner that their authors would exclaim, 'Well done, but it is not what we wrote!' Rewriting is not our business. We may take it for granted that Isaiah knew his Hebrew quite well. Nor did he consult us as to the arrangement of his thoughts.[43]

In addition, advanced critics avoid the difficult task of discerning "relevancy, continuity, coherence" in, for example, a book of prophecy. Instead, they resort to the easier procedure of breaking up "a text into atoms."[44]

"Radical" critics were accustomed to describe their enterprise as an open, scientific quest that would successfully free Biblical study from the

---

it." (See chapter 1.) Margolis' classes in Bible, no less than those in Hebrew grammar and syntax, seem to have been organized in line with that initial promise. These courses also appear to be consistent with what Kaufmann Kohler meant by "Bible exegesis." When Margolis returned to HUC in 1905, this may have been one of the few areas in which he and Kohler were in basic agreement; after all, Kohler never accused Margolis of infusing too much, or too little, higher criticism into the classroom. Nor did Margolis and Cyrus Adler, his "boss" for over two decades at Dropsie, clash over this issue.

[41] Margolis delivered this address, titled "Our Own Future: A Forecast and a Programme," on December 27, 1923; it was published in *JBL* 43 (1924), 1–8. Portions of this speech are quoted below and also in chapter 2.

[42] For the term "advanced," see Margolis, *History*, 739; for "radical," see Margolis, *Hebrew Scriptures*, 45; for "conservative" and "cautious," see a review by Margolis, *JQR* n.s. 1, 547; for "sane," see a review by Margolis, *JQR* n.s. 3, 113; for "more moderate," see Margolis, *Hebrew Scriptures*, 48. (These and other, similar expressions are, of course, found elsewhere in Margolis' writings as well.)

[43] Margolis, "Programme," 7.

[44] *Ibid.*

limitations imposed by the dogmas of tradition. In Margolis' view, such scholars were deluding themselves (and the public), for in reality they were "indulging in [a] pseudo-science," which was "woefully lacking in [the] self-criticism" that formed an integral part of truly scientific inquiry.[45] It was in this respect, Margolis correctly observed, that advanced criticism ("Untradition") and Tradition, which diverged at almost all other points, "seemed to be at one":

> Tradition, or that which passes for it, and Untradition, which goes by the name of criticism, are quite apart in their results. But in one respect they seem to be at one. Both know by whom and when every book of the Scriptures, nay, every chapter and verse and every infinitesimal bit of the sacred text, was written; they know also the sequence of the writings in the process of public recognition. Tradition may be shown to rest upon scriptural data, perhaps imperfectly understood, and therefore to constitute mere opinion; Untradition operates with evidence likewise derived from the Scriptures, possibly more successfully apprehended, and tends to be hardened into a tradition of the critical school unquestioned by its followers.[46]

Margolis frequently made this same point in his book reviews; for example:

> The [hyper]critical position has become the orthodox one; but neither orthodoxy nor fashion is a measure of scientific achievement. Where the issues are so momentous, cool and unimpassioned judgment is exceedingly difficult. But undignified expressions are as much out of place with the traditionalists as they are with the critics. . . . Criticism can ill afford to rest on foundations which cannot stand a fresh test with regard to their solidity.[47]

He also attempted to alert the public to the dangers of "a criticism hardened into a tradition":[48] "There are fashions also in Bible study. It is fashionable to hold certain opinions on the Bible today [, but] true criticism never acquiesces in dogmatic assertions."[49]

As Margolis saw it, "true criticism will act as its own corrective."[50] He spoke of a return to "'first principles,' by which questions seemingly disposed of are reopened." This "regress" to basics constitutes "criticism's

---

[45] Margolis, "Programme," 6.

[46] Margolis, *Hebrew Scriptures*, 52.

[47] Max L. Margolis, "Review of Harold M. Wiener, *Essays in Pentateuchal Criticism*," *JQR* n.s. 1 (1910/11), 561f.

[48] The phrase, "a criticism hardened into a tradition," comes from Margolis, "Programme," 6.

[49] Max L. Margolis, "Bible Study and Bible Reading," *B'nai B'rith News* January 1913, 10.

[50] *Ibid.*

safest corrective when in forgetfulness of its own origin it shows itself
ready to relapse into dogmatism."[51] Such an "injection of a measure of
'learned ignorance' will at least save us from the dogmatic assurance
which clings to traditionalists and untraditionalists alike."[52]

The traditional dogmatist was, at least, respectful of the text. He was,
moreover, convinced that the passage of time had done nothing to
diminish the Bible's value; it was as worthy of study in the twentieth
century as it had been in the second. In Margolis' view, no such respect
was to be found among adherents of the "radical" school. Indeed, their
failure (as Margolis wrote about Wellhausen) "to do justice to the trust-
worthiness [and "worthwhileness"] of sacred literature" constituted their
most serious and characteristic shortcoming:[53]

> A presentation of the Old Testament religion [Margolis stated in his
> presidential address] which winds up with the skepticism of Koheleth
> fails significantly in insight. And, worst of all, neither Jahveh nor his
> words seem to be able to live down their past. So we have passed on the
> word . . . that the Old Testament as seen in the light of today is
> decidedly not worthwhile. . . . If the Scriptures lack worthwhileness,
> why then study them?[54]

These "students of the Scripture" are in fact "hostile to them or even
indifferent. . . . [They] have profaned the holy, yielding to the unrest
which has loosened what was bound and dishallowed what was hal-
lowed."[55]

"An unreasonable measure of skepticism," Margolis had noted
elsewhere, permitted the "radical school" to "operate quite recklessly"
with the received text.[56] As an example, Margolis pointed to the radicals'
views on the "prophetic books as they stand in the Scriptures":

> A very small proportion in the volumes of the prophets antecedent to
> the fall of the state (pre-exilic prophets) may be ascribed to the men
> whose names they bear. By far the greater amount is late accretion,
> dating from post-exilic times, nay, largely from the Maccabean period.[57]

[51] Max L. Margolis, "Review of B. D. Eerdmans, *Alttestamentliche Studien*," *JQR* n.s. 1 (1910/11), 554.

[52] Margolis, *Hebrew Scriptures*, 53.

[53] The statement about Wellhausen comes from Margolis, *History*, 739. For "worth-whileness," see the quotation from "Programme" that follows directly below.

[54] Margolis, "Programme," 5f.

[55] Margolis, "Programme," 6.

[56] The phrase, "an unreasonable measure of skepticism," comes from Margolis' review of Wiener (see above), p. 561; "radical school" and reckless operation are phrases Margolis used in *Hebrew Scriptures*, 45.

[57] Margolis, *Hebrew Scriptures*, 45.

As to the writings of the third division, which in the Jewish tradition includes the book of Psalms,

> the writings of the entire third division are pronounced to be products of the post-exilic period, that is from the concluding decades of the Persian domination clear almost to the Romans. Over against the moderate position that certain Psalms are post-exilic and possibly even Maccabean, the exaggerated claim is made that none of the Psalms is of pre-exilic date.[58]

The Torah, although the earliest material "elevated to scriptural rank," was "by no means . . . the earliest written book."[59]

In opposition to the radicalism of the advanced school—but fully in accordance with Margolis' own exegetical position—is "a more moderate school, which, while at one with the methods of modern criticism as applied to the Scriptures, refuses to accept the conclusions in their entire range."[60] Elsewhere, he described the attitude of those who adhere to this school as "a conservative and cautious one; while acknowledging the fulness of information which criticism has laid bare, they shrink from following its conclusions of the more advanced type and express a mild doubt as to the cogency of the argument from internal evidence."[61] In still another place, scholars in this group are said to accept the results of higher criticism, without being "bound hand and foot to all of its vagaries."[62]

These authors (as Margolis said about Rudolf Kittel) exhibit "sober judgment and respect for tradition"[63] and write "with sympathy and respect."[64] They may dissect and dissever, "but the parts do not become infinitesimal." This sort of scholar "concedes much to a sane criticism, [but] he is emphatic in having to give up nothing that is vital in the value of the Old Testament."[65] The books produced by this school are "refreshing" in that "the religion of the Hebrew Scriptures [is] taken at its highest, the tendency of pure historical criticism with its analytic dissection and its regress to beginnings operating for the most part in the opposite direction."[66]

[58] Margolis, *Hebrew Scriptures*, 46f.
[59] Margolis, *Hebrew Scriptures*, 47.
[60] Margolis, *Hebrew Scriptures*, 48.
[61] Max L. Margolis, "Review of *The Temple Dictionary of the Bible*," *JQR* n.s. 1 (1910/11), 547f.
[62] Max L. Margolis, "Review of H. C. O. Lanchester, *The Old Testament*," *JQR* n.s. 3 (1912/13), 107.
[63] Margolis, *History*, 739.
[64] Margolis' review of Lanchester (see above), 108.
[65] Margolis' review of Lanchester (see above), 108.
[66] Max L. Margolis, "Review of John Adams, *"Israel's Ideal, or Studies in Old Testament Theology*," *JQR* n.s. 1 (1910/11), 571.

As an example of the cautious criticism characteristic of this school, Margolis might have cited S. R. Driver, whose Cambridge Bible commentary on the book of Exodus he commended in a brief review published in 1912: "Driver's strength lies in his intimate acquaintance with the language and his cautious criticism." A "worthy expounder of Exodus," Driver accepted "as historical . . . the *outline* of the narratives concerning the exodus and the person of Moses."[67] A year or so earlier, Margolis had similarly praised the revised edition of Driver's *Introduction to the Literature of the Old Testament*:

> The vagaries of the 'advanced school' are rejected; there is a chariness in subscribing to the views of those who find in the prophetic books but meager kernels belonging to the pre-exilic seers, all else being post-exilic frame-work; nor is meter accepted as an all-sufficient guide to distinguish the genuine from the spurious after the fashion of Duhm and his followers.[68]

Margolis did not do so, but it is certainly the case that he could have cited himself as another cautious scholar of the more moderate school. In the Introduction to his 1907 commentary on Micah, Margolis included a long excursus on higher or "literary" critics, whose "preconceived notions," "fatal flaws," and "preposterous pronouncements" he sought to expose:

> The unity of authorship which, in keeping with tradition, is here assumed for the entire book has been challenged by the exponents of the higher or 'literary' criticism. As applied to prophetic writers, literary criticism is a quarter of a century old, its principles having been set forth in 1881, in . . . a 'pioneering' article by the late Professor Stade. . . . The underlying conception is that the prophetic books . . . constitute the result of the literary activity of generations of students at whose hands the pre-exilic prophets received substantial additions (insertions, interpolations) mirroring the beliefs and ideas, but particularly the hopes and wishes, of the post-exilic community. Advanced critics do not hesitate to assign large portions of the prophetical literature to as late a period as the Maccabean. Especially the eschatological sections . . . are in bulk pronounced to be the fabrications of post-exilic scribes, parasitic after-growths, which must be removed in order that the genuine pre-exilic prophecies may be laid open to view. The arguments upon which literary criticism bases its results are mainly drawn from incoherencies in the sequence of thought, differences of vocabulary and style, and difficulties of an antiquarian character. It is found that the

[67] Max L. Margolis, "Review of S. R. Driver, *The Book of Exodus*," *JQR* n.s. 3 (1912/13), 135f.
[68] Max L. Margolis, "Review of S. R. Driver, *An Introduction to the Literature of the Old Testament* (new edition, revised)," *JQR* n.s. 1, 549.

transition from the denunciatory to the consolatory prophecies . . . is often abrupt, unprepared, and psychologically inconceivable in one and the same writer.[69]

In responding to these "principles" of higher criticism, Margolis made at least seven points:[70]

(1) and (2) "No room seems to be allowed for the free play of the imagination, which is certainly capable of bridging over the gulf yawning between periods widely apart; nor is it remembered that abruptness and a certain amount of obscurity are characteristic of prophetic style."

(3) "Literary criticism . . . operates with a preconceived notion that we possess in the prophetic books full verbal reports of the prophetic utterances, while the opposite is rather true, that from the outset we have but echoes of the actual speeches, fragments loosely strung together and coming from different periods in the activity of the same prophet."

(4) "It is a fatal error of literary criticism to assume that, because a certain idea meets us for the first time in a late literary production, it is necessarily late itself." This "fatal error" should be less likely in the future, Margolis remarked, thanks to "a newer school of criticism (headed by Gunkel)."

(5) "As for differences of vocabulary, it is well to remember that the transformation which a language undergoes is usually in the nature of a slow process. . . . It is preposterous to pronounce [certain verses] to be late merely because some of the words . . . are frequent in late writings."

(6) "The judgment of style is a matter of subjective taste; unless supported by weightier arguments, the evidence therefrom is inconclusive."

(7) "Antiquarian difficulties are naturally of greater moment, but in view of the imperfect knowledge of historical circumstances a cautious attitude is imperative."

For the edification of his readers, Margolis "subjoined" a table that showed "the extent of the additions or interpolations which advanced criticism assumes in the book of Micah."[71] Among the scholars who "assumed" numerous interpolations were Ewald, Wellhausen, Stade, and Marti; one or another of these "advanced" critics variously dated the additions anywhere from 722 to 103 B.C.E. Margolis felt that it was "impossible . . . to discuss the merits of such criticism, unsubstantiated as its reasonings are in most cases"; "the more serious difficulties," however, did "claim [his] attention."[72] Margolis considered these diffi-

[69] Margolis, *Micah*, 8f.

[70] The material quoted below is taken from Margolis, *Micah*, 9.

[71] The table is found on p. 10 of Margolis, *Micah*. The description of this table is quoted from p. 9.

[72] Margolis, *Micah*, 11.

cult passages (e.g., 2:12f, 4:1-14, 6:7) at some length, taking into account traditional Jewish sources and modern scholarship alike.[73] In the end, none of the suggested interpolations posed an "insurmountable" difficulty to "the unity of authorship which, in keeping with tradition," Margolis himself had "assumed for the entire" book of Micah.[74]

In his popular *Hebrew Scriptures in the Making*, which appeared in 1922, Margolis turned to the difficulties of dating certain Biblical books. His own observations here (as was also the case in Micah) are consistent with the "conservative," "cautious" approach he urged others to adopt. According to tradition, Margolis noted, "Job, the Psalter, Koheleth were written in the times of Moses, David, Isaiah." There is "great difficulty," he observed, "in dating these books with anything like accuracy. We shall probably not accept the traditional dates. But when left to ourselves, we have so little to go upon."[75] He then examined these three books one by one.

Margolis realized that there was no simple answer to the question: "When was Job written?" "The moderns are quite divided in their answers ["in the seventh century . . . in the sixth . . . in the fifth. . . ."]," but feel nonetheless that certainty is possible.[76] For his part, Margolis preferred to emphasize the necessarily uncertain nature of any quest to provide a precise date for the book of Job:

> The poet makes allusion quite generally to the movements of nations away from their homes . . . but such dislocations were as old as the history of the Orient, and there is no evidence that the fate of Israel or Judah was before the author's mind. . . . [Most other references are] no less vague. . . . Job curses the day of his birth (3:3) and so does Jeremiah (20:14), but who will tell which of the two, if either, is dependent on the other? Nor does the problem with which the book deals shed light on the time of its composition. It is [an] ever-recurring question. . . . It touches a universal experience of mankind and may have arisen at any time. All that can be said is that it belongs to the sphere of wisdom. . . . The poet understood all too well that his theme belonged to all ages, and he wisely refrained from dealing with it in terms of his own place and time.[77]

Margolis dealt next with the difficult process of attempting to date the Psalms:

> It is the essence [of the Psalter's] lofty piety that, though its manifestation is conditioned by circumstances of place and time, it lifts itself so

---

[73] Margolis, *Micah*, 11–14.
[74] Margolis, *Micah*, 13, 8.
[75] Margolis, *Hebrew Scriptures*, 70.
[76] *Ibid.*
[77] Margolis, *Hebrew Scriptures*, 70f.

far out of touch with life's affairs as to transcend both, and great
difficulty will always attach to dating a psalm purely from its contents. It
seems reasonable to suppose that Psalm 137 was not penned before the
Babylonian captivity. Psalm 79 and several others in which reference is
made to the defiling of the Temple and the martyrdom of the saints
might date from the events which led to the Maccabean uprising, but an
earlier occurrence may fit the veiled allusions just as well. . . . It is a
preposterous contention that no psalm dates from pre-exilic times.[78]

In any consideration of the date of Koheleth, Margolis noted, "the
strongest point . . . is the evidence from language."[79] Margolis then
quoted, with apparent approval, the dictum, "If the Book of Koheleth be
of old Solomonic origin, then there is no history of the Hebrew language." To this dictum, Margolis immediately appended two interesting
provisos—one from tradition and one from linguistic research. "Tradition," he remarked, "does not ascend that high [i.e., to an 'old Solomonic
origin' for Koheleth]; it brings the 'writing' down to the age of Hezekiah."
More to the point (since "the strongest point . . . is the evidence from
language"), Margolis queried, "Now what do we actually know about the
fortunes of the Hebrew language?" Responding to his own question, he
wrote:

We are barely able to distinguish two periods: a golden and a silver age.
In the latter certain grammatical forms, syntactical constructions, and
words, especially particles, approach the state of the language of the
Mishna. But as students of language know, it often takes centuries for a
new coinage, at first employed sparingly, to pass into general use. We
must not on the basis of one word or turn of speech pronounce upon the
date of a writing. Cumulative evidence alone leads to results which may
be said to have convincing power. Moreover, subject-matter has always
much to do with style. Prayers cannot be composed in the style of legal
enactments, and a philosophical treatise must perforce take on diction
foreign to both.

These general comments, Margolis felt, had a direct bearing on
Koheleth:

Koheleth may have been written in the Grecian or in the late Persian
period, but conceivably also at an earlier point; the writer would simply
have been forced to create the appropriate style when he needed it. He
really could not write his book in the language of Isaiah or Deuteronomy.

[78] Margolis, *Hebrew Scriptures*, 73–75.
[79] Margolis' discussion of Koheleth is found on pp. 76f of *Hebrew Scriptures*. The material
quoted in this paragraph is taken from those pages.

As can be seen from this discussion, Margolis, although he apparently preferred a fairly early date for Koheleth, was open to any view that could be supported by informed scholarship. Less well-structured scholarship usually met with a firm rebuke. On one occasion, however, he somewhat more gently chided a writer who held that "the whole tone and substance and manner of the book [Koheleth] is like Solomon's old age": "I fear [wrote Margolis] that readers who are a bit more familiar with the history of the Hebrew language than the author shows himself to be . . . will be tempted to smile at the well-intentioned but naively absurd theory with which we are here regaled."[80]

Margolis had been unable to determine, to his own satisfaction, precise dates for the writing of Job, Psalms, or Koheleth. For the book of Daniel, similar difficulties did not arise:

> There is one book in the third division, Daniel, the date of which we may establish with accuracy by the aid of the historical perspective, which is brought down to the stirring events in which it was published. It opens up a novel genre of literature of which there arose numerous imitations. It is an *apocalyptic* writing. . . . Whatever older materials the writer may have used, particularly in the first part of the book, he certainly wrote in full view of the persecution under Antiochus Epiphanes.[81]

Margolis titled chapter 7 of *Scriptures in the Making,* "The Higher Unity of the Torah." Among the many topics he covered in that chapter is the problem of identifying the book found in the Temple at the time of Josiah. Margolis began his discussion of this matter with a statement that probably startled many readers, even conservative, moderate ones:

> The book found and promulgated in the reign of Josiah is identified even by Graetz with Deuteronomy. But it need not have been any other than the same Torah Ezra placed before the people for their ratification. [On the extent of Ezra's Torah, Margolis stated earlier in chapter 7: "That Ezra's Torah contained the whole Pentateuch ought to be beyond debate."] The Book was really found; it had actually been lost.[82]

Josiah, as is well known, was moved by the discovery of "the book of law" (2 Kings 22:8) to institute a number of reforms. Margolis points out that the abuses Josiah dealt with are not found exclusively in the book of Deuteronomy. And yet, as Margolis was of course aware, the centraliza-

---

[80] Max L. Margolis, "Review of F. Ernest Spencer, *A Short Introduction to the Old Testament*," *JQR* n.s. 3 (1912/13), 109.

[81] Margolis, *Hebrew Scriptures,* 77f.

[82] Margolis, *Hebrew Scriptures,* 99f.

tion of sacrificial worship in Jerusalem was a unique feature of Josiah's reformation and "the law of the single Sanctuary . . . is characteristic of the Code of Deuteronomy."[83] As Margolis also knew, it was commonly held that a passage like Deuteronomy 12:13 (on centralized worship) "cannot very well be brought into consonance with" the material contained in Exodus 20:21ff (which takes for granted the existence of a number of altars for sacrificial worship).[84] Supported by observations such as these, the majority of scholars maintained "that these two contradictory laws could not have been found in the Book of Josiah."[85] Margolis, who based his position on the same Biblical material, came (as noted above) to a very different conclusion: Josiah's Torah contained the whole Pentateuch, the laws of Exodus as well as the legislation of Deuteronomy.

To begin with, Margolis notes, these two laws "co-exist . . . in our Pentateuch"—"quite peaceably," in his opinion: "The so-called compiler found no difficulty in reconciling them."[86] However, even if

we . . . grant that the two codes [Exodus and Deuteronomy] disagree, we contend . . . that had the Book of Josiah been confined to the Deuteronomic Code alone, as is generally maintained, it would have met with instant opposition of a nature to preclude acceptance. The priests of the country sanctuaries might have pointed to the Exodus legislation. It was obviously imperative to mark the rival code as repealed. This could be accomplished only by having the two codes in one and the same book. Both were allowed to stand as Mosaic; only the Exodus Code was dated from the beginning of the wanderings . . . while the Deuteronomic Code was the final legislation set forth. . . . Where they differed, the Second Law was manifestly in force. A body of narrative became necessary to indicate that there was a sequence in time. Hence the two Codes must have been encased in a framework of history, which, of course, means that Josiah's Book resembled our Pentateuch.[87]

Margolis, then, concluded that "the Torah of Josiah most probably had" both the Exodus Code and the Deuteronomic Law, "just as we have them to-day."[88] "But," Margolis continued, "at some period in the

[83] Margolis, *Hebrew Scriptures*, 102.
[84] Margolis, *Hebrew Scriptures*, 103.
[85] Margolis, *Hebrew Scriptures*, 105.
[86] *Ibid.*
[87] Margolis, *Hebrew Scriptures*, 106f.
[88] Margolis, *Hebrew Scriptures*, 108.

background they must have existed by the side of each other as independent versions of the Mosaic Torah":

> From Joshua 24.26 and I Samuel 10.25 we know that the ancient shrines had their archives. In each there must have been a copy of the Torah, here shorter and there longer, alike in subject-matter, but with differences in detail according to the attitude of the local priesthood.[89]

In evaluating different codes, Margolis contended, it will not do to set some against others on the grounds that this one is all ritual, that one all morality: "For it is neither all ritual nor all morality that meets us in any of them."[90] In no code are ritual matters ignored; "what is still more important is that no hostile attitude is taken to them."[91] The lawgiver is described by Margolis as a "priest-prophet," who believed "in the whole of the religious life, in an organized piety which leaves nothing undone."[92] Tradition, of course, identified this lawgiver with Moses.

In Margolis' day, the existence of any single lawgiver was being increasingly thrown into doubt by modern scholarship's emphasis (or, as Margolis put it, "overemphasis") on disagreements in the Pentateuchal text.[93] Such differences should be noted, as they were by medieval Jewish commentators,

> but when all of these [differences and modifications] have been taken into account, there is a residue common to one Code with the other, and the agreement covers not only essentials, but extends to the very language. The presumption is therefore forced upon us that we are dealing with a body of law and tradition antedating the divergences of the disparate versions and ascending to the Mosaic age. Whether the Pentateuch as we have it *is* the Mosaic Torah may be a matter of debate. That it *has* the Mosaic Torah, which is neither in this strand nor in the other but 'dispersed in them all,' must be the conclusion of sound criticism.[94]

Margolis never published a sustained theological treatment of the Hebrew Bible nor did theology as such occupy a central position in his teaching. Early in his career he did produce a ten-page study of "The Theology of the Old Prayer-Book."[95] Several years later, in 1903, he

[89] *Ibid.*
[90] Margolis, *Hebrew Scriptures*, 109.
[91] Margolis, *Hebrew Scriptures*, 111.
[92] *Ibid.*
[93] On this tendency to "overemphasize," see Margolis, *Hebrew Scriptures*, 116f.
[94] Margolis, *Hebrew Scriptures*, 119.
[95] Max L. Margolis, "The Theology of the Old Prayer-Book," *Central Conference of American Rabbis Year Book* 7 (1898), 1–10 (Appendix A).

delivered a lengthy address, titled "The Theological Aspect of Reformed Judaism," at the annual meeting of the Central Conference of American Rabbis.[96] This extended theological investigation on the part of Margolis was not received well in all quarters, and it has been suggested that criticisms directed against this work (especially by Kaufmann Kohler) were a significant factor in dissuading Margolis from venturing again "into the thorny ground of theology."[97] Be that as it may, in the absence—for whatever reason—of a more comprehensive statement of Margolis' theological understanding of the Bible, brief statements such as the following constitute valuable evidence for this scholar's theological position—a stance that complements well the "conservative," "cautious," "sane," and "more moderate" approach that Margolis advocated toward the study of all aspects of the Old Testament:

> The Torah may be a composite work. It lacks unity of the mechanical sort. It has unity, nevertheless, and that in a much higher sense. We have observed how it keeps itself above the contending parties. It takes sides neither with Judah nor with Joseph. North and South may own it, pluralists and the proponents of centralization, ritualists and moralists, Ezra and Sanballat. The Torah when viewed as a whole transmits to the last generation the piety of the patriarchs and even of the righteousness that preceded them. . . . It sums up all the movements in the religious life of the nation, imposing a lasting peace upon them all. No extreme views are permitted to prevail. . . . In this sum all the strife of the contests is hushed, for the highest has been attained, that which for ever made the Torah for Israel 'life and length of days' and constitutes that unity of purpose which dominates every part of it.[98]

[96] This address was printed as an article in *Central Conference of American Rabbis Year Book* 13 (1903), 185–308, and as a separate publication a year later (Baltimore, 1904).

[97] See Silberman, "Theology and Philosophy," 392. Silberman devotes an entire section of his essay (pp. 388–392) to "Max Leopold Margolis and *The Theological Aspect of Reformed Judaism*." References to Margolis' work are also found in Silberman's next section (pp. 392–398), "Kaufmann Kohler and His *Jewish Theology Systematically and Historically Considered*."

[98] Margolis, *Hebrew Scriptures*, 119f.

BIBLIOGRAPHY OF THE WORKS OF MAX L. MARGOLIS*

Compiled by Joseph Reider

Prefatory Note

This annotated bibliography of the scientific and general works of the late Professor Max L. Margolis is as complete as possible. There may be some brief articles or notes from his early student days in New York that escaped my ken, but these no doubt were ephemeral in character. At any rate, I am absolutely certain that none of his scientific work, of permanent importance, has been overlooked here.

It was deemed advisable to keep apart his various literary activities, and therefore I subdivided this bibliography into three sections, as follows: A) Scholarly books and papers, B) Reviews of books, and C) Popular articles in periodicals.

Of the first class I have listed practically everything, whether large or small, be it book, article or note. Here I included also the typewritten "Notes on the Translation of the Holy Scriptures," multigraphed for private circulation only; and a book in manuscript on Andreas Masius, which is finished and complete and has been in the hands of the publisher for many years.

Of the second class, the reviews, I have indexed all those that, besides the enumeration of the contents, contain also some sort of judgment or opinion on the book reviewed. Mere summaries of contents were omitted.

The same holds true of the third class, the popular articles: I have listed only those that are worthwhile and have some measure of permanent value.

I wish to thank Dr. Joshua Bloch of the Jewish Division in The New York Publc Library for his help with regard to the last section, especially in ferreting out some early and little known items.

It is well known to his intimates that Margolis assisted young scholars with valuable notes and suggestions, some signed by his initials; but since these proved extremely difficult to locate and, besides, would have swelled the

---

This Bibliography originally appeared in *Max Leopold Margolis: Scholar and Teacher* (Philadelphia: Alumni Association, Dropsie College for Hebrew and Cognate Learning, 1952). It is reprinted here with permission. Minor corrections have been introduced.

bibliography to unreasonable proportions, it was decided to omit them altogether.

In this connection it should be mentioned that in the Margolis files there is a vast amount of manuscript material, scattered here and there on library cards and plain sheets, as well as on the margins of his books, full of valuable data and suggestions in Bible exegesis and Hebrew grammar, in Septuagint readings and versional reconstruction generally. If only these *disiecta membra* could be gathered together and saved from oblivion!

J. R.

ABBREVIATIONS

AH — American Hebrew
AJYB — American Jewish Year Book
AJSL — American Journal of Semitic Languages and Literatures
APA Pr. — Proceedings of the American Philological Association
APS Pr. — Proceedings of the American Philosophical Society
BBM — B'nai B'rith Magazine
BBN — B'nai B'rith News
CCARYB — Central Conference of American Rabbis Year Book
HUCA — Hebrew Union College Annual
JAOS — Journal of the American Oriental Society
JBL — Journal of Biblical Literature
JE — Jewish Encyclopedia
JIRB — Jewish Institute of Religion Bulletin
JPOS — Journal of the Palestine Oriental Society
JQR — Jewish Quarterly Review
JQR n.s. — Jewish Quarterly Review, new series
Mac — The Maccabean
MJ — Menorah Journal
ZAW — Zeitschrift für die alttestamentliche Wissenschaft

A. SCHOLARLY BOOKS
AND PAPERS

Commentarivs Isaacidis Qvatenvs ad Textvm Talmvdis Investigandvm Adhiberi Possit, Tractatv 'Ervbhin Ostenditvr. Dissertatio Inavgvralis qvam consensv et avctoritate Amplissimi Philosophorvm Ordinis in Collegio Colvmbiae ad Svmmos in Philosophia Honores rite impetrandos scripsit Max. Leopoldvs Margolis, A.M. Novi Eboraci, MDCCCXCI. pp. 72.

An attempt to improve the damaged text of the Talmud through reference to variant readings in Rashi's Commentary on the Talmud, demonstrated through the tractate Erubhin. A thesis, written entirely in Latin, presented to Columbia University in New York City for the attainment of the degree of Doctor of Philosophy. Contains a brief life of the author on the last page.

The Columbia College Ms. of Meghilla (Babylonian Talmud). Examined . . . With an autotype facsimile. New York, 1892. pp. 14.

A collation of one third of a Ms. tractate Megilla in Columbia College, corresponding to the printed text fol. 2a-12a, with four other Mss. listed in Rabbinovicz's *Dikduke Soferim* and the *editio princeps* (Pesaro 1516). The disagreements prove to be considerable, amounting to 1751 cases in the ten folios.

An Elementary Text-Book of Hebrew Accidence Arranged in Typical Examples with Concise Explanations referring especially to the Modification of Sounds. . . Cincinnati, 1893. pp. xv + 149 + [1].

A practical method to teach the intricate details of Hebrew accidence by a set of examples carefully selected and properly classified, each representative of a whole category of phenomena and so presented that it must associate itself in the mind of the trained observer with its underlying linguistic principle. The method is paradigmatic, but is followed at the end by a summary of the principles of the modifications of sound. One of the chief aims of the book is to teach the reading of unpointed Hebrew to the uninitiated.

"Notes on Semitic Grammar. I: The First Vowel of the Imperfect Tense-Stem." In *Hebraica*, X (1893–1894), 188–192.

Aims to prove that the Semitic form *yaqtul* presupposes an earlier form of the type *yaqutul*, with a vowel between the first and second radicals.

"Notes on Semitic Grammar. II: The Feminine Ending T in Hebrew." In *AJSL.*, XII (1895–1896), 197–229.

Hebrew grammars treat of feminine nouns ending either in *at* or simply in *t*. The author considers only the former as genuinely Hebrew, the latter being due to the prevalence of the Aramaic method of inflection in Hebrew. He finds no trace in Hebrew of a consonantal termination *t*, and consequently he regards such formations as Aramaic deflections from nouns with *at* endings.

"Another Haggadic Element in the Septuagint." In *AJSL.*, XII (1895–1896), 267.

A note recording that the Septuagint version of Am. 1.11 finds its explanation in Norzi's commentary ad loc.

"Dogmatic Influences in our Vocalization." In *AJSL.*, XIV (1897–1898), 208.

Adduces proof that the vocalization and accentuation of the Bible texts often betray the dogmatic predispositions of the age in which the traditional reading and cantillation assumed their final and permanent form.

"Notes on some Passages in Amos." In *AJSL.*, XVII (1900–1901), 170–171.

The notes are on 3.12, 4.3.5, and 5.6 of the Book of Amos.

"Accents in Hebrew." In *JE.*, I (1901), 149–158.

A pithy and succinct account of the complicated accents and their symbols in the Hebrew Scriptures, illustrated by examples.

"Judg. 11.37." In *ZAW.*, XXI (1901) 272.

Explains the meaningless וירדתי as a doublet of ורעיתי at the end of the verse.

"A Passage in Ecclesiasticus." In *ZAW.*, XXI (1901), 271–272.

Identifies the Septuagint version of Ecclus. 34.16 and 17 with the newly found Hebrew text of Ecclesiasticus published by G. Margoliouth in *JQR.*, XII (1899–1900), 4, lines 8a, 10b, 10a, 8b.

"Interpretation of the Book of Job." In *Papers Presented at the Fifth Annual Session of the Summer Assembly of the Jewish Chautauqua Society,* Philadelphia 1902, pp. 55–70.

A syllabus of seven lectures given at Atlantic City, N.J., July 7 to July 28, 1901, in the interpretation of one of the most difficult books of the Bible.

"Notes on Semitic Grammar. III: An Abnormal Hebrew Form." In *AJSL.*, XIX (1902–1903), 45–48.

Discusses the abnormal וּבְצָעַם in Am. 9.1, sometimes vocalized וּבְצָעַם, showing that it is absolutely normal in the light of Semitic punctuation.

The Theological Aspect of Reformed Judaism. In *CCARYB.*, XIII (1903), 185–308. Reprinted as a separate in book form: Baltimore 1904, pp. VII + 142.

Discusses the creeds and dogmas of Judaism as formulated in the past from Maimonides onwards, and then states the creeds and dogmas of Reformed Judaism under these headings: Theology (and Cosmology), Anthropology, Psychology, and Ecclesiology. Favors an ecclesiastical organization, such as a Synod, as the key-stone of Reformed Judaism.

"The Plural of Segolates." In *APA Pr.*, XXXV (1904), liii–liv.

The vowel *a* between the second and third radicals in the plural of Hebrew segolates (e.g. *malk: melakim*) is explained as due to the circumstance that this plural is not an ordinary plural, but a plural of a plural (namely *malk* first gave rise to a broken plural *malak*, and this in turn gave rise to another plural *melakim*).

"Ecclus. 3.25." In *ZAW.*, 25 (1905), 199–200.

The difficult word ומתחולל is emended to ומתהולל on the basis of the Septuagint and Peshitta.

"Ecclus. 6.4." In *ZAW.*, 25 (1905), 320–322.

The incomprehensible תשינם is emended to תַּצִּינֵהוּ with reference to Jer. 51.34 and Job 17.6. The aberration is explained as phonetic.

"Ecclus. 7.6d." In *ZAW.*, 25 (1905), 323.

Proposes פצע for בצע on the basis of the Septuagint and Peshitta.

"Entwurf zu einer revidierten Ausgabe der hebräisch-aramäischen Äquivalente in der Oxforder Concordance to the Septuagint and the other Greek Versions of the Old Testament." In *ZAW.*, 25 (1905), 311–319.

A criticism of the Oxford *Concordance to the Septuagint* by Hatch and Redpath and a draft of a revised edition of this work, in which instances of *quid pro quo* and other false identifications would be removed, composita would be listed with the simple words, unidentified passages designated by obeli would be traced to their Hebrew originals and solved as much as possible. Also the minor Greek versions would receive their Hebrew-Aramaic equivalents, and similar improvements. As a sample the article μένειν is presented with all its composita.

"χαίειν (einschliesslich der Komposita und Derivata) und seine hebräisch-aramäischen Äquivalente im Gräzismus des A.T." In *ZAW.*, 26 (1906), 85–90.

Another example of the contemplated revision of the Oxford *Concordance to the Septuagint* by Hatch and Redpath, carried out along the lines indicated in the above article.

"ΛΑΜΒΑΝΕΙΝ (including Compounds and Derivatives) and its Hebrew-Aramaic Equivalents in Old Testament Greek." In *AJSL.*, XXII (1906), 110–119.

Another criticism of the Oxford *Concordance to the Septuagint* by Hatch and Redpath and a repetition of the plan to reissue a revised edition of that work with all the improvements enumerated above. The article λαμβάνειν serves this time as a sample, with all its compounds and derivatives.

"Studien im griechischen alten Testament." In *ZAW.*, 27 (1907), 212–270.

In his desire to produce a critical revision of the *Concordance to the Septuagint* by Hatch-Redpath, Margolis continues here his studies in the Greek Old Testament under the following rubrics: inner-Greek aberrations due to various causes, mannerisms in translation, linguistic knowledge and exegesis of the translators, the original Hebrew text (Vorlage) and the problems of identifications. Each rubric contains numerous examples from the entire Old Testament.

"Zu Seite 142 des vorigen Jahrgangs." In *ZAW.*, 27 (1907), 276–277.

A reply to Israel Lévi's strictures on Margolis' comments on Ecclus. 6.4 in *ZAW.*, XXV (1905), 320ff.

טעיות סופרים בתרגום השבעים. In the *Festschrift zu Ehren des Dr. A. Harkavy* aus Anlass seines ... siebzigsten Lebensjahres (St. Petersburg 1908), Hebrew section, pp. 112–116.

Lists a number of inner Greek errors in the Septuagint version of the Bible, which very often are mistaken as departures from the Hebrew masoretic text.

Micah. (The Holy Scriptures with Commentary). Philadelphia, 1908. Pp. 104.

Intended as a specimen of a popular commentary series on the Scriptures contemplated by the Jewish Publication Society of America. The text in English is given above, and a brief factual commentary follows below. The book opens with a concise historical-critical introduction and closes with additional notes dealing with special problems. Characteristic of this commentary are its freshness and originality, above all suggested improved readings.

"The Character of the Anonymous Greek Version of Habakkuk, Chapter 3." In *Old Testament and Semitic Studies in Memory of William Rainey Harper*, I (1908), 133–142.

This version differs from that of the Septuagint, Aquila, Symmachus, Theodotion, and the other minor Greek versions. It is paraphrastic and Targumic in character, hence the conclusions that its author must have been a Jew.

"Short Notes on the Greek Old Testament." In *AJSL.*, XXV (1908–1909), 174.

Claims that the Septuagint must have read וְצֹרֹנֵךְ instead of והרנך in Gen. 3.16, and נפתלי נחל שלח הנותן תַּמְרֵי שפר ibid. 49.21.

"The Greek Preverb and its Hebrew-Aramaic Equivalent." In *AJSL.*, XXVI (1909), 33–61.

Conclusions: 1) The Greek preverb corresponds to a Hebrew-Aramaic root. 2) Certain Hebrew-Aramaic roots may be the equivalents of more than one Greek preverb, according to the nature of the complementary preposition following. 3) The preverb may correspond to no radical element in the Hebrew-Aramaic verb, its employment being conditioned by the prepositional complement which it anticipates or by the general context.

"The Pronunciation of the שׁוא according to New Hexaplaric Material." In *AJSL.*, XXVI (1909), 62–72.

The new Hexaplaric material is that discovered by Mercati and others and excerpted in the second Supplement to the Oxford *Concordance to the Septuagint*. These transcriptions reveal a state of pronunciation by no means fixed. In some instances the Masoretic rules are substantiated, but in others the current Ashkenazic pronunciation seems to be followed.

"The Particle ἤ in Old Testament Greek." In *AJSL.*, XXV (1909), 257–275.

Generally speaking, ἤ corresponds to Hebr. אוֹ, less frequently to וְ. Other cases discussed are ἤ interrogative, ἤ comparative, and ἤ alternating with a negative.

A Manual of the Aramaic Language of the Babylonian Talmud. Grammar, Chrestomathy and Glossaries. München, 1910. Pp. xvi + 184.

The first scientific presentation of the grammar of the East-Aramaic idiom spoken in Upper Babylonia until the ascendancy of Arabic. For the sake of accuracy use was made not only of old editions but also of important Mss. of the Talmud. The book forms the third volume of the *Clavis Linguarum Semiticarum*, edited by Hermann L. Strack, and was published also in German under the following title: *Lehrbuch der aramäischen Sprache des babylonischen Talmuds*.

"Complete Induction for the Identification of the Vocabulary in the Greek Versions of the Old Testament with its Semitic Equivalents: Its Necessity and the Means of obtaining it." In *JAOS.*, XXX (1910), 301–312.

Whether the student of the Septuagint aims at restoring the Greek original as it left the translator's hands, or, more ultimately, at a recovery of the Semitic "Vorlage", he is always face to face with problems of identification. In his attempt to identify the Greek version with the Semitic original not only a knowledge of the style of the individual Greek translator is necessary, but also a knowledge of the style of the individual Semitic writer. Nevertheless, in order to discover the total sum of criteria and make retroversion comparatively reliable, complete induction from the whole of the Greek Old Testament is requisite, and this can be secured only by two methods of procedure which can be easily combined: lexical equations and grammatical equations.

"The Grouping of the Codices in the Greek Joshua." In *JQR.*, n.s., I (1910–1911), 259–263.

This is the first hint that Margolis was preparing a critical edition of the Greek text of the Book of Joshua. Based chiefly on transliterations in Holmes-Parsons the following six groups of Mss. are evolved: Complutensian, Aldine, Oxford, Hesychian, Catenae, and Sixtine. These are further reduced to two main divisions: Egyptian (B and its satellites) and Palestino-Syrian (A and its satellites). The new edition is to be printed in two columns: one containing the Egyptian and the other the Palestino-Syrian text, and each is to be accompanied by a double set of notes: one embodying Hexaplaric matter, the other the critical grounds for the readings adopted in the text. The hope is expressed that in this way the original Septuagint version may be recovered and consequently also the pre-Masoretic Hebrew text.

"The Scope and Methodology of Biblical Philology." In *JQR.*, n.s., I (1910–1911), 5–41.

Deals with the problem of interpretation of the biblical text from every possible angle: comparative philological, lexical, grammatical, syntactical, masoretic, versional, contextual, literary, historical, archeological, allegorical, midrashic, etc. As a concrete example he adduced the problematic verse Job 3.3.

A Note on Wilhelm Bacher's review of Margolis' book *A Manual of the Aramaic Language of the Babylonian Talmud*, which appeared in *JQR.*, n.s., I (1910–1911), 265–273. The note follows the review, ibid. p. 274.

"The K Text of Joshua." In *AJSL.*, XXVIII (1911), 1–55.

The letter K designates Codex Tischendorfianus II of the Leipzig University Library, which has been classed in the past with the Mss. of the Lucianic recension. Margolis found in it a close affinity with the cursives 54.75.118. In this edition of K the Greek text is accompanied by three sets of notes giving the variants of different Mss. and versions, and these are followed by a running textual commentary.

"The Place of the Word-Accent in Hebrew." In *JBL.*, XXX (1911), 29–43.

Against the statement in Gesenius' *Hebrew Grammar* that ultimate or *milra'* accentuation predominates in biblical Hebrew, evidence is furnished that, genetically considered, penultimate or *mil'el* accentuation predominates in Hebrew. The proportion of *mil'el* to *milra'* is shown to be 6:3.

"Ez. 27.4." In *ZAW.*, 31 (1911), 313–314.

Believes that the Septuagint read נבלים instead of נבוליך and transcribed it ΓΟΒΕΛΕΙΜ, which subsequently became corrupted to τω βεελειμ.

"ἡνία, χαλινός." In *ZAW.*, 31 (1911), 314.

Thinks that αἱ ἡνίαι of the Septuagint in Nah. 2.4, corresponding to Hebr. פלדת, implies a reading פגדת, "bridles" in Syriac.

"The Washington MS. of Joshua." In *JAOS.*, XXXI (1911), 365–367.

On the basis of a fresh collation of the Washington MS. known as Θ, Margolis arrives at the same conclusion as Sanders, its first collator, namely that this MS. is very close to A though in a number of cases it follows B against A. Moreover, he finds Θ more accurate than A.

"Ps. 69.11." In *ZAW.*, 31 (1911), 314.

Reads וָאֶכֹּף instead of ואבכה on the basis of καὶ συνέκαμψα of the Septuagint.

"Ps. 74.3." In *ZAW.*, 31 (1911), 315.

Reads הדום instead of הרימה rendering "The stool of thy feet hath become eternal ruins."

"Ps. 85.9." In *ZAW.*, 31 (1911), 315.

The suggestion is made that instead of ואל ישובו לכסלה the Septuagint seems to have read ואלי שָׁבֵי לֵב סֶלָה.

"The Elephantine Documents." In *JQR.*, n.s., II (1911–1912), 419–443.

An elaborate and learned review of Eduard Sachau's edition of the Aramaic Papyri of Elephantine of the fifth pre-Christian century (Leipzig, 1911), in which some improved readings are suggested, especially in the Aḥikar text.

"'Man by Man,' Joshua 7.17." In *JQR.*, n.s., III (1912–1913), 319–336.

Aims to show that the verse-half 17b was present in the Septuagint and that furthermore the translator read in his Hebrew text לבתים instead of the incongruous לגברים.

"The Mode of Expressing the Hebrew 'A'ID in the Greek Hexateuch." In *AJSL.*, XXIX (1913), 237–260.

The Hebrew construction in which a relative pronoun or adverb is resumed by a demonstrative pronoun or adverb (Arabic 'a'id) is quite frequent in Septuagint Greek and especially in the minor Greek versions. It is interesting that Deissmann discovered it in Hellenistic Greek generally. Margolis finds the ratio of the Hellenistic-Hebraic construction as against the classical construction as follows: Genesis 1:1; Joshua 4:3; Exodus and Leviticus 2:1; Numbers and Deuteronomy 4:1.

"τῶν ἐνδόξων Josh 4.4." In *Studies in Jewish Literature,* issued in honor of Professor Kaufmann Kohler (Berlin, 1913), pp. 204–209.

The Hebrew is אשר הכין, and the conclusion is therefore that the rendering is paraphrastic.

"Additions to Field from the Lyons Codex of the Old Latin." In *JAOS.,* XXXIII (1913), 254–258.

Lists Hexaplaric elements in the Old Latin of the first nine chapters of the Book of Joshua, which were unknown hitherto.

"τετροπωμένους Joshua 11.6." In *JBL.,* XXXIII (1914), 286–289.

Defends this suspected free reading of the Septuagint for Hebrew חללים on the basis of another free reading, namely ἐν τῇ τροπῇ for אל חלליהם in Josh. 13.22.

"Hexapla and Hexaplaric." In *AJSL.,* XXXII (1915–1916), 126–140.

Endeavors to shed some light on the difficult question: which manuscripts of the Septuagint are hexaplaric, i.e. copied from the fifth column of Origen's Hexapla with its additions and subtractions? As is well known, the necessary criteria, the asterisks and obeli, had disappeared at an early date.

"Ai or the City? Joshua 8.12, 16." In *JQR.,* n.s., VII (1916–1917), 491–497.

Discusses a difficult textual problem, whether in the two passages mentioned above we are to follow the Ketib לעיר and בעיר or the Kre לעי and בעי.

The Holy Scriptures, according to the Masoretic Text; a new translation; with the aid of previous versions, and with constant consultation of Jewish authorities, Philadelphia, 1917. Pp. 1136.

Margolis prepared the fundamental version: "In preparing the manuscript for consideration by the Board of Editors, Professor Margolis took into account the existing . . . versions. Due weight was given to the ancient versions as establishing a tradition of interpretation, notably the Septuagint, and the versions of Aquila, Symmachus, and Theodotion, the Targums, the Peshitta, the Vulgate, and the Arabic version of Saadya. Talmudic and midrashic allusions and all available Jewish commentators, both the great mediaeval authorities, like Rashi, Kimhi, and Ibn Ezra, and the moderns S. D. Luzzatto, Malbim, and Ehrlich, as well as all the important non-Jewish commentators, were consulted. On this basis, a manuscript was prepared by the Editor-in-Chief [Margolis] and a copy sent to every member of the Board of Editors". — From the Preface. The Board consisted of Doctors Solomon Schechter, Cyrus Adler, Joseph Jacobs, Kaufmann Kohler, David Philipson, and Samuel Schulman, with Doctor Israel Friedlaender substituting one year for Doctor Schechter. All the proposals of the manuscript and many additional suggestions were considered. The committee spent seven years or 160 working days to discuss the new translation. See below "Notes on the New Translation of the Holy Scriptures."

The Story of Bible Translations. Philadelphia, 1917. Pp. 135.

The Bible translations examined here are the Aramaic Targum, the Septuagint and the minor Greek versions, the Syriac Peshitta, the Latin Vulgate, Jewish translations in the Middle Ages, the Luther and King James versions, modern translations by Jews and Christians. The brief volume serves as an auxiliary to the English version of the Bible published by the Jewish Publication Society of America.

"The Aldina as a Source of the Sixtina." In *JBL.,* XXXVIII (1919), 51–52.

Based on a study of the Greek Book of Joshua the suggestion is made that the editors of the Sixtina may have placed before the typesetters as 'copy' the Aldina into which they had entered the variants from the Vaticanus.

"*Le'iš ḥasideka,* Deut. 33:8." In *JBL.,* XXXVIII (1919), 35–42.

Discusses at length the awkward construction of this phrase (and the proposed emendation *le'iš ḥasdeka*), which might lead to the Maccabean origin of the whole Levi blessing, but proves conclusively that this pericope is really of Israelitish origin.

"A New Uncial of the Greek Psalter." In *AJSL.,*XXXVI (1919–1920), 84–86.

Criticizes Henry A. Sanders' edition of the Washington Manuscript of the Psalms, forming Part II of *The Old Testament Manuscript in the Freer Collection* (New York, 1917).

Notes on The New Translation of the Holy Scriptures (Published in 1917 by the J.P.S.A.). Prepared by the Former Editor-in-Chief Max L. Margolis. (For Private Circulation Only). Edited and Typewritten by H. S. Linfield. Philadelphia, 1921. Pp. 646.

These multigraphed notes contain a wealth of data and quotations from the ancient versions, medieval Jewish grammarians and exegetes, and modern commentators. They were gathered primarily for use in the new English translation of the Scriptures published in 1917.

The Hebrew Scriptures in the Making. Philadelphia, 1922. Pp. 131.

A popular description of the origin of the Scriptures, in which the point is made that the tripartite division of Scriptures was not consecutive and subordinate but coexistent and coordinate. The book forms an introduction to the English version of the Bible published by the Jewish Publication Society of America.

"Our Own Future: A Forecast and a Programme." In *JBL.,* XLIII (1924), 1–8.

A presidential address, delivered at the annual meeting of the Society of Biblical Literature and Exegesis at the Jewish Institute of Religion in New York City, December 27, 1923. The burden of this address is the neglect of biblical studies in school and church, which is ascribed to an overemphasis of Bible criticism and an underrating of Bible exegesis. The speaker appeals for the creation of an American biblical science, whose foundation, contrary to foreign biblical science, should be old-fashioned exegesis.

"How the Song of Songs entered the Canon." In *The Song of Songs*. A Symposium . . . Before the Oriental Club of Philadelphia. Wilfred H. Schoff, Editor. Philadelphia, 1924. Pp. 9–17.

Asserts that the seemingly secular Song of Songs must have been admitted into the Canon at an early date, when the later and more rigorous notions had not yet obtained. Canonization was a long process, and its beginning very likely ascends to the popular religion unrefined by prophetism, uncurbed by legalism, in reality to the Canaanite religion itself.

"Transliterations in the Greek Old Testament." In *JQR.*, n.s., XVI (1925–1926), 117–125.

A review of Franz Wutz's *Die Transkriptionen von der Septuaginta bis zu Hieronymus* (Leipzig 1925), in which close examination is made of Wutz's theory that the Greek translators made their version not directly from a Hebrew copy of the Scriptures but from a secondary exemplar in which the entire text was written out in Greek letters. Margolis does not favor this view, though he is willing to admit that the transliterated words originally stood in the margin of the translation as it issued from the hands of the translators and were subsequently dragged into the text by copyists either beside or in the place of the translated words.

"Presidential Address, Delivered at the Twenty-first meeting of the Palestine Oriental Society, January 8th, 1925." In *JPOS.*, V (1925), 61–63.

With the aid of the ancient Greek versions, this address aims to establish in the Book of Joshua a new place name along the border line between the tribes of Judah and Benjamin, namely Ai of Mount Ephron.

לוחות לדקדוק לשון עברי מאת מרדכי יום טוב מרגליות. Two-Leaf folder, fol. Jerusalem, 1925.

Tables of Hebrew grammar prepared for use in lectures on Hebrew Grammar delivered by Professor Margolis at the Hebrew University on Mount Scopus during his stay in Jerusalem in 1924–1925.

"Oriental Research in Palestine." An address delivered at the opening exercises of the Jewish Institute of Religion, Monday, October 5, 1925. In *JIRB.*, Vol. III, No. 2, November 1925, 17 pages.

Reviews recent scholarly research and archeological discoveries in Palestine; then describes personal experiences in the holy land during 1924–1925, when the writer was annual professor at the American School of Oriental Research as well as professor at the newly established Hebrew University in Jerusalem.

"ΧΩΡΙΣ." In *Oriental Studies* published in Commemoration of the Fortieth Anniversary of Paul Haupt as Director of the Oriental Seminary of the Johns Hopkins University (Baltimore 1926), pp. 84–92.

Endeavors to explain the meaning of the above word in the phrase παντες χωρις, which is met with on the margin of certain manuscripts of the Septuagint: it seems quite certain that it signifies "addition."

A History of the Jewish People. By Max L. Margolis and Alexander Marx. Philadelphia, 1927. Pp. xxii + 823 + [1] + 16 maps.

A concise and authoritative history of the Jews from their very beginning down to 1925, in which the greater part of the numerous facts and data were supplied by Marx but the composition and actual writing of the whole was executed by Margolis.

"Specimen of a New Edition of the Greek Joshua." In *Jewish Studies in Memory of Israel Abrahams*, New York, 1927, pp. 307–323.

The sum of witnesses yields four principal recensions, PCSE, and in addition a number of mixes Mss. designated by M. P is the Palestinian recension, i.e. the Eusebian edition of the Septuagint column in Origen's Hexapla-Tetrapla; C is a recension current in Constantinople and Asia Minor; S is the Syrian or Antiochian recension; E is the Egyptian recension preserved principally in B. The scope of this edition is to restore critically the original form of the Greek version. The restored text is printed at the top of the page; below follow the forms assumed in the four classes E, S, P, CM. Omissions and contractions of the text receive a rubric of their own. Then follow individual variations of class members, such as leave the characteristic class reading undisturbed in its main features. Lastly marginal readings in so far as they have not been embodied above.

"Textual Criticism of the Greek Old Testament." In *APS Pr.*, LXVII (1928), 187–197.

The Mss. of the Septuagint are notoriously corrupt. This paper discusses some of the corruptions, the so-called singular readings, which on occasion may have some value but in most cases are corrupt. Their greatest use consists in furnishing a clue for the grouping of manuscripts.

צפניה עם פירוש מדעי. נדפס בספר תורה נביאים וכתובים עם פירוש מדעי, יוצא בהשתתפות למדנים מומחים על ידי אברהם כהנא. נביאים: ספר תרי עשר, חלק שני. תל־אביב תר״צ. דף צ״ב־קט״ז.

מלאכי עם פירוש מדעי. נדפס בספר תורה נביאים וכתובים עם פירוש מדעי, יוצא בהשתתפות למדנים מומחים על ידי אברהם כהנא. נביאים: ספר תרי עשר, חלק שני. תל־אביב תר״צ. דף קצ״נ־רי״ב.

These commentaries, written in Hebrew, are rationalistic and factual, strictly grammatical and versional, though based chiefly on Jewish sources and tradition. The exegesis is straightforward, and there is no recoiling from *non possumus*. The standpoint taken is that there is nothing esoteric or supernatural in the Bible and some passages are difficult only because for some reason or another we have lost the proper key to their understanding.

"Corrections in the Apparatus of the Book of Joshua in the Larger Cambridge Septuagint." In *JBL.*, XLIX (1930), 234–264.

These corrections, running into the hundreds, were accumulated in the course of the preparation of a new critical edition of the Book of Joshua in Greek.

"Notes on 'Fifth Ms. of Ben Sira'". In *JQR.*, n.s., XXI (1930–1931), 439f.

Some pertinent remarks and improved readings to a new fragment of the Hebrew Ben Sira discovered by Rabbi Joseph Marcus and published in the same volume of the *JQR.*, pp. 223ff.

The Book of Joshua in Greek. According to the Critically Restored Text with an Apparatus Containing the Variants of the Principal Recensions and of the Individual Witnesses. Edited by Max L. Margolis. (Publications of the Alexander Kohut Memorial Foundation). Parts I, II, III, IV. (pp. 384). Paris, 1931.

A definitive edition of the Greek book of Joshua. The text as it appears on the top of the page is the nearest approach to the Greek original as it left the hands of the translator. Below the text is the apparatus, consisting of the many variants of the principal recensions ESPC(M). E is the Egyptian recension, S is the Syrian recension, P is the Palestinian recension, and C is the Constantinopolitan recension, each with its affiliates and satellites. M stands for a mixed group of Mss. not affiliated with any of the groups enumerated above. Owing to the numerous sigla and mixed quotations the work was photostated from the author's own manuscript instead of being set in type.

This book was Margolis' *magnum opus*, the achievement of his ambition. Unfortunately it was not completed in print: four parts were issued in quick succession by the firm of Paul Geuthner in Paris, covering the text to 19.38. The rest of the book, reserved for another part, as well as the introduction, was never published, due to the untimely death of the author in 1932, before the finishing touches could be put to the introduction.

Andreas Masius and his Commentary on the Book of Joshua.

In his work on the Greek text of the Book of Joshua Margolis had occasion to use the commentary on the Book of Joshua by the Belgian scholar Andreas Masius (Andrew Du Maes, 1515–1573). This great commentary, containing the Greek version with an accompanying Latin translation and copious exegetical notes, was published at Antwerp in 1574 and was subsequently excerpted in the *Critici Sacri* (Francofurti ad Moenum 1695ff.). Its importance stems from the fact that Masius used the famous Syriac manuscript written in 606, which afterwards belonged to

D. E. Jablonsky and is the only one that preserved the readings of Joshua as given by Origen in his Hexapla. Margolis was so impressed by it that he decided to write a monograph on it, in which the manner of the construction of the Greek text was most minutely discussed. This work was accepted by the Harvard Theological Studies for publication, but for some unknown reason it has not yet been published.

B. REVIEWS

Die Abhandlung des Abû Hâmid al-Gâzzali . . . Nach mehreren Handschriften herausgegeben und erläutert von Heinrich Malter (Frankfurt a. M. 1896). In *AJSL.*, XIV (1897–1898), 213–215.

Der Text des Buches Hiob. Untersucht von Georg Beer (Marburg 1895–1897). In *AJSL.*, XIV (1897–1898), 279–282.

Historisch-comparative Syntax der hebräischen Sprache. Schlussteil. Von Ed. König (Leipzig 1897). In *AJSL.*, XV (1898–1899), 248–251.

Die Massorah der Östlichen und Westlichen Syrer in ihren Angaben zum Propheten Jesaia nach fünf Handschriften des British Museum in Verbindung mit zwei Tractaten über Accente herausgegeben und bearbeitet von Gustav Diettrich (London 1899). In *AJSL.*, XVII (1900–1901), 125–127.

A Dictionary of the Targumim, the Talmud Babli and Yerushalmi, and the Midrashic Literature. Compiled by M. Jastrow (New York 1886–1900). In *AJSL.*, XVIII (1901–1902), 56–58.

Whilhelm Gesenius' Hebräische Grammatik, Völlig umgearbeitet von E. Kautzsch. Sieben and zwanzigste, vielfach verbesserte und vermehrte Auflage (Leipzig 1902). In *AJSL.*, XIX (1902–1903), 159–170.

Ecclesiasticus. The Greek Text of Codex 248. Edited with a textual commentary and prolegomena by J. H. A. Hart (Cambridge, 1909). In *JQR.*, n.s., I (1910–11), 403–418.

The Temple Dictionary of the Bible by W. Ewing and J. E. H. Thompson (London 1910). In *JQR.*, n.s., I (1910–11), 547–8.

An Introduction to the Literature of the Old Testament. By S. R. Driver. New edition, revised (New York, 1910). In *JQR.*, n.s., I (1910–11), 548–552.

Einleitung in das Alte Testament. Von E. Sellin (Leipzig, 1910). In *JQR.*, n.s., I (1910–11), 548–552.

Old Testment History and Literature. By B. H. Alford (London, 1910). In *JQR.*, n.s., I (1910–11), 548–552.

The Story of the Bible from the standpoint of modern scholarship. By Walter L. Sheldon. Second edition (Philadelphia, 1909). In *JQR.*, n.s., I (1910–11), 548–552.

History of Old Testament Criticism. By Archibald Duff (New York, 1910). In *JQR.*, n.s., I (1910–11), 552–554.

The New Bible-Country. By Thomas Franklin Day (New York, 1910). In *JQR.*, n.s., I (1910–11), 552–554.

Alttestamentliche Studien. Von B. D. Eerdmans. I. Die Komposition der Genesis. II. Die Vorgeschichte Israels. III. Das Buch Exodus (Giessen, 1908–10). In *JQR.*, n.s., I (1910–11), 554–562.

Essays in Pentateuchal Criticism. By Harold M. Wiener (Oberlin, 1909). In *JQR.*, n.s., I (1910–11), 554–562.

The Origin of the Pentateuch. By Harold M. Wiener (Oberlin, 1910). In *JQR.*, n.s., I (1910–11), 554–562.

Das Deuteronomium. Eine literarkritische Untersuchung. Von A. Filemon Puukko (Leipzig, 1910). In *JQR.*, n.s., I (1910–11), 554–562.

Die Nachtgesichte des Sacharja. Studien zur Sacharjaprophetie und zur jüdischen Geschichte im ersten nachexilischen Jahrhundert. Von J. W. Rothstein (Leipzig, 1910). In *JQR.*, n.s., I (1910–11), 563–568.

Die Bücher Esra (A und B) und Nehemja, textkritisch und historisch-kritisch untersucht. Mit Erklärung der einschlägigen Prophetenstellen und einem Anhang über hebräische Eigennamen. Von G. Jahn (Leiden, 1909). In *JQR.*, n.s., I (1910–11), 563–568.

Ezra Studies. By Charles C. Torrey (Chicago, 1910). In *JQR.*, n.s., I (1910–11), 563–568.

Geschichtlich und literarkritische Fragen in Esra 1–6. Inaugural-Dissertation von Johannes Theis (Münster i. Westf., 1910). In *JQR.*, n.s., I (1910–11), 563–568.

Aegypten und die Bibel. Die Urgeschichte Israels im Licht der aegyptischen Mythologie. Von Daniel Voelter. Neubearbeitete Auflage (Leiden, 1909). In *JQR.*, n.s., I (1910–11), 568–569.

Israel und Aegypten. Die politischen Beziehungen der Könige von Israel und Juda zu den Pharaonen. Nach den Quellen untersucht von Albrecht Alt (Leipzig, 1909). In *JQR.*, n.s., I (1910–11), 568–569.

Die Bedeutung des Namen Israel. Eine quellenkritische Untersuchung. Von Eduard Sachsse (Bonn, 1910). In *JQR.*, n.s., I (1910–11), 569.

The Early Religion of Israel. By Lewis Bayles Paton (Boston, 1910). In *JQR.*, n.s., I (1910–11), 569–570.

Israel's Ideal, or Studies in Old Testament Theology. By John Adams (Edinburgh, 1909). In *JQR.*, n.s., I (1910–11), 570–571.

Isaias. Diligenter revisus iuxta massorah atque editiones principes cum variis lectionibus e mss. atque antiquis versionibus collectis a C. D. Ginsburg (Londinii, MCMIX). In *JQR.*, n.s., I (1910–11), 571–575.

Specimina Codicum Graecorum Vaticanorum. Collegerunt Pius Franchi de' Cavalieri et Iohannes Lietzmann (Bonnae, MCMX). In *JQR.*, n.s., I (1910–11), 571–575.

Mitteilungen des Septuaginta-Unternehmens der Königlichen Gesellschaft der Wissenschaften zu Göttingen. Heft I: Der Lukiantext des Oktateuch. Von Ernst Hautsch (Berlin, 1910). In *JQR.*, n.s., I (1910–11), 571–575.

Studien zur Geschichte der Septuaginta. Die Propheten. Von O. Procksch (Leipzig, 1910). In *JQR.*, n.s., I (1910–11), 571–575.

The Octateuch in Ethiopic according to the text of the Paris codex, with the variants of five other manuscripts. Edited by J. Oscar Boyd. Part I. Genesis (Leyden, 1909). In *JQR.*, n.s., I (1910–11), 572–575.

The Authorized Version of the Bible and its Influence. By Albert S. Cook (New York, 1910). In *JQR.*, n.s., I (1910–11), 575–578.

Randglossen zur hebräischen Bibel. Von Arnold B. Ehrlich. I. Genesis und Exodus. II. Leviticus, Numeri, Deuteronomium. III. Josua, Richter, I. und II. Samuelis (Leipzig, 1908–10). In *JQR.*, n.s., I (1910–11), 575–578.

Die Heilige Schrift des Alten Testamentes . . . übersetzt und herausgegeben von E. Kautzsch. Dritte, völlig neubearbeitete Auflage. I & II (Tübingen, 1909–1910). In *JQR.*, n.s., I (1910–11), 575–578.

A Critical and Exegetical Commentary on Genesis. By John Skinner (New York, 1910). In *JQR.*, n.s., I (1910–11), 576–578.

A Critical and Exegetical Commentary on the Book of Chronicles. By Edward Lewis Curtis and Albert Alonzo Madsen (New York, 1910). In *JQR.*, n.s., I (1910–11), 576–578.

The Analyzed Bible. By G. Campbell Morgan. The Prophecy of Isaiah (New York). In *JQR.*, n.s., I (1910–11), 576–578.

The Hebrew Prophets for English Readers . . . Edited by Francis H. Woods and Francis E. Powell. Vol. I.—Amos, Hosea, Isaiah (1–39), and Micah. Vol. II.—Zephaniah, Nahum, Habakkuk, and Jeremiah (Oxford, 1909–1910). In *JQR.*, n.s., I (1910–11), 576–578.

The Book of the Prophecies of Isaiah. By John Edgar Mcfayden (New York, 1910). In *JQR.*, n.s., I (1910–11), 576–578.

Selections from the Old Testament. Edited with introduction and notes by Fred Newton Scott (New York, 1910). In *JQR.*, n.s., I (1910–11), 578–579.

The Old Testament Narrative . . . edited by Alfred Dwight Sheffield (Boston, 1910). In *JQR.*, n.s., I (1910–11), 578–579.

The Narrative Bible. Edited by Clifton Johnson (New York, 1910). In *JQR.*, n.s., I (1910–11), 578–579.

Bible Stories to Tell Children. By William D. Murray (New York). In *JQR.*, n.s., I (1910–11), 578–579.

The Old Jewish-Aramaic Prayer. The Kaddish. By David De Sola Pool (Leipzig, 1909). In *JQR.*, n.s., II (1911–12), 281–284.

A Dictionary of the Bible. By John D. Davis . . . Third edition, revised throughout and enlarged (Philadelphia, 1911). In *JQR.*, n.s., III (1912–13), 101.

Thesaurus totius Hebraitatis et veteris et recentioris. Auctore Eliezer Ben Iehuda. I, II, III. In *JQR.*, n.s., II (1911–12), 591–595.

Hebräisches und aramäisches Wörterbuch zum Alten Testament. Von Eduard König (Leipzig, 1910). In *JQR.*, n.s., II (1911–12), 595–598.

Vorstellung und Wort "Friede" im Alten Testament. Von Wilhelm Caspari (Gütersloh, 1910). In *JQR.*, n.s., II (1911–12), 598.

Neue Beiträge zur semitischen Sprachwissenschaft. Von Theodor Nöldeke (Strassburg, 1910). In *JQR.*, n.s., II (1911–12), 599–604.

Gesenius' Hebrew Grammar. As edited and enlarged by E. Kautzsch. Second English edition. Revised in accordance with the twenty-eighth German edition (1909) by A. E. Cowley (Oxford, 1910). In *JQR.*, n.s., II (1911–12), 605.

Hebräische Grammatik. Von Hermann L. Strack. Zehnte und elfte, sorgfältig verbesserte und vermehrte Auflage (München, 1911). In *JQR*., n.s., II (1911–12), 605–606.

Grammatik des Biblisch-Aramäischen. Von Hermann L. Strack. Fünfte Auflage (München, 1911). In *JQR*., n.s., II (1911–12), 606.

Kurzgefasstes Lehrbuch der speziellen Einleitung in das Alte Testament. Von Karl Holzhey (Paderborn, 1912). In *JQR*., n.s., III (1912–13), 101 ff.

Practical Handbook for the Study of the Bible and of Bible Literature. By Michael Seisenberger. Translated from the sixth German edition by A. M. Buchanan and edited by Thomas J. Gerrard (New York, 1911). In *JQR*., n.s., III (1912–13), 101ff.

Knowing the Scriptures. By Arthur T. Pierson (New York, 1910). In *JQR*., n.s., III (1912–13), 105.

Introduction to Bible Study: The Old Testament. By F. V. N. Painter (Boston, 1911). In *JQR*., n.s., III (1912–13), 105.

The Great Epic of Israel. By Amos Kidder Fiske (New York, 1911). In *JQR*., n.s., III (1912–13), 105–107.

The Old Testament. By H. C. O. Lanchester (New York, 1911). In *JQR*., n.s., III (1912–13), 107–108.

A Short Introduction to the Old Testament. By Ernest Spencer (London, 1912). In *JQR*., n. s., III (1912–13), 108–110.

Reasonable Biblical Criticism. By Willis J. Beecher (Philadelphia, 1911). In *JQR*., n. s., III (1912–13), 110–111.

Wider den Bann der Quellenscheidung. Von Wilhelm Moeller (Gütersloh, 1912). In *JQR*., n. s., III (1912–13), 111–113.

Über die Doppelberichte in der Genesis. Von Arthur Allgeier (Freiburg im Breisgau, 1911). In *JQR*., n. s., III (1912–13), 113.

I. Mose 14. Eine historisch-kritische Untersuchung. Von D. Johannes Meinhold (Giessen, 1911). In *JQR*., n. s., III (1912–13), 113.

An Introduction to the Pentateuch. By A. T. Chapman (Cambridge, 1911). In *JQR*., n. s., III (1912–13), 113–114.

Egypt and Israel. By W. M. Flinders Petrie (London, 1911). In *JQR.*, n. s., III (1912–13), 114–115.

Grundsteine zur Geschichte Israels. Alttestamentliche Studien von Martin Gemoll (Leipzig, 1911). In *JQR.*, n. s., III (1912–13), 115–116.

Die Indogermanen im Alten Orient. Von Martin Gemoll (Leipzig, 1911). In *JQR.*, n. s., III (1912–13), 115–116.

The Source of the Christian Tradition. By Edouard Dujardin. Revised edition, translated by Joseph McCabe (London, 1911). In *JQR.*, n. s., III (1912–13), 116–118.

Sociological Study of the Bible. By Louis Wallis (Chicago, 1912). In *JQR.*, n. s., III (1912–13), 118–120.

Geschichte der Alttestamentlichen Religion. Kritisch dargestellt von Eduard Koenig (Gütersloh, 1912). In *JQR.*, n. s., III (1912–13), 120–122.

Die Dämonen und ihre Abwehr im Alten Testament. Von Anton Jirku (Leipzig, 1912). In *JQR.*, n.s., III (1912–13), 122.

La durée de L'année biblique, et l'origine du mot שנה   Par S. Ferares (Paris, 1912). In *JQR.*, n. s., III (1912–13), 123.

Das Buchwesen in Altertum und im Byzantinischen Mittelalter. Von V. Gardthausen. Zweite Auflage (Leipzig, 1911). In *JQR.*, n. s., III (1912–13), 124–125.

Papyri Graecae Berolinenses. Collegit Wilhelm Schubart (Bonnae). In *JQR.*, n. s., III (1912–13), 125.

The Old Testament in Greek. According to the text of Codex Vaticanus, supplemented from other uncial manuscripts, with a critical apparatus containing the variants of the chief ancient authorities for the text of the Septuagint. Edited by Alan England Brooks and Norman McLean. Volume I. The Octateuch. Part I. Genesis. Part II. Exodus and Leviticus. Part III. Numbers and Deuteronomy. (Cambridge, 1906–11). In *JQR.*, n. s., III (1912–13), 125–128.

Codex Zuqninensis Rescriptus Veteris Testamenti . . . Edité avec introduction et notes par Eugène Tisserant (Roma, 1911). In *JQR.*, n. s., III (1912–13), 128–129.

Septuaginta-Studien. Herausgegeben von Alfred Rahlfs. 3. Heft: Lucians Rezension der Königsbücher. Von A. Rahlfs (Göttingen, 1911). In *JQR.*, n. s. III (1912–13), 129–130.

Fragmente einer griechischen Übersetzung des samaritanischen Pentateuchs. Von Paul Glaue und Alfred Rahlfs. . . . (Berlin, 1911). In *JQR.*, n. s., III (1912–13), 130–131.

A Coptic Palimpsest containing Joshua, Judges, Ruth, Judith and Esther in the Sahidic dialect. Edited by Herbert Thompson (London, 1911). In *JQR.*, n. s., III (1912–13), 131.

Untersuchungen über die Peschitta zur gesamten hebräischen Bibel. Von Ch. Heller. Teil I (Berlin, 1911). In *JQR.*, n. s., III (1912–13), 131–132.

Die aussermasorethischen Übereinstimmungen zwischen der Septuaginta und der Peschittha in der Genesis. Von Johannes Haenel (Giessen, 1911). In *JQR.*, n. s., III (1912–13), 132–133.

An Interpretation of Genesis. Including a translation into present-day English. By F. P. Ramsay (New York, 1911). In *JQR.*, n. s., III (1912–13), 134–135.

La Nuit de Penouel. Étude de philologie, d'histoire et de mythologie israélites. Par Alfred-B. Henry (Paris, 1911). In *JQR.*, n. s., III (1912–13), 135.

The Book of Exodus. In the Revised Version. With introduction and notes. By S. R. Driver (Cambridge, 1911). In *JQR.*, n. s., III (1912–13), 135–136.

The Book of Numbers. In the Revised Version. With introduction and notes. By A. H. McNeile (Cambridge, 1911). In *JQR.*, n. s., III (1912–13), 135–136.

The Hebrew Prophets, or Patriots and Leaders of Israel. By Georgia Louise Chamberlin (Chicago, 1911). In *JQR.*, n. s., III (1912–13), 138–139.

The Composition of the Book of Isaiah in the Light of History and Archaeology. By Robert H. Kennett (London, 1910). In *JQR.*, n. s., III (1912–1913), 139–140.

The Book of the Prophet Isaiah. With introduction and notes. By G. W. Wade (New York, 1911). In *JQR.*, n. s., III (1912–13), 140.

Das Buch Jesaia. Nach dem Forschungssystem Samson Raphael Hirschs übersetzt und erläutert von Julius Hirsch (Frankfurt a. M., 1911). In *JQR.*, n. s., III (1912–13), 140–141.

A Critical and Exegetical Commentary on Micah, Zephaniah, Nahum, Habakkuk, Obadiah and Joel. By John Merlin Powis Smith, William Hayes Ward, Julius A. Bewer (New York, 1911). In *JQR*., n. s., III (1912–13), 141.

Jefeth b. Ali's Arabic Commentary on Nahum. Edited by Hartwig Hirschfeld (London, 1911). In *JQR*., n. s., III (1912–13), 141–142.

The Book of Habakkuk. Introduction, translation, and notes on the Hebrew text. By George C. V. Stonehouse (London, 1911). In *JQR*., n. s., III (1912–13), 142.

Die Schriften des Alten Testaments. In Auswahl neu übersetzt und erklärt. Dritte Abteilung. Erster Band. Lyrik (Psalmen, Hoheslied und Verwandtes). Von W. Staerk (Göttingen, 1911). In *JQR*., n. s., III (1912–13), 143–144.

Die Psalmen. Hebräisch und deutsch. Mit einem kurzen wissenschaftlichen Kommentar. Von Nivard Schloegel (Graz und Wien, 1911). In *JQR*., n. s., III (1912–13), 144–145.

Life, Death, and Immortality: Studies in the Psalms. By W.O.E. Oesterley (London, 1911). In *JQR*., n. s., III (1912–13), 145.

The Hebrew Personification of Wisdom. Its Origin, Development and Influence. By Charles Everett Hesselgrave (New York, 1910). In *JQR*., III (1912–13), 145–146.

Eine babylonische Quelle für das Buch Job? Eine literargeschicht liche Studie. Von Simon Landersdorfer (Freiburg im Breisgau, 1911). In *JQR*., n. s., III (1912–13), 146–147.

Commentary on the Book of Job. By George A. Barton (New York, 1911). In *JQR*., n. s., III (1912–1913), 147–148.

Das älteste Liebeslied der Welt. Das Hohelied Salomons. Von M. Epstein (Frankfurt a. M., 1911). In *JQR*., n. s., III (1912–13), 148.

Das dritte Buch Esdras und sein Verhältnis zu den Büchern Esra-Nehemia. Von Edmund Bayer (Freiburg im Breisgau, 1911). In *JQR*., n. s., III (1912–13), 148–149.

Les Psaumes de Salomon. Introduction, texte grec et traduction. Par J. Viteau (Paris, 1911). In *JQR*., n. s., III (1912–13), 149–150.

The Culture of Ancient Israel. By Aaron P. Drucker (New York, 1911). In *JQR*., n. s., III (1912–13), 150.

The Story of Israel and Judah. From the Call of Abraham to the Death of Nehemiah. By H. J. Chaytor (London, 1911). In *JQR.*, n. s., III (1912–13), 150–151.

Prophecy, Jewish and Christian. By Henry Wace (London, 1911). In *JQR.*, n. s., III (1912–13), 152–153.

The Parting of the Roads. Studies in the development of Judaism and Early Christianity. With an introduction by W. R. Inge. Edited by F. J. Foakes Jackson (New York, 1912). In *JQR.*, n. s., III (1912–13), 153–154.

The Hope of Catholick Judaism: An Essay towards Orientation. By J. H. A. Hart (Oxford, 1910). In *JQR.*, n. s., III (1912–13), 154–155.

Mountain Pathways. A study in Ethics of the Sermon on the Mount. With a new translation and critical notes. By Hector Waylen. Second edition: revised and enlarged (London, 1912). In *JQR.*, n. s., III (1912–13), 155.

"The Son of Man," or Contributions to the Study of the Thoughts of Jesus. By Edwin A. Abbott (Cambridge, 1910). In *JQR.*, n.s., III (1912–13), 155–157.

Neutestamentliche Grammatik. Das Griechisch des Neuen Testaments im Zusammenhang mit der Volkssprache. Dargestellt von Ludwig Radermacher (Tübingen, 1911). In *JQR.*, n. s., III (1912–13), 158.

An Atlas of Textual Criticism. Being an attempt to show the mutual relationship of the authorities for the text of the New Testament up to about 1000 A.D. By Edward Ardron Hutton (Cambridge, 1911). In *JQR.*, n. s., III (1912–13), 159.

The Commentaries of Isho'dad of Merv, Bishop of Hadatha, in Syriac and English. Edited and translated by Margaret Dunlop Gibson (Cambridge, 1911). In *JQR.*, n. s., III (1912–13), 159–160.

The Modern Speech New Testament. An idiomatic translation into everyday English from the text of "The Resultant Greek Testament." By Richard Francis Weymouth. Edited and partly revised by Ernest Hampden-Cook (New York). In *JQR.*, n. s., III (1912–13), 160–161.

La date de "l'épitre de Barnabé." Par Michel d'Herbigny (Paris, 1910). In *JQR.*, n.s., III (1912–13), 161–162.

Die Oden Salomos. Aus dem Syrischen übersetzt, mit Anmerkungen. Von A. Ungnad und W. Staerk (Bonn, 1910). In *JQR.*, n. s., III (1912–13), 162.

Das Verständnis der Oden Salomos. Von Wilhelm Frankenberg (Giessen, 1911). In *JQR.*, n. s., III (1912–13), 162.

Les Odes de Salomon. Une oeuvre chrétienne des environs de l'an 100–120. Traduction française et introduction historique. Par J. Labourt et P. Battifol (Paris, 1911). In *JQR.*, n. s., III (1912–13), 162.

Die Oden Salomos. Syrisch-hebräisch-deutsch. Ein kritischer Versuch. Von Hubert Grimme (Heidelberg, 1911). In *JQR.*, n. s., III (1912–13), 162.

A Fountain Unsealed (London, 1911). In *JQR.*, n. s., III (1912–13), 163–164.

Records of the English Bible. The documents relating to the translation and publication of the Bible in English, 1526–1611. Edited, with an introduction, by Alfred W. Pollard (London, 1911). In *JQR.*, n. s., III (1912–13), 164.

The International Bible Dictionary. Based on Wm. Smith's one-volume work. Edited by F. N. Peloubet, assisted by Alice D. Adams (Philadelphia, 1912). In *JQR.*, n. s., IV (1913–14), 249.

The Life of William Robertson Smith. By John Sutherland Black and George Chrystal (London, 1912). In *JQR.*, n. s., IV (1913–14), 250–251.

Lectures and Essays of William Robertson Smith. Edited by John Sutherland Black and George Chrystal (London, 1912). In *JQR.*, n. s., IV (1913–14), 250–251.

Nieuw licht over het Oude Testament. Van G. Wildeboer (Haarlem, 1911). In *JQR.*, n. s., IV (1913–14), 252–255.

Stand und Aufgabe der Alttestamentlichen Wissenschaft in der Gegenwart. Von D. Karl Marti (Bern, 1912). In *JQR.*, n. s., IV (1913–14), 255.

The Scientific Study of the Old Testament. By Rudolf Kittel. Translated by J. Caleb Hughes (New York, 1910). In *JQR.*, n. s., IV (1913–14), 255–257.

A History of the Literature of Ancient Israel. From the earliest times to 135 B. C. By Henry Thatcher Fowler (New York, 1912). In *JQR.*, n. s., IV (1913–14), 257.

Zur Einleitung in das Alte Testament. Von Carl Heinrich Cornill (Tübingen, 1912). In *JQR.*, n. s., IV (1913–14), 257–258.

Zur Einleitung in das Alte Testament. Von E. Sellin. Eine Erwiderung auf die gleichnamige Schrift C. H. Cornills (Leipzig, 1912). In *JQR.*, n. s., IV (1913–14), 257–258.

Pentateuchal Studies. By Harold M. Wiener (Oberlin, 1912). In *JQR.*, n. s., IV (1913–14), 259–260.

Textkritische Materialien zur Hexateuchfrage. Von Johannes Dahse. I. Die Gottesnamen der Genesis. Jakob und Israel. P in Genesis 12–50 (Giessen, 1912). In *JQR.*, n. s., IV (1913–14), 260–261.

De naam Gods in den Pentateuch. Door A. Troelstra (Utrecht, 1912). In *JQR.*, n. s., IV (1913–14), 261.

Alttestamentliche Studien. Von B. D. Eerdmans. IV. Das Buch Leviticus (Giessen, 1912). In *JQR.*, n. s., IV (1913–14), 261–263.

The Antiquity of Hebrew Writing and Literature or Problems in Pentateuchal Criticism. By Alvin Sylvester Zerbe (Cleveland, 1911). In *JQR.*, n. s., IV (1913–14), 263.

The Deciding Voice of the Monuments in Biblical Criticism. By Melvin Grove Kyle (Oberlin, 1912). In *JQR.*, n. s., IV (1913–14), 263–264.

A History of Civilization in Palestine. By R. A. S. Macalister (Cambridge, 1912). In *JQR.*, n. s., IV (1913–14), 264–265.

Die jüdischen Exulanten in Babylonien. Von Erich Klamroth (Leipzig, 1912). In *JQR.*, n. s., IV (1913–14), 265–266.

The Scholastic View of Biblical Inspiration. By Hugh Pope (Rome, 1912). In *JQR.*, n. s., IV (1913–14), 267.

The Ethics of the Old Testament. By Hinckley G. Mitchell (Chicago, 1912). In *JQR.*, n. s., IV (1913-14), 267.

Bibel und Naturwissenschaft. Von E. Dennert (Halle a. S., 1911). In *JQR.*, n. s., IV (1913–14), 267.

Mose und die ägyptische Mythologie. Nebst einem Anhang über Simson. Von Daniel Völter (Leiden, 1912). In *JQR.*, n. s., IV (1913–14), 268.

Mose und seine Zeit. Ein Kommentar zu den Mose-Sagen. Von Hugo Gressmann (Göttingen, 1913). In *JQR.*, n. s., IV (1913–14), 268–269.

Hebräische Grammatik. Von Arthur Ungnad (Tübingen, 1912). In *JQR.*, n. s., IV (1913–14), 271–272.

The Principles of Hebrew Grammar. With examples and exercises for the use of students. By D. Tyssil Evans. Part I. Signs and Sounds. Words and their Inflections (London, 1912). In *JQR.*, n. s., IV (1913–14), 272.

Florilegium Hebraicum. Locos selectos librorum Veteris Testamenti in usum scholarum et disciplinae domesticae adiuncta appendice quinquepartita edidit Hub. Lindemann (Friburgi Brisgoviae, MCMXII). In *JQR.*, n. s., IV (1913–14), 272.

The Formation of the Alphabet. By W. M. Flinders Petrie (London, 1912). In *JQR.*, n. s., IV (1913–14), 272–273.

A Research into the Origin of the Third Personal Pronoun Epicene in the Pentateuch and its Connexion with Semitic and Indo-European Languages. By J. Iverach Munro (London, 1912). In *JQR.*, n. s., IV (1913–14), 273.

De poesia Hebraeorum in Veteri Testamento conservata. Auctore V. Zapletal. Editio altera, emendata (Friburgi Helvetiorum, 1912). In *JQR.*, n. s., IV (1913–14), 273–274.

The Early Poetry of Israel in its Physical and Social Origins. George Adam Smith (London, 1912). In *JQR.*, n. s., IV (1913–14), 274.

The Poets of the Old Testament. By Alex. R. Gordon (New York, 1912). In *JQR.*, n. s., IV (1913–14), 274–275.

Wurzelforschungen zu den hebräischen Synonymen der Ruhe. Von Julius Cohen (Berlin, 1912). In *JQR.*, n. s., IV (1913–14), 275.

. L'erreur de traduction prouvée par le mot   בשל Par S. Ferarès (Paris, 1912). In *JQR.*, n. s., IV (1913–14), 276.

Der alttestamentliche Prophetismus. Von Ernst Sellin (Leipzig, 1912). In *JQR.*, n. s., IV (1913–14), 278–279.

Die Konstanz-Weingartener Propheten-Fragmente. In phototypischer Reproduction. Einleitung von Paul Lehmann (Leiden, 1912). In *JQR.*, n. s., IV (1913–14), 279–280.

The Book of Isaiah. I–XXXIX by George Buchanan Gray. Vol. I. Introduction and commentary on I–XXVII (New York, 1912). In *JQR.*, n. s., IV (1913–1914), 280.

The Mines of Isaiah Re-explored. By T. K. Cheyne (London, 1912). In *JQR.*, n. s., IV (1913–14), 280–281.

The Veil of Hebrew History. By T. K. Cheyne (London, 1913). In *JQR.*, n. s., IV (1913–14), 280–281.

The First Twelve Chapters of Isaiah. A new translation and commentary. By George S. Hitchcock (London, 1912). In *JQR.*, n. s., IV (1913–14), 281–282.

The Twelve Prophets. By Bernhard Duhm. Authorized translation by Archibald Duff (London, 1912). In *JQR.*, n. s., IV (1913–14), 282.

The Psalms. Translated from the Latin Vulgate, and with the other translations diligently compared, being a revised and corrected edition of the Douay Version. By Francis Patrick Kenrick (Baltimore). In *JQR.*, n. s., IV (1913–14), 283–285.

Erläuterungen zu dunkeln Stellen im Buche Hiob. Von Georg Richter (Leipzig, 1912). In *JQR.*, n. s., IV (1913–14), 285–286.

Das Buch Qoheleth. Ein Beitrag zur Geschichte des Sadduzäismus. Kritisch untersucht, übersetzt und erklärt von Ludwig Levy (Leipzig, 1912). In *JQR.*, n. s., IV (1913–14), 286–287.

De theologie van Kronieken. Door Jelte Swart (Groningen, 1911). In *JQR.*, n. s., IV (1913–14), 287.

The Wisdom of Jesus the Son of Sirach, or Ecclesiasticus. In the Revised Version, with introduction and notes. By W. O. E. Oesterley (Cambridge, 1912). In *JQR.*, n. s., IV (1913–14), 288.

The Book of Wisdom. With introduction and notes. Edited by A. T. S. Goodrick (London, 1913). In *JQR.*, n. s., IV (1913–14), 288–290.

The Book of Enoch, or I Enoch. Translated from the editor's Ethiopic text, and edited with the introduction, notes, and indexes of the first edition wholly re-cast, enlarged, and rewritten. By R. H. Charles (Oxford, 1912). In *JQR.*, n. s., IV (1913–14), 290–292.

The Ezra-Apocalypse. Being chapters 3–14 of the book commonly known as 4 Ezra (or 2 Esdras). Translated from a critically revised text . . . By G. H. Box (London, 1912). In *JQR.*, n. s., IV (1913–14), 292.

Griechisch-deutsches Wörterbuch zum Neuen Testamente. Von Heinrich Ebeling (Hannover und Leipzig, 1913). In *JQR.*, n. s., IV (1913–14), 293–294.

The New Testament Manuscripts in the Freer Collection. Part I. The Washington Manuscript of the Four Gospels. By Henry A. Sanders (New York, 1912). In *JQR.*, n. s., IV (1913–14), 294–295.

Neue Fragmente und Untersuchungen zu den judenchristlichen Evangelien. Von Alfred Schmidtke (Leipzig, 1911). In *JQR.*, n. s., IV (1913–14), 295–296.

The Syriac Forms of New Testament Proper Names. By F. C. Burkitt (London, 1912). In *JQR.*, n. s., IV (1913–14), 296–297.

Bible Reading in the Early Church. By Adolf Harnack. Translated by J. R. Wilkinson (New York, 1912). In *JQR.*, n. s., IV (1913–14), 297.

The Odes and Psalms of Solomon. Published from the Syriac Version. By J. Rendel Harris. Second edition, revised and enlarged (Cambridge, 1911). In *JQR.*, n. s., IV (1913–14), 297–299.

Light on the Gospel from an Ancient Poet. By Edwin A. Abbott (Cambridge, 1912). In *JQR.*, n. s., IV (1913–14), 299–300.

The People of God. An inquiry into Christian origins. By H. F. Hamilton (London, 1912). In *JQR.*, n. s., IV (1913–14), 300–301.

Materialien zur Bibelgeschichte und religiösen Volkskunde des Mittelalters. Von Hans Vollmer. Band I. Ober- und mitteldeutsche Historienbibeln (Berlin, 1912). In *JQR.*, n. s., IV (1913–14), 301–302.

The Rule of Life and Love. An exposition of the Ten Commandments. By Robert Lawrence Ottley (London, 1913). In *JQR.*, n. s., IV (1913–14), 302.

The Faith of Israel. A Guide for Confirmation. By H. G. Enelow (Cincinnati 1917).—A Manual for Teaching Biblical History. By Eugene Kohn (New York 1917). In *Mac.* for July 1918, p. 208.

The Old Testament Manuscripts in the Freer Collection. Part II. The Washington Manuscript of the Psalms. By Henry A. Sanders (New York, 1917). In *AJSL.*, XXXVI (1919–1920), 84–86.

C. POPULAR ARTICLES

Peter Smolenskin. In *AH*. for December 11, 1891, pp. 131–132.

An evaluation of the great Hebrew writer and Jewish nationalist Perez Smolenskin (1842–1885), in which his attitude toward Reform Judaism is stressed.

The Theology of the Old Prayer Book. In *CCARYB*., VII (1898), 1–10.

Traces the dogmas, doctrines, beliefs and hopes, of the oldest elements of our Prayer Book to their original sources in the Bible, especially the book of Deuteronomy.

The Church and the Individual. In *HUCA*., 1904, pp. 134–137.

Reformed Judaism, nurtured in the bosom of the Evangelical Church, borrowed from it its theological attitude, scorning the slavery of authority and glorifying the freedom of the individual. The writer pleads for the abandonment of this attitude and advocates a strong ecclesiastical government, even at the risk of a few heresy trials.

The Mendelssohnian Programme. In *JQR*., XVII (1905), 531–544.

In reply to Mr. Lucien Wolf on "the Zionist peril", an attempt is made to show that the Mendelssohnian programme of assimilation, while it may have proved beneficial to the Jews, has been disastrous to Judaism, whose only salvation lies in downright conservatism, in the centripetal tendencies of the Zionist creed rather than in the centrifugal tendencies of the assimilationist programme.

The Message of Moses. In *Mac*. for February, 1907, pp. 41–46.

Interprets the message of Moses in the light of a nationalist movement in ancient Israel, thus justifying the principles of nationalism or Zionism in present-day Jewish life.

Professor Max Margolis a Zionist. In *Mac*. for March 1907, pp. 97–99.

Contains a letter from Professor Margolis to Dr. Harry Friedenwald, President of the Federation of American Zionists, in which the writer announces his adhesion to the Zionist movement and sets forth his reasons in detail.

The Return. In *BBN*. for September 1909, p. 11.

A clarion call to the Jewish people to discard their differences and antagonisms and unite under one banner for the benefit of Judaism. "Let us all unite in the one supreme endeavor to preserve the Jewish people and the Jewish religion intact, and attune hearts and minds to the ancient prophetic cry 'Return'."

Are We Disintegrating? In *BBN*. for October 1909, p. 9.

In reply to an article by Ray S. Baker in the *American Magazine* claiming that the Jews in America are disintegrating, the assertion is made that while this may be true to a certain extent there is also a reinvigoration of Jews and Judaism going on at the same time. "The body of Israel, it is safe to predict, will outlive the modern heresies, on the left and on the right."

The Jewish Culture. In *BBN*. for November 1909, pp. 1–2.

In connection with a Congress of Jewish Culture to be convened in Hamburg, the German term *Kultur* and its English equivalent "civilization" are defined distinctly and the suggestion is made that the low level of Jewish culture in America might be raised through improvement of Jewish education.

The Maccabean Victory. In *BBN*. for December 1909, p. 6.

Tells the story of the festival of Hanukkah, how the Maccabees saved the Jews and Judaism from perdition, and predicts the same auspicious result from the similar crisis facing present-day Jewry.

The Bible as a Text Book. In *BBN*. for January 1910, p. 9.

In a heated discussion among rabbinical authorities whether the Bible should or should not be used as a text-book in Jewish schools, the writer expresses his opinion that by all means the Bible, the supreme book of moral and religious education, should be used as a text-book, and preferably in its original, not an abbreviated, form.

The Jewish Consciousness. In *BBN*. for February 1910, p. 5.

In reply to a query, the term "Jewish consciousness" is minutely defined in both its individual and corporate connotation.

The Season of our Freedom. In *BBN*. for March–April 1910, p. 22.

An exposition of the festival of Passover in all its phases, natural, historical, social and political.

What Are We? In *BBN*. for March–April 1910, p. 3.

Deals with the question: Are we a race, a nationality, or a religious body? The answer is: We are a distinct race, though mixed to a certain extent; at the same time we are a nation, though in abeyance; and of course we are a distinct religious body. "Nowhere in the whole world is the threefold cord of race, nationality and religion as strong as with us."

Abraham Geiger. In *BBN*. for May–June 1910, p. 20.

On the centenary of Geiger's birth an appraisal is given of his master mind and his profound learning which redounded to the glory of the Torah and Jewish Science.

Church and State. In *BBN*. for September 1910, p. 3.

Asserts that Church and State must be divided about us as well as in our own midst, if the Jewish people is to survive.

The Inward Peace. In *BBN*. for October 1910, p. 5.

In face of ubiquitous clashing and wrangling the observation is made that true, inward peace, comes home once a year to penitent Israel, during the high holidays.

The Historical Perspective. In *BBN*. for November 1910, p. 5.

"The historical perspective teaches us that Israel is possessed of a strong personality which is the same amidst the fluctuating events of the centuries".

Straight to the People's Heart. In *BBN*. for December 1910, p. 5.

Maintains that true prophets and conscientious leaders always speak straight to the people's heart, and hence people love and adore them; while false prophets and leaders are generally abhorred and forgotten.

"Understanded of the People." In *BBN*. for January 1911, p. 5.

Discusses popular literature which appeals to the masses and generally proves to be great literature, as e.g. the Scriptures.

"The Past and the Present." In *BBN*. for February 1911, p. 10.

In reply to a pronouncement of some liberal Jews "The past is no concern of ours; our only care is the present", this cogent answer is made: "The normal Jew has his ideals in the hoary past and distant future; the present can only be provisional . . . this is Judaism".

The Right Nationalism and the Wrong. In *BBN*. for March 1911, p. 10.

The burden of this article is that the only kind of Jewish nationalism is modern Zionism, which aims to establish an independent Jewish state in Palestine.

The Tercentenary of the English Bible. In *BBN.* for April 1911, p. 10.

On the occasion of the tercentenary of the English Bible the great share of the Jews in the Bible is pointed out and their contributions to the religion and ethics of the world are dwelt upon.

Strange Gods. In *BBN.* for May 1911, p. 10.

In the face of a resuscitated desire for polytheism from time to time, stress is laid once more on the great value of monotheism, which is the cornerstone of Judaism and the gift of the Jews to the world.

The Destiny of the Jewish People. In *BBN.* for June 1911, p. 14.

Basing himself on two ethnological works dealing with the destiny of the Jews, one in an affirmative and the other in a negative sense, the writer insists that the Jews are immortal, an eternal people, and that though they lose a certain amount of their membership in each age through assimilation and apostasy they will never disappear altogether from the face of the earth.

All-Israel. In *BBN.* for September 1911, p. 5.

Meditations for the Day of Atonement, the day of penitence and humiliation, concord and peace for All-Israel.

The Root of the Matter. In *BBN.* for November 1911, p. 5.

The root of the matter, the nerve of our dilemma is: to be a Jew and at the same time a man among men.

Judaism and Hellenism. In *BBN.* for December 1911, p. 10.

In connection with the feast of Hanukkah the everlasting struggle between Judaism and Hellenism is dealt with once more, and the conclusion is reached that it is a combat between two points of view which may complement each other admirably but which must forever remain apart.

Mendelssohnian Judaism. In *BBN.* for January 1912, p. 10.

Criticizes Mendelssohn's declaration that Judaism knew no dogmas, no articles of a creed: if the Jews are to persist and persevere they must cultivate a number of things which will be distinctively their own.

Power. In *BBN.* for March 1912, p. 10.

"Power exercised over men has a brutalizing effect, but power which men exercise over things means enlarging the domain of the spirit" (through exploration and research).

"Judentaufen". In *BBN*. for April 1912, p. 10.

In connection with Werner Sombart's book *The Jews and the Economic Life*, which gave rise to considerable discussion, above all on the subject of assimilation of the Jews through conversion and mixed marriages, a warning is sounded that under no circumstances should we tolerate a deserter or an apostate: the deserter should be stigmatised as a traitor and the apostate should be shunned as a plague.

The Chapters of the Fathers. In *BBN*. for May 1912, p. 10.

An evaluation of the wise sayings or Ethics of the Fathers, which form part of the Mishnah and are recited in the long Sabbath afternoons of the summer.

The New Theology. In *BBN*, for June 1912, p. 10.

Criticizes the new theology of the Christian clergy which is built on a sociological basis and implies that God ministers to the masses but not to the individual.

Lay and Cleric. In *BBN*. for September 1912, p. 10.

The distinction between laity and clergy, customary in the Christian Church, is foreign to the Synagogue, where everyone has a right to read and understand the word of God.

Like Them. In *BBN*. for October 1912, p. 10.

Criticises a sermon by a Reformed rabbi which claimed that "outside our house of worship we are in every way 'like them' and in our house of worship our mode of service differs but little from theirs". Instead of undermining the Jewish separateness it behoves the appointed shepherds of Israel to strengthen the Jewish consciousness, to teach their flock to be more and more "like ourselves", faithful to our traditions and institutions, to our ideals and hopes, to our beliefs and religion.

Religion and Nationalism. In *BBN*. for November 1912, p. 10.

Argues that these two terms are not antagonistic, but supplement each other: the word of God shall come out of Zion for all mankind, and at the same time there is room for a Jewish nation which is for the Jew alone.

The Future of the Jews. In *BBN.* for December 1912, p. 10.

The title is that of Werner Sombart's book, which provoked a good deal of harsh criticism but which is reviewed here objectively and without bias, attention being called to its good points.

Bible Study and Bible Reading. In *BBN.* for January 1913, p. 10.

Contrary to medieval Christian usage, Bible reading and even Bible study was obligatory to the Jews everywhere and it is only in modern times that this practice came in abeyance. Still we are in need of both, the former for the religious inculcation of the young, the latter for the scientific research of the professional.

Congregation and Community. In *BBN.* for February 1913, p. 10.

Argues in favor of both congregational and communal organization, as in European countries, since one supplements the other. "Let the congregations in each city assist in the upbuilding of Jewish communal work on systematic and modern lines".

The Beginnings of the Egyptian Diaspora. In *BBN.* for March 1913, p. 10.

Tells the story of the Jewish colonies of Assuan and Elephantine in Upper Egypt, where Aramaic documents had been found concerning a Jewish military community and their life and practice there.

Passover Reflections. In *BBN.* for April 1913, p. 10.

Assuming that Passover marks our birth as a nation as well as the birth of our religion, the writer stresses the fact that it is not enough to contemplate the Passover of Egypt, but that our attention must be directed toward the Passover of the Future, the great day of deliverance which is to come.

A Jewish Translation of the Scriptures. In *BBN.* for May 1913, p. 10.

Gives reason for the need of a new English version of the Scriptures, undertaken by the Jewish Publication Society of America in conjunction with other learned bodies.

The New Conscience. In *BBN.* for June 1913, p. 10.

In connection with Jane Addams' book *The New Conscience*, laying bare the immorality of our poor populations in the slums of the large cities, an appeal is made to the Jews to return to their old morality as mirrored in the Scriptures and rabbinic writings and to accomplish this through an efficient system of education.

A Statute Unto Israel. In *BBN*. for September 1913, p. 10.

Reflections on the two holidays of the autumn, the New Year and the Day of Atonement, of which it is said that they are "a statute unto Israel and ordinance unto the God of Jacob".

"Our Enemies Being Judges". In *BBN*. for October 1913, p. 10.

On the occasion of the trial of Mendel Beilis in Kiev for ritual murder the viciousness and groundlessness of this charge throughout the ages are hammered in once more with great force.

Religion and the History of Religions. In *BBN*. for November 1913, p. 10.

Maintains that Judaism as it is lived and practiced is of prime importance, not what the modern histories of religions say concerning its origin, whether Egyptian or Babylonian.

The Bible in the Making. In *BBN*. for December 1913, p. 10.

Describes the Bible as it was formed into a tripartite canon by scribes and Pharisees.

The First Psalm. In *BBN*. for January 1914, p. 10.

A characterization of the Psalter through an analysis of the first psalm, which contrasts the saint and the sinner and thus seizes upon an eternal truth.

The Nations Rage. In *BBN*. for February 1914, p. 10.

With war on the horizon a warning is sounded to the raging nations to embrace the prophetic doctrine of peace and the Jewish hope for a society of federated nations.

Unreligious Moral Instruction. In *BBN*. for March 1914, p. 10.

Maintains that moral instruction, to be effective, must be based on religion. Religion is inclusive of morality, but it transcends it even as it sanctifies it. "The only kind of moral instruction for Jewish children is and remains the Jewish one", with religion as its fulcrum.

A Gap in our Educational System. In *BBN*. for April 1914, p. 10.

Deplores the gap existing in our system of education between the elementary Talmud Torah and the advanced theological school, without any provision for a secondary school to carry on Jewish education through the period of adolescence.

"Hebrew Classics" and Jewish Literature. In *BBN*. for May 1914, p. 10.

Justifies the publication of Hebrew Classics, i.e. the choicest productions of Hebrew literature, with exact translations into English, with short notes and introductions, and, above all, in attractive form and portable size.

The Fifty-First Psalm. In *BBN*. for June 1914, p. 10.

An analysis of this great psalm, known to Christians as *Miserere*, which depicts the contrition of a great sinner and his stricken conscience before the Lord.

Sins of Nations. In *BBN*. for September 1914, p. 10.

In the face of the first World War the nations are excoriated for their incessant greed and imperialistic ambitions and the hope is expressed that universal peace, as desiderated by the prophets of Israel, may soon be restored.

Nationalism and Imperialism. In *BBN*. for October 1914, p. 10.

The contention is made that nationalism and imperialism, the two principles which are at the root of the policy of modern states, are incompatible, and that imperialism must give way to the internationalism which does not destroy nationalities but affords them equally ample scope each within its legitimate boundaries.

The War and the Bible. In *BBN*. for November 1914, p. 10.

Nietzsche, the prophet of young Germany, teaches that might is right, but the Bible teaches the opposite, that right is might, and unless men hearken to the peaceful message of the Bible they are doomed to extinction.

The Servant of the Lord. In *BBN*. for December 1914, p. 10.

Deals with a group of poems in the second part of the book of Isaiah, which go by the name of the above title and which always served as an inspiration to Israel in the gloomiest periods.

A Prophetess of Jewish Nationalism. In *BBN*. for January 1915, p. 10.

An appraisal of George Eliot and her remarkable novel *Daniel Deronda*, in which she predicted the establishment of a new Jewish State in Judea and the definitive solution of the vexing Jewish question.

The Twilight of Hebraic Culture: The Transition from Hebraism to Judaism. In *MJ*. for January 1915, pp. 33–38.

Describes the living Hebraic culture as mirrored in the books of the Bible and its decline at the close of the Second Jewish Commonwealth, when it was superseded by bookish Judaism.

The Logic of Instinct. In *BBN.* for February 1915, p. 10.

Although we have been dispersed for more than two thousand years over all countries of the globe, instinct tells us to concentrate in certain favorable localities for the preservation of our identity.

Hyphenated Jews. In *BBN.* for March 1915, p. 1.

The Jews of America, like the Jews of other countries, cannot help but be hyphenated, since they come from different parts of the world, but this does not impair their American patriotism or make them less devoted to the country which offered them asylum in their distress.

Ehrlich's Monumental Work. In *BBN.* for April–May 1915, p. 8.

An appreciation of the great exegetical work of Arnold B. Ehrlich of New York on the occasion of the completion of his monumental work *Randglossen zur hebräischen Bibel* (Leipzig 1908–1914).

The Jewish Defense of the Bible. In *BBN.* for June 1915, p. 10.

Deals with the need of a Bible commentary in English by competent Jewish scholars, who would make it their task to defend the Hebrew Scriptures against their Christian detractors, on scientific lines.

At the Crossroads. In *MJ.* for February 1916, pp. 17–25.

Deals with the period between the Maccabean and the Bar Kochba revolts, the period of the shaping of later Judaism, when Philo, Paul, Josephus, Johanan ben Zakkai, and Akiba had their being. Of these, Akiba the scholar and patriot and his successors are singled out as the true sons of Israel, the true builders.

The Talmud. In the University Edition of the Warner Library of *The World's Best Literature*, XXIV (New York 1917), 14453–14468.

A clear and lucid exposition of the Talmud and its variegated contents, written primarily for non-Jews who are entirely unfamiliar with this type of literature. The article is accompanied by numerous illustrations from the Talmud.

The New English Translation of the Bible. In *AJYB.*, 5678 (1917), 161–193.

A description of the new English translation of the Hebrew Scriptures, its origin and chief characteristics, based upon the preface of the new translation, the statements published from time to time by the Jewish Publication Society of America, and the records kept by the Society. It is certain that this article was written by Margolis, in his capacity as Editor-in-Chief of this Translation and Secretary to the Editorial Board, though not signed by his name.

Zionism and Reform. In *Mac.* for May 1917, pp. 226–228.

Though Zionism and Reform seem to be unalterably opposed to one another, the writer insists that in view of the course of events they must come to terms and work together for Zion Restored.

The Leadership of Herzl. In *Mac.* for August 1917, p. 23.

A reassertion of the Zionist aims and the Basle program and a glowing tribute to the great man who at great personal sacrifices laid the foundation for political Zionism.

Hour of Deliverance has Struck. In *Mac.* for December 1917, p. 423.

Likens the Balfour Declaration to the edict of Cyrus in biblical times and rejoices over the political restoration of Zion.

Ben Yehudah—Gatherer of Dispersed Words. In *Mac.* for April 1918, pp. 111–112.

A glowing appraisal of the monumental work of Eliezer Ben Yehudah of Jerusalem, namely his many-volumed Dictionary of the Hebrew Language along historical lines, written on the occasion of his sixtieth birthday.

Hermann Cohen. In *Mac.* for May 1918, pp. 132–133.

Following the death of Professor Cohen an appraisal is given of his Neo-Kantian philosophy and mode of thinking generally, especially his Jewish convictions and his adherence to conservative Judaism.

Shabuot-Festival of Revelation. In *AH.* for May 17, 1918, p. 34.

Dwells on Shabuot as the festival of revelation and the giving of the Law, rather than the harvest festival, when the first sickle was put to the standing corn and the barley was reaped.

Utopian Dreams—and the Inexorable Reality. In *MJ.* for June 1918, pp. 151–152.

In a symposium entitled "Palestine Regained—What Then?", initiated soon after the Balfour Declaration, the writer warns to face stern reality and not to expect a Utopia: the road to Zion will be arduous though safe and assured, but Jewish life all over the world will go on as before.

The Sound of the Horn. In *AH.* for September 6, 1918, p. 439.

Expatiates on the significance of the blowing of the shofar on New Year's day in time of war.

Jewish Nationalism. In *BBN.* for January 1919, p. 6.

The Election of Israel. In *BBN.* for February 1919, p. 6.

Jewish Apologetics. In *BBN.* for March 1919, p. 9.

Judaism in the Western World. In *BBN.* for April 1919, p. 10.

The Third Party. In *BBN.* for May 1919, p. 9.

At the Dawn of Kingdoms. In *Mac.* for May 1919, pp. 117–118, 135.

Discusses the miracle of the revival of the Jewish people caused by the Balfour Declaration and its analogues in the millennial Jewish history, whenever there was a momentous change in the history of the world.

Earthly and Heavenly. In *BBN.* for June 1919, p. 4.

The Lord's Day. In *BBN.* for September 1919, p. 10.

On Atonement: Let the Cord be strengthened that knits all Jewry together.

The Three Faiths. In *BBN.* for October 1919, pp. 8 and 12.

A true Jew cannot be a Modernist; Judaism must be anchored in the past. Actually a review of Moore's History of Religion. Vol. I.

The Inevitable Middle Course. In *BBN.* for November 1919, p. 13.

A scrutiny of the history of Judaism which, though it was not written with that purpose in mind, may well indicate the manner in which political and industrial problems of the day eventually will be solved.

The Aftermath. In *BBN.* for December 1919, p. 8.

An analysis of post-war conditions and a prediction in favor of sanity.

On the Doorposts of Thy House. In *BBN.* for January 1920, pp. 8 and 11.

Describes the significance of the Mezuzah as a visible outward symbol of the Jewish house.

Seeking Unto the Dead. In *BBN.* for February 1920, p. 7.

The role of spiritualism in religion is discussed. "Religion deals with the realm of the spiritual. But spirituality is not spiritualism".

Freedom of the Spirit. *BBN.* for March 1920, pp. 8 and 12.

A Passover article pleading for an endeavor to understand the Bible from Jewish premises.

The Soul of the Stranger. In *BBN.* for April 1920, pp. 8 and 13.

A review of Katzowitz.

The Broad Synagogue. In *BBN.* for May, 1920, p. 8.

Schechter introduced the terms "High Synagogue" and "Low Synagogue" to designate two sub-divisions of the Jewish religious community. Margolis now adds "The Broad Synagogue" to designate a third sub-division.

A Communal Meeting House. In *BBN.* for June 1920, pp. 8 and 15.

Advocates the use of the synagogue as the Community's meeting house where communal affairs be cleared and Jewish thought clarified.

The Great Misunderstanding. In *BBN.* for September 1920, p. 12.

A review of the first volume of the Beginnings of Christianity by Foakes-Jackson and Kirsopp Lake.

The Great Misunderstanding, II. In *BBN.* for October 1920, p. 10.

The Great Misunderstanding, III. In *BBN.* for November 1920, p. 10.

The Great Misunderstanding, IV. In *BBN.* for December 1920, p. 10.

The Great Misunderstanding, V. In *BBN.* for January 1921, p. 10.

The Great Misunderstanding, VI. In *BBN.* for February 1921, p. 10.

The Great Misunderstanding, VII. In *BBN.* for March 1921, p. 10 and 12.

The Great Misunderstanding, IX. In *BBN.* for April 1921, p. 10.

The Great Misunderstanding, X. In *BBN*. for May 1921, p. 10.

Despising the Old Mother. In *BBN*. for June 1921, p. 10.

A defense of traditional Judaism against the charge that it is "forbidding".

The Origins of Judaism, I. In *BBN*. for September 1921, p. 10.

"A plain narrative and a still plainer discussion . . . of the origins of Judaism".

The Origins of Judaism, II. In *BBN*. for October 1921, p. 4.

The Origins of Judaism, III. In *BBN*. for November 1921, p. 6.

The Origins of Judaism, IV. In *BBN*. for December 1921, p. 4.

The Origins of Judaism, V. In *BBN*. for January 1922, p. 9.

The Origins of Judaism, VI. In *BBN*. for February 1922, p. 9.

The Origins of Judaism, VII. In *BBN*. for March 1922, p. 9.

The Origins of Judaism, VIII. In *BBN*. for April 1922, p. 9.

The Origins of Judaism, IX. In *BBN*. for May 1922, p. 9.

The Origins of Judaism, X. In *BBN*. for May 1922, p. 9.

The Story of Our People. In *BBN*. for September 1922, p. 9.

The Story of Our People, II. In *BBN*. for October–November 1922, p. 21.

The Story of Our People, III. In *BBN*. for December 1922, p. 12.

The Story of Our People, IV. In *BBN*. for January 1923, p. 14.

The Story of Our People, V. In *BBN*. for February 1923, p. 14.

The Story of the Jew. A Study in the Writing of History. In *MJ*. for February 1923, pp. 10–19.

This is the fourth Annual Zunz Lecture, delivered under the auspices of the Intercollegiate Menorah Association, at the University of Pittsburgh, December 13, 1922. It deals with Jewish historiography throughout the ages, as found in the Bible, Josephus, the medieval chronicles, Basnage and other Christian historians, Jost, Graetz, Dubnow, et al., and voices the need for a fresh history today by a corporate body of competent scholars.

The Story of Our People, VI. In *BBN*. for March 1923, p. 15.

The Story of Our People, VII. In *BBN*. for April 1923, p. 14.

The Story of Our People, VIII. In *BBN*. for May 1923, p. 12.

The Story of Our People IX. In *BBN*. for June–July, 1923, p. 12.

The Truth About the Jew. In *BBN*. for September 1923, pp. 5 f.
   Deals with certain misunderstood and unknown facts about the Jews.

The Truth About the Jew, II. In *BBN*. for October 1923, pp. 41 f.

The Truth About the Jew, III. In *BBN*. for November 1923, pp. 86–88.

The Truth About the Jew, IV. In *BBN*. for December 1923, pp. 109 f.

The Truth About the Jew, V. In *BBN*. for January 1924, pp. 152 f.

The Truth About the Jew, VI. In *BBN*. for February 1924, pp. 184 f.

The Truth About the Jew, VII. In *BBN*. for March 1924, pp. 212 f.

The Truth About the Jew, VIII. In *BBN*. for April 1924, pp. 249 f.

The Truth About the Jew, IX. In *BBN*. for May 1924, pp. 281 f.

The Truth About the Jew, X. In *BBN*. for June 1924, pp. 307 f.

A Year in the Holy Land, I–II. In *BBN*. for October 1924, pp. 8–10, 44–45.

A Year in the Holy Land, III. *BBN*. for November 1924, pp. 74, 86.

A Year in the Holy Land, IV. In *BBN*. for December 1924, pp. 106–107.

A Year in the Holy Land, V. In *BBN*. for February, 1925, pp. 167, 182–183.

The Talmud. In Columbia University Course in Literature, Vol. 1: The Wisdom of the East, New York, 1928, pp. 138–151.

INDEX OF SUBJECTS

INDEX